SOMETHING OF
THE NIGHT

SOMETHING OF THE NIGHT

A JOURNEY INTO THE DARKNESS
OF THE BRITISH ISLES

IAN MARCHANT

**SIMON &
SCHUSTER**

London · New York · Sydney · Toronto · New Delhi

A CBS COMPANY

First published in Great Britain by Simon & Schuster UK Ltd, 2012
This paperback edition published by Simon & Schuster UK Ltd, 2013

A CBS Company

1 3 5 7 9 10 8 6 4 2

Simon & Schuster UK Ltd
1st Floor
222 Gray's Inn Road
London WC1X 8HB

www.simonandschuster.co.uk

Simon & Schuster Australia, Sydney
Simon & Schuster India, New Delhi

A CIP catalogue for this book is available
from the British Library.

ISBN: 978-1-84739-779-9
ISBN: 978-0-85720-218-5 ebook

Typeset by Hewer Text UK Ltd, Edinburgh
Printed and bound by CPI Group (UK) Ltd, Croydon CR0 4YY

For Hilary

'The Law is not the same at morning and at night'

George Herbert

Night

We're moonlit, raw-eyed with insomnia –
the woman whose body bled away her child,
the man whose boss no longer meets his eyes,
the teenage boy still fizzing with desire.
We feel like freaks, we press our eyelids shut
and yearning for the sledgehammer of sleep
we count achievements, lies, commitments, sheep –
all useless. Let's stop fretting, and get up,

and gather in a street sugared with frost
then steal a minibus and drive for miles.
Let's all link hands under the glittering stars
and pity those for whom the night is lost.
We'll celebrate the earth's celestial hood
and greet the Great Bear, roaring in our blood.

Catherine Smith

NEIL

One morning in early November, I drove the 300 and some odd miles from Belfast to West Cork through endless pouring rain to spend a night in company with Neil.

Neil is a pal of mine and an astute reader.

'Oh, I loved *The Longest Mile*,* brilliant that was,' he'd told me, months ago, in the garden of The Duke's Arms in Presteigne, in the no longer extant Welsh county of Radnorshire.

'Cheers, Neil.'

'Man, I'd have loved to have come with you to all those pubs.'

'We could have hired a coach and sold tickets to all the blokes who wanted to come . . .'

'I bet you could. What are you working on now?'

'I'm writing this book about the night. It's about all kinds of things that happen at night.'

'Like what sort of thing?'

---

* I think he was referring to my last book, *The Longest Crawl*.

'Like, anything that can happen at night,' I said.

'Like, what?'

'Like, anything.'

'Can I come on this one?'

'Sure. So long as you're up for anything . . .'

'I am. Ian, I really am. Please can I come?'

Of course you can, Neil. I don't know where I'm going, or what I'm doing, except that I'll be trying to see in the dark. But of course you can come, and welcome.

ANYTHING COULD HAPPEN

When I was a kid, anything could happen in the night.

It very seldom did; but it could.

In the night, I could play centre-back for Brighton and England. I could replace Macca on the bass guitar in the re-formed Beatles.

I could say 'Hello' to Jackie Sinclair, the girl of my dreams.

In the night, Jackie Sinclair might drop by, unannounced. I could write a triple concept album based on her visit, and hire an all-girl band to record it at Rockfield Studios. At night anything was possible.

When I was a kid, I loved going to bed, because it meant that I would be alone. I wasn't there to sleep; I was there to read, and play, and dream. I was one of those spoddy kids who read under the covers; when I was seven, to my eternal shame, my mum caught me crying my eyes out to Enid Blyton's *Five Bad Boys* by torchlight. Later on, I was similarly mortified when My Old Feller caught me relaxing with a copy of *Parade* which I'd had away from my paper round. Nights just got better the older you got.

Year after year and minute by minute, I stayed awake a little longer each night. I discovered that I was a night owl, though if there are day owls, I haven't heard them hoot.

A friend of mine, a devoted adherent of evolutionary psychology, tells me that my ancestors were probably the kind of cavemen who sat around keeping the fire going, telling stories, and generally guarding the women-folk. So, I've never been much of a one for sleeping at night. Daytime has always been my preferred downtime, a fact which goes some way to explain a series of still embittered ex-employers.

Night is therefore my most productive time, and I've tried to turn it to my advantage. In the early 80s, I nearly hacked a precarious living as a rock singer, and I still head off now and then to do the odd gig. For a musician or an actor, this ability to be awake and perky at night is something of a *sine qua non*. If you like to be tucked up by nine, you can forget that ambition to be the next Olivier or John Lydon. As a single parent, night time was always the time that I could work; it was the time when I taught myself to write, while the kids slept.

Night is still a time of work; 20 per cent of workers in the industrialised world work at night. The kids and the punters are tucked up in bed, so the shelves can be stacked, the Tube de-fluffed, and the motorways repaired. There is a special quality to night-shift work; indeed, night-shift workers see themselves as superior to the daytime bods.

And night is our time of greatest playfulness and freedom, of love and romance. We go to pubs, nightclubs, and all-night drinking dens; we go to cinemas, theatres and bingo halls. We go to night classes, dance lessons, the football and the dogs.

Nightingales sing in Berkeley Square. We fall in and out of love. Our culture is full of the romantic playful night.

But perhaps as a result of increased playfulness and freedom, the night has become heavily politicised, as the idea that inner-city areas are given over to drunken youth blossoms unchecked in the press and broadcast media. Still, there is truth mixed with the hysteria. It can be horrible out there at night. There's a half-eaten kebab, its gizzards strewn across the precinct slabs; there are hen parties in skimpy dresses and fairy wings being slammed into the back of a police van; there are young lads heaving up outside the KFC; Belisha beacons and ATMs are flashing on and off for no one; a faraway ambulance wails the estate to prayers and to bed. Crime is rife in the city night.

So the night is also the site of our greatest danger. It is a time of crime, and of transgressive sexuality. Prostitutes walk the streets; doggers crack off in the car parks of daytime beauty spots. Businessmen go to lap-dancing clubs to forget what waits at home. The police helicopter chatters overhead, chasing after lads hurdling garden walls. Dealers deal in shadowy corners. The A&E department is full of the walking and aggressively drunk wounded. Night is when we are most likely to die, to commit suicide.

And the night is the time of our greatest fears: of ghosts and ghouls, and vampires, and werewolves, of night terror and night sweats, of bogeymen hiding in the wardrobe. Monks chant compline in freezing cloisters to keep us safe from the old powers of the dark.

Still, despite the horrors, the night is our time of rest and recuperation. We take up a hot-water bottle, pull on our jim-jams, snuggle under the duvet and blankets, breathe in the freshly laundered bedclothes, drink a soothing mug of Ovaltine, and read our Dan Browns. By day, bed is itself transgressive, naughty, forbidden. It's where we steal a nap, and it's where mum entertains the milkman. At night, bed becomes our refuge, a harbour from the dark and the cold fear of the looming unknown. And I may go late to bed, but when I do go, I sleep like a baby on barbiturates. Metallica could play outside my bedroom, and I wouldn't notice; in fact, Metallica might be put off their chops by the volume of my snoring. At least I don't talk in my sleep any more.

We sleep to dream. In dreams, our unconscious is loose, and doing what it will. We need sleep; we have evolved so that we need the night. Our circadian rhythms mean that our biological clocks are reset and our cells regenerate. We are born again, night after night. This we share with all life on the planet. The night is alive; the real night owls, the consumptive badgers, the eels that run up our rivers, the hateful slugs, invisible by day, all kinds of creatures live their lives by night.

During the day, our sense of wonder can be diminished. On the odd day when the clouds break, the blue of the sky serves as a reassuring ceiling which lets us focus on our lives. At night, we are confronted with the infinite nature of the universe, as count-less billions of stars mock us with our insignificance. It is the stars that remind us of our microscopic size. The night sky can confront us with the sheer pointlessness of our existence; the things that seem to matter so much in the sun hardly matter at all by starlight. Paul Bowles makes this point the central image of his novel *The Sheltering Sky*: 'The sky hides the night behind it, and shelters the people beneath from the horror that lies above.'

So unboundaried can our insignificance make us feel that we become gripped by night sweats, panic attacks, by the heebie-jeebies. I could die. I could stop breathing. How do you know that this breath isn't the last one? We can be over-whelmed by our imminent death. Philip Larkin knew that the darkest hour is just before dawn. In one of his last poems, 'Aubade', he comes awake 'in soundless dark' to see death a day nearer. Perhaps if he had been more of a night owl, his childhood would have been less boring, and the nights less full of horror.

Thinking about the night, meeting people at night, travelling by night, I realised that most of the important events in my life had happened under cover of darkness. I wasn't just a bit of a night owl; I was a full-on creature of the night. As I've changed, so have my nights; and as I talked to people, and read, and wrote, my story and the story of the night became indistinguish-able in my thinking. This is the story of my nights, and not, I suppose, everybody's. It must be faced: I have something of the night about me, as I came to understand.

Take, for example, crime. Who should I talk to about night crime? Criminals, obviously. But where to find them? I hunted around for a while to find a criminal who would talk, and found a few. But this approach came to seem artificial. After all, some of my best friends are criminals. Most of them, now I come to think of it. Me too. Have been for years, since the night I met my great friend Perry Venus in a student disco at St David's University College, in the mid-Wales town of Lampeter one night in 1976.* What better way to begin, then, than by committing a crime?

So here I am, one morning in early November, driving the 300 and some odd miles from Belfast to West Cork through endless pouring rain to spend a night in company with Neil, pal, astute reader and weed farmer – and to buy an ounce of his excellent home-grown spliff.

* I tell the story of our meeting in my book *Parallel Lines*. Perry was my travelling companion for *The Longest Crawl*. It isn't necessary for you to have read my other books in order to understand this one, but it is necessary that you buy them.

IN DORSET?

My old car, 125,000 miles already on the clock, is lapping up the road, but the journey is dull as the ditchwater which tips from the sky. It's pretty much motorway all the way from Belfast to Cork, apart from a gap in the north between Lisburn and Newry, and another in the south between the end of the M7 and the start of the M8. The M8 is proper in clear weather: fast and mostly empty of traffic, and so newly opened that it doesn't yet seem to exist on any maps, as it carves through the valley between the Galtee and Knockmealdown mountains. I know the mountains are there, through that thick mist, I can sense them as the light starts to fail. But in the rain, there is nothing to see and less to hear; I channel hop between dozens of radio stations, but they are all indistinguishable from one another, except for the Irish-language channel, where they chat away, I'm sure, about intelligent and interesting things in Irish Gaelic, and where also they play traditional Irish music, which I loathe above all things on earth. The English-language stations are mercifully free of Irish music, but otherwise they are without all merit. This is what happens on Irish radio: a genial host plays unchallenging pop music, and chats on the phone to Irish celebrities about Irish things; mostly, today, *X Factor*, and the fate of the Irish Grimes twins, the hateful 'Jedward', hopefully, by the time you read this, condemned to the dustbin of history on their way to the landfill site of oblivion.

Also, people phone in to talk about their ill children, and the host says, 'Oh, Noreen, you're in our prayers.'

The sports news is about Liverpool, Manchester United, Celtic, and hurling.

There are no service stations on any of the motorways, so in order to get a coffee, you have to pull off and follow the signs to the nearest town, but I am late, and anxious, so I keep driving through that rain, hungry and thirsty and headachy from want of caffeine until I get the other side of Cork, out on the N71 towards Bandon, where I stop and grab a sandwich and a coffee, and phone my man to tell him I'm a bit late.

'That's alright, Ian,' says Neil. 'I'm always happy to wait in a bar.'

Shit. This is exactly what I'd hoped to avoid. Neil doesn't smoke his own home-grown. Neil's drug of choice is beer, and lots of it. Sometimes he doesn't drink at all; he'll go a fortnight, three weeks without touching a drop; and then he'll decide to go on a massive five-day drunk. I worry I might catch the start or, worse still, the end of one of his marathon binges.

I'm about twenty miles away from the bar where Neil is waiting for me, sinking pint after pint; it is dark now, has been since before Cork, and I'm on the back roads, and the rain is still falling in filthy sheets. I want to get to Neil as soon as I can, to try to connect with him before the tenth pint, which is where things can start to get confused. I'm going too fast on these twisty roads; no faster than I would in the hills of home, but too fast for these uncertain, unfamiliar roads. Coming down a long straight, I see the yellow and black chevrons which the Irish use to show a tight bend, just perceptible through the gloom; I brake, perhaps too hard, and exercise a slow skid; I arc across the oncoming carriageway, glide into the entrance of a driveway which joins the road at that point, and come to a halt, my headlights lighting the wet road, facing again in the direction I want to go. That there had been no traffic coming the other way, and no traffic behind me; that there was a driveway at that exact point which I could skid off into, all struck me as miraculous.

I thought, 'God doesn't want me to die tonight.'

Not tonight. On the radio, the genial presenter is telling Aoife that he hopes her troubles end soon, and that she is in all the listeners' prayers.

'And after a song from Westlife, I'll be talking to Jedward's cousin about last night's thrilling results show . . .'

I drive into the little West Cork town where I have arranged to meet Neil. It looks orderly and quietly prosperous, but the high tide of wealth which washed all over the country during the 'Celtic Tiger' years has now receded down the beach of Ireland's increasingly rickety economy, leaving shuttered bars and half-finished housing developments in its wake. I park the car, and walk into The Shamrock. There is no sign of Neil. The barmaid smiles.

'I'm looking for a mate of mine,' I tell her. 'His name's Neil.'

'Oh sure, and he's just gone to the jakes,' she says, and Neil emerges from the Gents, zipping up his fly against his ample belly. We shake hands, his slightly damp.

'I'm sorry I'm so late,' I say. (Two hours.)

'Mate, I told you. I'm always happy to wait in a bar.'

Neil is English, like lots of people out here. There is a legendary community out in these hills, called simply the Mountain, which in its time attracted dozens of disaffected English hippy travellers. Neil's ex was one such; she had come out here in the 80s, looking for an alternative lifestyle, and had ended up on the Mountain, living in a homemade bender with Neil, when he wasn't on a bender himself. They had a son together, and she moved away, unable to cope with Neil's drinking, leaving Neil in the bender. She and her son now live in the same old town as I do, and they are both good friends of mine. Neil rarely sees his son Mac these days, but when he comes to Wales to visit him, Neil always stays with me. I like Neil lots.

I've heard of the Mountain from other sources. After the Battle of the Beanfield,* lots of people in the Peace Convoy

---

* The Battle of the Beanfield took place on 1 June 1985. Over a thousand officers from Wiltshire Police cornered the Peace Convoy in a beanfield on the edge of Savernake Forest, and smashed their vehicles to pieces. *The Observer*'s Home Affairs correspondent Nick Davies was there. He wrote: 'There was glass breaking, people screaming, black smoke towering out of burning caravans and everywhere there seemed to be people being bashed and flattened and pulled by the hair . . . men, women and children were led away, shivering, swearing, crying, bleeding, leaving their homes in pieces . . . Over the years I had seen all kinds of horrible and frightening things and always managed to grin and write it. But as I left the Beanfield, for the first time, I felt sick enough to cry.' There was an ITN news crew present. The reporter, Kim Sabido, speaking to the camera, said, 'What we – the ITN camera crew and myself as a reporter – have seen in the last thirty minutes here in this field has

who had been brutalised by the British state hopped onto the boat to Ireland, and came out to the Mountain for a while. My friend Panit Dave was one such.

'We got off the boat at Rosslare with a goat and three chickens in the back of the van,' Panit Dave told me, 'and Customs waved us through. And then we headed out to West Cork, and stayed for three years.'

I'd met other travellers through Panit who were still out here, running businesses in Kinsale or Bantry, doing alright, one of them telling me at length about his reading of Gaddaffi's *Green Book*, oddly enough. They only keep the van now for the long annual trip to Pilton. But at the core of the West Cork hippy life is still the Mountain. So after all I've heard about this place, it's fascinating to be here, in Little Alternative England.

I take timid soundings, and find out that Neil's only had three pints, which is well within the comfort zone. He buys me a pint of Murphy's, the great drink of Cork, and we sit and chat while he has pint four. Then I buy him pint five, and pint two for me.

A grinning man, not as young as he looks, comes up to Neil in the bar.

'Orlright, Neil?' he says.

'Hello, Gareth,' says Neil. 'I thought you were in England.'

'I am, man. In Weymouth.'

'In Dorset?' I ask, helpfully. Gareth grins at me, but is unable to spot a music hall set-up line when he hears one.

---

been some of the most brutal police treatment of people that I've witnessed in my entire career as a journalist. The number of people who have been hit by policemen, who have been clubbed whilst holding babies in their arms in coaches around this field, is yet to be counted . . . There must surely be an inquiry.' No such inquiry was ever held.

'In Dorset, yeah. But the trial's tomorrow, and the Gardai have flown me back, and put me up in a hotel, but they haven't given me any money. They told me not to go out, and not to get pissed, but I smuggled two bottles of vodka through, and now I've given 'em the slip and come down here to see if anybody will buy me a pint.' Neil sighs, and buys a pint for Gareth and number six for himself. He offers me a third, but I decline, given that we still have to drive out to Neil's place on the Mountain, and also given that, although God doesn't want me to die tonight, I don't want to push my luck.

Gareth takes the pint, still grinning. It's a grin I recognise: a junk grin, a vacuous empty grin with malice, even evil behind it.

A group of Irish people come into the bar, dressed in suits.

'Hello, Mr Quinn,' says Neil to the youngest of the group. 'If you're wearing a suit, you're either getting married, or been in court . . .'

'I've been to my grandad's funeral, Neil.'

Neil laughs. 'Oops,' he says.

'Ooof,' I say.

'Time to go?' says Neil.

We walk down to the supermarket and buy some steak mince, a jar of Dolmio spaghetti sauce, and a twelve-pack of Stella. I do my sums. Six pints, plus a twelve-pack; that's a fair bit, even by Neil's standards.

I ask Neil if he is alright driving, and he snorts contemptuously, as though six pints were hardly going to impair a chap's ability to drive home from the pub. I get back into my car, and follow Neil in his as we drive out of town towards the Mountain.

We turn up lanes which grow narrower and steeper with each bend, and whose surfaces grow more rutted the higher we go; and finally we turn up a precipitous cinder track, and climb the side of the Mountain, my old car rumbling along in first gear. Neil lives in a house now; or, rather, a two-bed granny annexe on the side of a rather grand farmhouse, where a friend of his who is prone to occasional psychotic episodes spends his days. As we get out of our cars, a tiny sheepdog, little more than a puppy, half collie and half Jack Russell maybe, comes panting and tail-wagging towards us.

'That's Billy,' says Neil. Billy licks my hands.

Below us, a long way below, are the lights of the little West Cork town we have just left. Above us, a sky bright with stars, now that the rain has been chased away to the north and east. Tomorrow will be clear.

MAUDLIN REGRET

Neil's place is just as you might expect. He moves some fishing rods so I can sit on the sofa in the kitchen. He's lived so long in West Cork that he's turned into an Irish bachelor farmer. He has fields and crops to tend.

He pops his first tinnie.

'I guess you'd like a smoke,' he says. I agree.

Neil, like any self-respecting drug dealer, is on invalidity benefit.

'It's the bread and butter,' he tells me. 'This stuff is like the jam.'

He hands me an ounce of bud. He and his organisation don't usually do anything under ten oz. I very much appreciate their kindness. I open the bag and sniff; early season, outdoor grown, it smells buzzy. I skin up. It *is* buzzy, I can tell at once; it's talking grass.*

---

* Cannabis ('spliff') comes in two main varieties, leaf and resin. Much of the leaf cannabis ('grass', 'bush', 'weed' etc.) that is available on the black market is now 'skunk', which is largely grown hydroponically indoors. It can be a bit strong, and make you want to stare at the wall and dribble. Neil's outdoor-grown grass, which is less strong than skunk, is giggly, and makes you want to chat. It's like having a couple of glasses of champagne, rather than ten pints of Guinness.

'What trial is that guy involved with?' I ask.

'Gareth? He was a witness to a murder. He was at a junkie party up in the hills, and this bloke turns up with a concrete cutter and starts threatening his ex-girlfriend with it. So these people at the party subdue him, and take the concrete cutter off him, and put him in a back room, and torture him to death.'

'And Gareth was at the party?'

'The Gardai found his statement really useful to their case.'

'Er . . . should he be out, then? I mean, isn't he in danger?'

Neil rubs his chins.

'Yeah,' he says. 'Good point.'

We talk about Neil's boy Mac, while Neil fries up the steak mince, heats up the Dolmio, and boils some spaghetti. Neil has had exactly the right amount of beer with which to kick off a small attack of maudlin regret re. his parenting skills, whilst I have had just the right amount of spliff to make me utterly convinced of my peculiar parenting genius.

'I was never really there, Ian,' says Neil, his stirring of the Dolmio slowing to almost nothing.

'No, but you are around much more now. He's eighteen; there's still time.'

Neil gives me a brave, toothless grin, and pops another tinnie.

'No, man, but you're such a great parent.'

Modesty insists I cast my eyes downwards. I start to skin up again.

'Yeah . . . I guess . . . I mean, I've been at it a long time,' I say.

'I mean, you were always there when it was your kids' bedtime.'

'Well . . . oftener than not . . . if not quite always.'

'You gave them baths . . .'

'I did.'

'Sang them songs, read them stories . . .'

'Sort of.'

'I never did any of that,' he says. 'Too pissed.'

'I need a piss, actually,' I say.

'Oh, just go outside in the yard.'

Outside the front door, Billy is waiting to lick my hands. I piss, looking up into the stars, and down at the little town in the valley. I am stoned.

Was I there for my kids, at bedtime, all night every night? What I'd said to Neil was probably true for my elder daughter Charley, oftener than not, and certainly untrue of my younger, Minnie. I regret the nights I wasn't there to comfort them to sleep.

There are as many kinds of night as there are dreamers, and one dream of night is that of the night as a time of comfort, rest, peace, safety and security, which are at least some of the qualities we associate with home and family, if we're lucky.

My earliest memories are all associated with night, and bedtime.

I can remember a tin bath in front of a fire, and a pleasant stiffness in what my mother called my 'dinky-doo'. I can remember warm towels after the bath; I can remember a tiny dark corridor, and my mother carrying me to a milk-scented cot, with bars painted in different colours. I can remember my companions in the cot: Lamby Blue Blues, who was a kangaroo knitted in blue wool by our next-door neighbour, Uncle Harold;

and Patty Paws, who was an ancient bear, stuffed with straw which herniated in patches on her hessian belly, and who was stripped of fur except behind her ears, where a golden fuzz showed what she must have looked like in her long-distant youth, when my mother was a baby and had cuddled Patty Paws in the bedroom she shared with her brother.

There are similarities between my own earliest memories of bedtime and my mum's. My bath was in a tin bath in front of the range; so was hers. She cuddled the same bear as me. Her mum came up and told her a bedtime story, though it was told by candlelight, rather than electric light bulb. The tiny cottage where she grew up was lit by gas only downstairs; upstairs it was candles. Just before the Second World War, children still had feather pillows, as I did when I was a kid. We can both remember pulling feathers from pillows and bright eiderdowns.

In fact, this feather plucking is one of the commonest memories of bedtime, at least amongst older people. In the autumn of 1999, the organisation Mass Observation asked its contributors to write in on the subject of sleep and dreaming, and I spent a happy few days in the Special Collections area of Sussex University Library going through boxes of the resulting letters. This memory of pulling feathers from pillows was the second most common observation, according to my unscientific survey. The most common was not remembering dreams.

Mass Observation was set up in 1937 by the anthropologist Tom Harrisson, the poet and communist sociologist Charles Madge, and the documentary film-maker Humphrey Jennings, at least in part in reaction to what its founders saw as the false view presented by the media of the abdication in 1936. Mass Observation recruited hundreds of diarists, who listened to what people said and noted these overheard conversations in their diaries. To its founders, Mass Observation seemed excitingly democratic, a chance for the ordinary people of Britain to be heard for the first time; to its critics, it marked a chance for neighbours to spy on neighbours, one of the opening salvos in the long battle to turn Britain into a surveillance society.

In 1949, Mass Observation morphed into a market research organisation, which was dead by the early 60s, merged with the British Market Research Bureau. In 1970, Mass Observation's remarkable archive of private diaries passed to the University of Sussex Library; and in 1981 somebody had the bright idea of starting it up again. You can become an observer yourself, by contacting the revived organisation via their website. Every three months you will be sent a 'directive' suggesting an area of your life that you might like to reflect on, and to write about. This might be, for example, attitudes to the Iraq War, or to food; in the autumn of 1999 the directive was that the observers should write about sleeping and dreaming. To sit and read this collection of letters and diary entries was a huge privilege, and I thank Sussex University Library for the opportunity to do what amounted to interviewing a couple of hundred or so people on their bedtime habits.

What made the experience particularly interesting was that by its nature, Mass Observation consists mostly of older observers, because younger people are posting these kinds of observations directly onto the interweb. So quite a few people, like my mother, remember going to bed by candlelight, in houses that were lit by gas only downstairs. Quite a few of the observers note that going to bed was something that they enjoyed, for the same reason that I did: it afforded privacy, quiet, a time to read and a time to dream. Wartime observers remember what it was like to go to sleep in an Anderson shelter, or under a dining-room table. A few observers note that this wartime experience led to a lifetime of night terrors, including one correspondent who became a Mogadon addict in the 1970s, because of the horror of war: lying under a table, or in the dank squalor of an Anderson shelter, hearing the doodlebug overhead, and the sudden silence of its engine, waiting to see if death would fall from the night sky. As one of the observers notes, 'the War changed the pattern of sleep forever'.

A few of the oldest of the observers remember sleeping on straw mattresses; one gentleman from Derby remembers sharing a straw mattress with his father in one bedroom, while his three sisters and his mother shared another two straw mattresses in the next. Even my mother, shocking though I find her stories of rural poverty, had a feather mattress. This same gentleman remembers the 'knocker-up' who, for 3d per week, would come and knock on your bedroom window with a pole to say that it was time for work, in his father's instance in the railway works in Derby.

It seems extraordinary that mattresses stuffed with straw would still have been used in poor households up until at least the 1930s, but it is nevertheless true. There were few alternatives until very recently. The rich would have slept on feather mattresses, but they were thought to be unhealthy; Leonardo da Vinci spurned the use of feather mattresses, and declined to 'lie upon the spoils of other dead creatures'. Hair was used from about the 1650s; some people swore by moss, which was said to have antiseptic qualities, and to see off mice. Beech leaves were popular in the 1840s, because they remained 'sweet and elastic', and from the late eighteenth century onwards carded wool was used. But the fact remains that for most of humanity's history, we have slept on straw. The *Encyclopaedia Britannica* of 1823 says that 'most of the peasants around Manchester lie on chaff at present, as do likewise the common people all over Scotland'. A feather mattress would have been a luxury right up until the early years of the twentieth century; and in 1920s Derby, it clearly still was. Patents for sprung mattresses date back to the 1770s, but they were still a novelty 100 years later. It was not until the twentieth century that the technical problems of making a sprung mattress were overcome, and beds became bouncy. Before that, they were damp, and saggy, and needed a daily shake to make sleeping on them bearable. In Arthur Ransome's children's novel of 1930, *Swallows and Amazons*, the Swallows take large mattress bags with them to Wildcat Island, to stuff with bracken, which made adequately comfortable beds, and seem to think nothing of it. Imagine a camping trip today which depended on finding bracken to stuff your mattress; now we have sleep mats, and inflatable beds, and we probably sleep the sounder, even if we have become more decadent.

Not all the Mass Observers came from deprived backgrounds. Several talk of being told stories at bedtime by their nannies; clearly this presupposes an adequate light source by the bedside, as well as an indulgent nanny. Another observer wrote that starched sheets were 'a pleasure that has long since vanished now that cotton sheets have given way to synthetic materials that don't take starching'. Presumably, this was a phenomenon restricted to children from well-to-do backgrounds. Bed-wetting, however, seems to have been endured by all social classes; most unfortunate was the boy who woke up at night to urinate in 'shoes, drawers and cupboards'.

Lots of the observers talk of sleeping with the light on, perhaps most notably the 37-year-old teacher who is not only scared of the dark, but sleeps in the same bed in the same room with the same teddy as he has always slept. The observers are anonymous, which is a shame, because I imagine his pupils would pay a great deal of money to know his identity. All I know is that he lives in Henley . . .

Few observers actively enjoyed sleeping alone, certainly as children. Many of the observers remember their teddies with great affection, and many admit to still owning them (my mum still has Patty Paws, wrapped up in tissue in her loft space). There are lots of teddies, and several cats, but perhaps the most eccen-tric bedtime companions are a wooden steam engine wrapped in a blanket, and a roll of pink flannelette known as Pinkie, without which its owner was unable to sleep. It's interesting to note how many of these bedtime experiences are held in common, and how vivid they remain for so many of the Mass Observers. I am far from alone in having bedtime as my earliest memory.

When I was four we moved to Farnborough, in Hampshire, into a modern terraced house that smelled of recently departed builders and warm plastic. It was the winter of 1962–63, and there is a black-and-white photo of me standing outside the front door up to my tiny waist in snow.

Talking to my mum years later, I learned that not only was this the first house that she had lived in that had a bathroom, but it was also the first house that I had lived in that was so luxuriously equipped. The tin bath, which I had for years been convinced was used only because I was so small, was in fact the only bath we actually had in the dark old house. Bath time in the new house seemed less magical, and I didn't really recover my enthusiasm for baths till the onset of girls.

My memories of the new house are of fear, and illness, and bad dreams. That house is where I became aware that at night, my mum mostly stayed in on her own with me, and that at the times when my dad was home, there was usually a lot of shouting. That house is where I had measles; I lay in bed with my mum, staring in stark terror at the ceiling, while all night the house was full of the sound of drumming, my earliest and so far most frightening hallucination. And in that house, I started to be visited by a recurring dream which subsequently haunted my childhood. Something heavy lumps down on the end of my bed. I start up in fear. Whatever is sitting on my bed is invisible; it nonetheless somehow forces me to follow it in darkness to the top of the stairs. I stand at the top of the stairs, and a great brightness dazzles up at me. I step down the stairs towards the light.

One night in that house, I woke up in darkness. I called out, but there was no reply. I clicked the light, but nothing worked. I called out and called out, and walked towards the top of the stairs, where I dreaded that I would see the dazzling light. But there was nothing. I called again, and still no reply, so I walked step by step down the stairs, holding on to the railing in the dark. I pushed open the door of the lounge, and clicked the light switch, but no light came and my parents had gone. I screamed; and the front door opened, and my dad came in with a lit candle. He took me back up to bed, and stayed with me till my mum came home.

They'd been to a cheese and wine party two doors down, and had been taking it in turns to pop back, when a power cut came, which was unfortunately the moment I'd woken up to find neither of them there. I've had a horror of cheese and wine parties ever since.

Two Englishmen in West Cork

Neil calls me back inside. He has glopped the Dolmio sauce onto the fried-up steak mince, and mixed it with spaghetti. We carry our plates through into the sitting room, which is half full of unpacked boxes, and where a wood stove is burning. On the coffee table in front of Neil's collapsing armchair is a laptop; Neil plugs in a guitar amp, calls up iTunes, and presses PLAY. Some good ol' boy country music starts to thump through the room. We suck up spaghetti, and do our best not to spray it over our clothes.

'What's this?' I ask Neil.

Neil and I are both musicians, and this is one of the things that two bloke musicians do when they spend time together, which is to play one another music. We come from traditions which only overlap here and there, like a Venn diagram where two circles only contain a small shared space. Neil is from the traditional Irish music, rootsy down-home acoustic-y tradition, while I'm from the thin white boys smacking electric guitars meets 60s girl band pop/soul/r'n'b/dub crossover, with a dash of over-produced bossa-esque psychedelia and a splash of post-Van Dyke Parks* surf, all stewed in funky vibes and dipped in a hot spicy loungecore salsa sauce tradition. The area where the circles on our Venn diagram overlap is mostly outlaw country music. This stuff Neil is playing is something I've never heard.

'It's called *White Mansions*. It came out in '78. It's a sort of double album with another thing called *Jesse James*. It's written by this English bloke, who got people like Waylon Jennings and Emmylou Harris to sing on it. Clapton plays guitar. It's great, isn't it?'

It is, as it goes, Clapton scepticism notwithstanding. Neil sucks up his spaghetti.

'It's like this concept album about the Confederacy.'

'Oh . . .'

'Listen to this.'

Neil plays me a song called 'Dixie Hold On', sung by Waylon Jennings, and it's great, but . . .

'I never got off on that sentimental Dixie thing,' I say. 'I mean, the good guys won, didn't they?'

'Well . . . yeah,' says Neil. 'But the Confederates had the best songs.'

'Well the Nazis had some good tunes, but the good guys won.'

'You can't compare the Confederates and the Nazis,' says Neil.

---

* Van Dyke Parks is a songwriter and lyricist. His 1968 collaboration with Brian Wilson on the unreleased *Smile* album marks the moment when The Beach Boys went a bit odd . . .

'Well . . . you can. The Confederate flag is just swastika lite.'

I told Neil about the last night of a country and western festival I'd been to in a caravan park in Silloth, on the Solway Coast of Cumbria, a place where great nights out are few and far between.

'The night ends with all these people in Confederate uniforms waving all these Confederate flags, to the sound of Elvis singing 'American Trilogy'. And they all stand to attention, and cry and that. It's the whitest thing I've ever seen, and I've been to Burgess Hill.'

Neil slurps up a string of spaghetti from his fleece.

'Yeah, but I still like the Confederacy,' he says.

'The good guys won. Of course they did. There's nothing sad about bad guys losing. That's your Bhagavad-Gita, innit?'

'Is it?'

'Yeah. It's better to fight evil, and live with the evil that you had to do to win, than not to fight at all, and let the greater evil prevail. Like the Battle of the Boyne. The good guys won.'

'Jaysus, but you'd better not say that in The Shamrock.'

'No, but it's true.'

'What about Cromwell? What about the Famine?' asks Neil.

'Nothing to do with it. The world would be a radically different place if James had won. King Billy is the whole point of the Civil War, and the final triumph of Parliament. By 1700, England was the most democratic, the most liberal and most advanced society on earth. The good guys won.'

'Are you not a Republican?' asks a clearly shocked Neil.

'No, man. I like living in the UK. I like the NHS, the BBC, I believe in a woman's right to choose. There's none of that down here.'

'No, but, it's their country, man . . .'

'Why, because they share a landmass? So do Serbia and Bosnia, but that wasn't great, was it? If I lived in the North, I'd vote to stay in the UK every time. Besides . . . I am *affianced* to a lady from the North.'

Neil puts down his fork, and leans towards me to grasp my hand.

'Congratulations, mate,' he says.

'Cheers, mate.'

'Is she, like, Protestant?'

'Don't sound surprised. I am myself.'

Neil nods. It must come as a shock. In the 70s and 80s, all right-thinking English radicals supported the idea of a united Ireland. I didn't, and don't.

'Why do you like it here so much?' I ask.

'The people, man. I love the people. I mean, they'll never love me, 'cos I'm English, but I love them. They hold their hands out to you in welcome, you know?'

'Is there anything you miss about England?'

Neil slurps up the last of his spaghetti.

'Fireworks,' he says. 'Fireworks are illegal here.'

'Really?'

'Yeah. That's why you get all those firework factory places as you cross over the border into the North.'

'I've often wondered.' I put down my empty plate, and pick up my big bag of grass.

'But is there nothing else you miss?' I ask.

Neil pops a tinnie, and sucks at the foam as it bubbles up from the can.

'No, man. Just the fireworks.'

OOH! AAH!

For Netty and Jim's wedding night, no expense had been spared, and the sky over the Wye valley was lit up, as were most of the guests.

Well: it's not quite true to say that *no* expense had been spared, because they had hired me as the wedding entertainment. If *no* expense had been spared, they'd have persuaded Led Zep to do a one-off, or brought Elvis back from the dead. If *almost* no expense were to be spared, they might have hired Tony Bennett and his Orchestra to croon through a few wedding-night favourites. No, if you hire me to sing at your wedding, clearly you are going to be sparing quite a bit of expense, as my keyboard-playing partner Chas and I are 500 nicker all in, including petrol money. And we bring our own PA. We are called 'Your Dad'.

That part of the expense which had not been spared, then, rather than finding its way to my threadbare pocket, was going up in the sky. Our set had been timed to end as the fireworks were due to begin, and as we finished our ground-breaking version of The Archies' plangent and moving 1969 hit 'Sugar Sugar', the guests rushed out from the marquee without so much as a backwards glance to stare up into the night sky. Behind a roped-off area, the pyrotechnicians were preparing to launch their fusillade. All the wedding guests (and the wedding singer) craned their necks as several thousands of the bride and groom's pounds scintillated in the sky. The middle of nowhere is a wonderful spot from which to watch a fireworks display. And if the borderlands between Radnorshire and Herefordshire are not the middle of nowhere, then I don't know where is.

I've lived in Radnorshire, on and off, since 1987, and if there is one thing to which Radnorshire residents become used, it is darkness. There is hardly any light pollution, because very few people live there. It is the least populated part of Britain south of the Scottish Highlands, the eastern edge of the empty quarter of Wales which people call The Great Green Desert. Night here is black. You can walk in the Radnor Forest at night and be actually unable to see your hand in front of your face; or you might turn a particular corner on a particular mountain track, and see a twinkle of cottage windows from a tiny hamlet in the valley bottom, the few faraway lights serving only to deepen the darkness, to frame it. Driving through Radnorshire at night, you might go miles without meeting another car, even on our only arterial road, the thrice-blessed A44, which crosses the county on its way from Woodstock to Aberystwyth. The darkness in Radnorshire is perfect, complete, entire.

Since 1974, Radnorshire has been part of the administrative fiction that is Powys, and in such a huge county with so few people, the council are always looking to save money. Recently, they have started to turn off some of the streetlights in the little town where I live, so that the perfect darkness has found its way back down from the hills into the streets of Presteigne, which has become increasingly spectral. Night seeps into the alleys and squares, gathers around the tower of St Andrew's Church. Stare up into the sky, even in the middle of the town, and the stars are still bright.

So for a firework display, you can do no better than to stand on the English side of the Wye and look across into Radnorshire, and watch as the chrysanthemums and dahlias and peonies explode against that unbroken night. The wedding guests oohed and aahed (it is compulsory at a fireworks display). I suspected that the pyrotechnicians might not have set their roped-off area quite far enough away from the spectators, as a few hot sparks from spent incendiary devices rained down on my big baldy head, which somewhat marred my enjoyment. After the fireworks were done, a DJ fired up an improbably large sound system, proving that fireworks are all but impossible to follow. Perhaps if he'd been a proper wedding DJ, playing proper wedding music (e.g. ABBA, 'More More More' by Andrea True Connection, 'I'm Every Woman' by Chaka Khan etc.), then the post-fireworks wedding audience might actually have danced. But instead he was a DJ in the modern sense, which is to say he played 'records' which sounded like a five-year-old child operating a pocket calculator next to a dishwasher full of nuts, tied cruelly together by a moronic four on the floor beat. The DJ even employed a rapper, by far the worst I've ever witnessed. Nobody was dancing. The wedding guests stood around drinking and smoking, and Chas and I packed up our gear, pocketed our modest fee, and drove back through the Radnorshire night to Presteigne, the light from the fireworks burnt into my retina like a lurid migraine aura.

A week later, and once again I had been hired to 'entertain', this time at the Abergavenny Food Festival. The Abergavenny Food Festival is the Cannes of food festivals, as Juliet, the organiser's wife, asserted to me one year over a cup of Vietnamese latte. By day the streets of the characterful old town heave with visitors come to enjoy the staggering array of different taste sensations from all around the world (such as Vietnamese latte). By night, the festival is centered on the area around Abergavenny Castle. There is a geodesic dome for a couple of bands, a smaller bar stage where unplugged acts play, and a dozen or so carefully chosen food outlets. Even in the middle of September, Abergavenny Food Festival always seems to get lucky with the weather, so the thousand or so festival-goers who buy tickets for this 'Party at the Castle' sit around drinking, eating fabulous food and listening to music. Strings of lights festoon the site. It is gorgeous, perhaps my favourite festival site of all. I am hired to perform a number of functions: a bit of stand-up, a bit of compering, a bit of interviewing food writers and C-list celebrity chefs if need be. And once again, for the second week in a row, my bit was curtailed by a fireworks display. In order to bring home the difficulty of following fireworks, a dreary lo-fi nu-folk act were scheduled to come on after the display, which is as good a way as any of saying the show's over.

I stood with my great friend Pete Mustill, as the festival-goers oohed and aahed for the twenty-minute display.

'I fucking hate fireworks,' said Pete.

'How can anyone hate fireworks? What's to hate?'

'I dunno. They're just dull. I don't like the bangs. What's anyone supposed to get out of them? If the organisers had given me that money, I could have booked some really classy acts.' (Pete was the promoter for the night.)

The fireworks ended, and I introduced the nu-folkies, to no huge enthusiasm from the audience, who wanted to get back to their eating and drinking after the fireworks had finished. I went and found Pete.

'I fucking hate folk music,' I told him. 'I'd much rather have fireworks than folk music.'

'Then you are wrong,' said Pete.

But to judge from the oohing and aahing enthusiasm of the crowd during the fireworks, and from the way they were ordering crepes and earth-oven-baked pizza and Vietnamese latte and drinking at the bar during the nu-folkies act, I am far from alone in my estimation of the relative merits of fireworks and folk music as forms of entertainment. After all, thousands of people will go to a fireworks display, while only a few dozen beardy types will sit about in the pub supping real ale and listening to some twat bleat on about how he was forced to work down the mine when he was nine, even though his name is really Crispin, and far from being an ex-child miner, in actuality he's a cost accountant from Kettering.

Fireworks, as I'm attempting to argue, are the perfect end to a night, the crowning blazing glorious conclusion to any celebration. There is a line in Peter Brook's film of the Indian epic *The Mahabharata* about a king who dreams of his wife with 'a joyful explosion of seed', a line which always reminds me of fireworks, joyful explosions seeding the sky with hope against the gathering night.

Their origin is obscure, but the clever money would place the genesis of fireworks in China. Almost certainly gunpowder was discovered in China. At least three centuries before mineralogy even began to be systematised in Europe, the Chinese had an understanding of the subject sophisticated enough to know what happened when saltpetre, sulphur and charcoal were combined; and, what's more, they knew how to mine and refine these necessary substances. There is evidence that by the late tenth century the Chinese were encasing gunpowder in paper or bamboo tubes in order to make a loud report, so that evil spirits might be chased away, and further evidence that they were using rockets in warfare by not much more than a century later. Pre-modern Chinese warfare had a strange ritual aspect to it; there was a degree of shame attached to killing even during battle. Chinese warfare therefore became 'projectile-minded', as death could be detached from the person who was doing the actual killing. As ever, the Chinese seem startling in their modernity.

Whether gunpowder was transmitted to Europe from China, or whether it was discovered independently, is a tricky issue. There is some evidence, for example, that the Emperor Diocletian enjoyed pyrotechnic displays, though it's doubtful that they used 'black powder'; if they did, there's no evidence that the Romans used it in warfare, and its use disappeared utterly as the Roman Empire collapsed. There are no accounts of fireworks in Europe until after the Crusaders returned to Christendom; but whether gunpowder came down trade routes from China, or was a consequence of Arabic alchemical experimentation, it is now all but impossible to say. But we do know for sure that by the mid-sixteenth century, pyrotechnics formed a part of court celebrations; for example, in 1533 at the wedding of Henry VIII and Anne Boleyn, 'there went before the Lord Mayor's barge a foyst or wafter full of ordnance which foyst also carried a great red dragon that spouted out wild fire and round about were terrible and monstrous wild men casting fire and making a hideous noise'.

The Holy Roman Emperor Charles V brought fireworks under regulation in 1535; according to George Plimpton in his book on fireworks, this was because Charles was a timid man, who was scared of mice, and who also wanted to stop things going BANG around him and shredding his already jumpy nerves even further. In 1613, at the marriage of Frederick the Elector of the Palatinate and Princess Elizabeth of England, four of the King's gunners provided 'a fiery drama which included a dragon, a lady, St George, a conjurer and an enchanted castle'. Many books on fireworks were published in the seventeenth century, and it is possible to gain some impression of the effects they achieved. Nye, the master gunner of Worcester, in his *Art of Gunnery* from 1648 says that 'it is a rare thing to represent a tree or a fountain in the air'. The displays could have moral purpose: Casimir Simienowicz in *The Great Art of Artillery*, published in Germany in 1650 and deemed so important a publication that it was translated into English by order of the Board of Ordnance, wrote that 'Princes may be very reasonably reminded of the incertitude of prosperity by a sight of The Wheel of Fortune'.

From the middle of the seventeenth until the early twentieth century, fireworks would be attached to flammable façades, such as wooden castles, which would be festooned with roman candles and rockets. These 'fire-engines' would often be floated on rivers or lakes, for safety as much as for the spectacle of seeing them go up in flames at the end of the display. Alas, safety could on occasion be hard to achieve. Handel's 'Music For The Royal Fireworks' was composed for a great display in London in 1749, designed to mark the end of the War of Austrian Succession. Eleven thousand fireworks were fixed inside a giant machine, 410 feet long and 114 feet high. So complicated were the procedures to ignite this great display that many of the pyrotechnicians got themselves into a bit of a state. The chief pyrotechnician, Gaetano Ruggieri, drew his sword on one of his assistants, and was carted off to the Tower. One end of the machine exploded; one of the technicians fell off the infernal engine to his death; another fell into the water and was drowned. And far from being a spectacular display, 25 tons of fireworks simply didn't ignite. Of course, *Blue Peter* viewers know that they must never go back to an unexploded firework, but in those benighted days people didn't yet have Val, John and Peter to give them sensible advice. The Duke of Richmond bought up the unexploded shells, and presented them at a private entertainment three weeks later. The writer Horace Walpole, who was present, wrote that 'Whatever you hear of the fireworks, that is short of the prettiest entertainment in the world, don't believe it; I have never passed a more pleasant evening.' And Horace's dad was the first Prime Minister, so it just goes to show that Pete Mustill is utterly wrong, and that fireworks really are much more fun than folk music.

The colour scheme in 1749 was not what the punters at Jim and Netty's wedding would have seen. The predominant colour would have been amber, caused by adding iron filings to the black powder. From the 1830s onwards, the development of chemical engineering began to offer pyrotechnicians a wider colour palette. Red is created by adding lithium or strontium carbonate; orange by various calcium salts; yellow by compounds of sodium; green by barium chloride; and blue, which according to George Plimpton was the last colour to be added to the pyrotechnic palette, by compounds of copper. Electric white and silver are created by burning flakes of aluminium, titanium or magnesium. It's good to know, isn't it, that the earth's limited supply of minerals is being spent on prettification of the night sky?

And if the different colours are produced by changing the chemical composition of the black powder, the effects of the explosions are caused by the characteristics of the shell casings: the peonies and dahlias and chrysanthemums (this really is what pyrotechnicians call the various effects of the various casings) are produced by mechanical rather than chemical means.

If you like fireworks (and, apart from Pete Mustill, who doesn't?), then apparently Malta is the best place to go. The Maltese use any excuse for any number of stunning displays. If you like your fireworks very scary, then Crete is a top spot, because there they dispense with black powder and just get down to tossing sticks of dynamite about the hillsides. But if we're honest, it's our own traditions we like best, and in the predominantly Protestant parts of England, it's mostly on November the 5th that we light up the sky (though in multi-cultural parts of Britain you can see fireworks at Eid and Diwali too). We send up rockets in memory of the night that Guido Fawkes and the Gunpowder conspirators were caught trying to blow up the Houses of Parliament. Incredibly, the thirty-six barrels of gunpowder (amounting to some 1.6 metric tonnes of explosive) had been hidden in a vault beneath the House of Lords under piles of coal and faggots of wood since the previous March; the plotters had waited for exactly the right moment, when the King was due to open Parliament, before ordering Fawkes to light the blue touchpaper and retire.

However much we might sympathise with the plotters (and one likes to imagine that all one's readers are anarchists at heart), the discovery of the plot was one of those signposts on the road to democracy that still seem worth celebrating, 400 and more years later. And if you want to celebrate Guy Fawkes Night in style, with lots of fireworks and hardly any folk music at all, then there is really only one place to be; and that's Lewes, in East Sussex.

BONFIRE BHOYS

When I was a kid growing up in East Sussex, the history of fireworks and Bonfire Night and what it was all about was immediate and current. In school we learned about Guy Fawkes and the Gunpowder Plot, of course, but we also knew that the fifth of November was the date of King William III's landing in Brixham, the night of the Glorious Revolution, the night England was saved from the wicked Papist King James II. More than that, it was the night we remembered the poor Protestant martyrs, who had been burnt at the stake by the wicked Papist Bloody Mary. When Valerie Singleton and John Noakes warned us on *Blue Peter* to keep our pets in for Bonfire Night, we had already been locking them up for weeks. Because Bonfire comes early to East Sussex. In my hometown of Newhaven our Bonfire Night was usually in October. Our little house stood on a bank overlooking the main street, and my brother and I would stand in our front garden and watch as the Bonfire Boys marched in torchlight procession through the closed-off streets. Bonfire Night, you see, wasn't just about a couple of fireworks in the back garden around a few feeble burning sticks with a half-assed guy smouldering away on top. Oh no. Bonfire was a mighty celebration of the nights when England was saved from Popish plotting.

To say that the Bonfire Boys wore fancy dress is like saying the Bullingdon Club get a bit smartened up for dinner. Every year, hundreds of characterful guisers paraded past our house accompanied by marching bands, including the band of the Newhaven Air Cadets, with whom we were all too familiar since they practised in our next-door neighbours' back garden. There were sumptuous Tudors, be-feathered Red Indians, and fearsome Vikings; most startling of all (and the least PC) were the Zulus, twenty or so earnest promenaders dressed in full Zulu battle rig, blacked up to the nines. They all held aloft their blazing torches, which were dropped into the gutter as they were spent, and replaced by marshals dressed as smugglers who hauled carts of new torches which were lit from the dying flames of the old. After the Torchlight Procession had passed, we would go with our mum and Old Feller down to Lewes Road Rec to see the actual Bonfire and watch the actual fireworks, while the bands played and the Bonfire Boys mingled with those of us who were merely standers-by.

As we got older, we learned more. Only a few of the Bonfire Boys were from Newhaven. Most of them came from other Sussex towns, as each town had its own Bonfire Society of Bonfire Boys, and each town had its own Bonfire parade, on different nights throughout the autumn. They had all come to Newhaven for our Bonfire Night, and then our Bonfire Boys went to theirs. The only exception was Lewes. Lewes didn't have *a* Bonfire society: it had seven. This was because the big bonfire, the Mother of all Bonfires, was in Lewes itself, on the night of the fifth of November. All the other parades were merely preludes to the big event.

As we got older still, we no longer went down to Lewes Road Rec with our mums and dads; we followed the procession and picked up guttering torches to hold them aloft for the few minutes' life they had left; we lit bangers and jumping jacks, and threw them at the feet of the watching crowds. Some of us who were really keen went and joined the Bonfire societies themselves; my pal Steve, who I walked with to school most mornings, was one such. As we grew through our teenage years, Steve would turn up at our house every Thursday night to collect waste newspaper, the first time I'd ever encountered recycling. The money that Newhaven Bonfire society raised from the sale of waste newspaper went towards the cost of staging our Bonfire celebrations; the procession used hundreds of torches, and fireworks don't come cheap. Sometimes Steve would talk to us about Bonfire on the way to school. He told us about *Foxe's Book of Martyrs*, which was compulsory reading for anyone who was serious about their bonfire. It recounted the stories of those Protestant martyrs that Bloody Mary had burnt. She was a bad lot, that Mary; so much every East Sussex child knows to a greater or lesser extent.

When in 1976 I moved away to go to university in the small mid-Wales town of Lampeter, I could no longer go to the Torchlight Procession, but when I moved back to Brighton in 1979 I made sure that I always visited my folks on Newhaven Bonfire Night. Never being quite as bonkers as a full-on Bonfire

Boy (at least half of the Boys are girls, I should perhaps make plain), I never fancied going up to Lewes for the fifth; but I never missed a night in Newhaven. After my daughter Charley was born, I always used to take her and her mother with me, and Charley would squeal as the marchers came by, hold her ears at the bands, and hide in my shoulder as the fireworks exploded. I was proud to show her off to those of my old school friends who would be lining the streets or marching with the Bonfire Boys; and proud to show Charley this part of my culture, something that was unique to my little part of the world.

On Saturday 13 October 1984, I took Charley to Newhaven Bonfire as usual. Her mother was working away, in Japan, but Charley and I took our place standing in a crush by the road-side, watching as the Tudors and Vikings and Zulus paraded past by torchlight. And suddenly, with a flash of incredulous horror, I finally understood what Bonfire was about. All the Bonfire societies hold up banners, so that the spectators can tell where they are from. On that night, I understood why the Cliffe Bonfire Society from Lewes had 'No Popery' written on their banner; and why another banner said 'Our Cause Is Just And Shall Prevail'. Suddenly, I understood it all. I understood what 'the cause' was, and against whom it was destined to prevail.

In the early hours of Friday 12 October 1984, I'd been at home in Brighton with Charley when I heard a muffled 'whump' from the direction of the seafront. I went into our back yard; and although this may be a false memory, I swear I could see a brightness in the sky somewhere between the two piers. And then the Brighton night was full of sirens. Something had happened, that much was clear, but in those days before rolling news and the interweb, it was impossible to find out what, unless I went down to the seafront to find out for myself, which I clearly wasn't going to do with a toddler sleeping upstairs.

Oh well, I thought. Perhaps I'll find out tomorrow.

Which, of course, I did. The IRA had bombed the Grand Hotel on Brighton seafront, a wedding cake of a hotel where most of the Tory cabinet had been staying, as the Conservatives were in conference in town that week. And now, the next night, I was watching the Bonfire parade in Newhaven, and understanding it, really for the first time. It was sectarian, straightforwardly so. King Billy landing in Brixham, or Guy Fawkes being thwarted in his attempt to blow up Parliament, were not necessarily occasions of great joy for Catholics.

I had stood by for much of my childhood and applauded and cheered as the Bonfire Boys carried an effigy of the Pope past our house, and cheered as he was thrown onto the Bonfire with Fawkes. Now I understood what the marching was all about. The IRA had brought the Troubles to East Sussex, but maybe they had been there all along. I had no Catholic friends. There might well have been a Catholic population in my part of the world, but where they lived, or went to school, I really had no idea. The darkness of Bonfire had been there for me to see all along (and, after all, I had studied seventeenth-century history at school), but I had been blinded to it, or had somehow ignored it.

I never took Charley to the Torchlight Procession again. A few years later, Newhaven Bonfire lost its organisers, and the thing petered out.

Over the intervening years, I lived all over the UK. For eleven years I lived in Lancaster. Lancashire was the part of England least enthusiastic about the Protestant Reformation. There were reputed to be villages in the Forest of Bowland which had never even pretended to convert. The great Catholic public school, Stoneyhurst, hidden in the Lancashire hills, was one place where Bonfire Night was never celebrated, even though it was illegal not to keep Guy Fawkes Night right up until 1959. So Bonfire Night in Lancaster always struck me as an actual damp squib. Although you might very occasionally see kids collecting their 'penny for the Guy', the night itself was anti-climactic. It was known as Fireworks Night, and there was usually a not terribly impressive display over Lancaster Castle. To a Sussex boy, even one who had become shocked by the nature of Bonfire Night celebrations, it was all a bit tame. The traditional *Blue Peter* warning about keeping your pets indoors hardly seemed fair on my old cat, who regularly went out on the fifth to carry on his traditional activities of catching rare migrant birds and shitting in the neighbours' flower pots. But living in a largely Catholic area did mean that I got to date a couple of Catholic girls, who were horrified by my ignorance about Catholics in Sussex.

'How do you think it feels?' said one. 'How would you like it if you lived in France and they held a big festival celebrating the St Bartholomew's Day Massacre?' (Marchant is reputed to be a Huguenot name.)

'Er . . . I'm not sure it's quite the same thing . . .' I said.

Nor is it. Guy Fawkes and James II really did try to do for our nascent democracy, and Mary I really did burn a lot of Prots at the stake. The Glorious Revolution still seems like something worth celebrating, though perhaps it is time to do away with some of the sectarian stuff.

So in 2008, I decided that I wanted to go to a proper bonfire, for the first time since that night in 1984. And Bonfire does not get more proper than Lewes.

I had arranged to meet a couple of writer friends outside Lewes station, the poet Catherine Smith and the novelist Monique Roffey. Catherine lives in Lewes and had arranged for us to go to a party in a flat overlooking the High Street.

'You really don't want to be standing down on the street,' said Catherine. 'It can get really scary. You'll be able to see everything from up in the flat, but you won't get bangers dropped on your feet.'

Monique had been the year before with Catherine, to another party in another flat.

'It's the scariest thing I've ever seen; much scarier than *jouve* at Trinidad Carnival.' *Jouve* is the dark heart of carnival, a night of thinly veiled voodoo excess, which even Trinidadian Monique finds hair-raising. But Monique might be expected to find Lewes Bonfire Night scary, because Monique is a Catholic. The two of them, one local and one left-footer, would make good guides to England's greatest anti-Catholic festival.

Outside the station, even at four in the afternoon, Bonfire was already under way. Sussex Police, and even the Lewes Bonfire societies, urge outsiders to stay away from Lewes on the great night. It is for Lewes people, not really for spectators from outside the town. But of course they come. Twelve thousand people are estimated to line the streets of Lewes during the parades and marches. Lewes, as I've said, has seven separate

Bonfire societies, representatives of the biggest of which stood outside the station selling programmes and tickets to the fireworks displays which end the night. Seven bonfires, and seven huge firework displays, and the societies vie for the greatest number of spectators.

Catherine took us to The John Harvey for a pre-Bonfire drink. Walking through town, we could already see lots of people in their fancy dress; not so much the Zulus, but plenty of Tudors, and lots and lots of smugglers. The smuggler costume is the most common, and common to all the societies. Each of the Lewes Bonfire societies wear a different-coloured striped sweater with white trousers and red caps; so that, for example, the Cliffe Society wear black and white striped sweaters, Lewes Borough wear blue and white, Commercial Square wear black and gold, and so on. Although the Boys in fancy dress (the 'Pioneers') are the most spectacular, it's the smugglers who seem to have the most fun, dropping endless fire crackers at the spectators' feet. As we stood drinking outside The John Harvey, the smugglers were already starting to set off . . . well, really rather terrifying bangs. My heart rate was starting to climb. This was not a place to come for a relaxed drink. I pointed out to Monique and Catherine a mini-bus parked up in the corner of the pub car park; a banner on its side proclaimed that it had brought a contingent from one of the Glasgow Orange Lodges.

Catherine announced that the time had come to make our way up into the town. It was 5 p.m., and the streets were being taken over by smugglers and cavaliers; the streets were owned by what Adam Ant would have been happy to call dandy highwaymen, since some of them were dressed as dandy highwaymen.

A couple dressed as Mongol tribesmen wandered past, pushing a buggy containing a sleeping baby Mongol wrapped in blankets.

'You don't see that every day,' said Catherine.

'Except perhaps in Ulan Bator,' I said.

The first of the processions happens in darkness; no torches are lit, and no music other than a muffled drum is played. At the culmination of this first procession, (or rather processions, because at this stage all the societies are processing independently), wreaths are laid at the War Memorial, to commemorate the thirteen Marian martyrs who were burnt outside The Star Inn.

'Lots of Catholics were burnt too,' said Monique.

'I know. But here in Lewes, it was the Prots who got torched. You can't blame people for wanting to commemorate their own local atrocity . . .' I said.

'It was a local atrocity for local people,' Catherine pointed out helpfully.

The societies started to arrive; one by one, they laid their wreaths and said their prayers for the martyred dead. The bands were all silent, except for one muffled drum each.

'It's quite dull, this bit,' said Catherine.

'Don't be cynical. It's very moving . . .' I said.

'Can't we go to the party?' asked Monique.

Catherine agreed, as she is a woman who is much keener on drinking white wine than bowing her head in prayer. We found the entrance down a small side alley, and climbed three flights of steps to the flat where the party was being held. Although the processions had not begun in earnest, window space was at a premium. Guests were kneeling by the windows, and standing, jostling for position, peering over one another's shoulders. I pulled rank. For some odd reason, people admire writers, and see writing as a noble trade. Perhaps it's the fact that we don't earn much money. Perhaps people accord us relatively high status because they see us as monkish figures who have sacrificed nonsense like a regular income for our vocation. Luckily, few of them realise that most writers do it because no one has ever seen fit to give them a proper job. Whatever the reason, when Catherine told our hostess Bobbi that I was writing a book, and that one of the chapters was going to be devoted to Lewes Bonfire, Bobbi made sure that I was propped up in one of the corners of the window and given a nice big glass of something. The pavements were packed; I could hear the first of the bands starting to play; I looked down the High Street to see the glow from the newly lit torches coming up the hill. Lewes' annual night of madness was about to begin in earnest.

'The villagers are coming,' I said, for that was how it looked, as hundreds of marchers came over the brow of the hill; just as though we were locked in Dracula's castle, and the very unhappy Transylvanian peasants were coming to torch us. A river of fire, torches held high, came by the window of the flat, carried by a huge cast of characters. There were scary clowns, Scottish high-landers, WWII soldiers, soldiers from the Boer War, Napoleonic soldiers and US Civil War soldiers, from both sides, both infantry and cavalry. There was a large group of Nelson's sailors, holding a banner saying 'England Expects'. There were countless smugglers, dropping fireworks at the feet of the crowd; the sound of the marching bands was punctuated by great explosions. Some of the smugglers (and, as I said, it always seemed to be the smugglers who were having the most fun) carried large structures covered in hundreds of firecrackers, which they would stop and ignite with a thunderous crackling roar, the smugglers carrying them looking as though they were drowning in fire.

The Cliffe Bonfire Society marched past, their banner saying 'No Popery', followed by dozens of highly authentic-looking Vikings, who I guess would have been opposed to Christianity in *all* its forms if they were off burning and pillaging and looting, as opposed to marching through the streets of Lewes. The Cliffe had a New Orleans marching band in their train, playing 'O When The Saints' to the percussive accompaniment of a thousand bangers and fire crackers, followed by more smugglers, dozens of them, some of them towing blazing tar barrels on a small cart. There were Mongolians (two of them still pushing their baby buggy) carrying aloft flaming crosses.

'Don't they know that only bad guys carry flaming crosses?' said Monique.

'I don't think they are actually going to lynch anybody,' I said.

'But still . . . it's the principle of the thing.'

There were Roman legionnaires, and Beefeaters, and firemen, and a group in medieval finery, and another lot of Boer War soldiers.

'It's like when you're a kid,' I said, 'and you play soldiers with lots of different armies . . .'

'Girls don't really play with soldiers,' said Monique.

'Unless you grew up in Colchester,' said Catherine.

'No, but it is. Say you've got a group of medieval archers, and some Romans, and some Napoleonic horsemen and some First World War Americans, and a load of Nazis. When you're a lad, you don't really discriminate about who goes where with who. You just lump them all in together, and get them fighting.'

'How do the archers do against the Nazis?' asked Catherine.

'Not always terribly well,' I admitted.

'Ooh look,' said Monique. 'It's the Aztecs of Burgess Hill.'

And so it was. Dozens of resplendent Aztecs were marching behind a banner proclaiming them as the Burgess Hill Bonfire Society, their head-dresses looking eerily authentic by torchlight. It was easy to imagine them carving out human hearts and holding them up dripping and hot for the approval of their fierce gods.

Then there were cowboys, and devils, and some Japanese ladies in kimonos hobbling along, trying to keep the sparks from their torches away from their costumes. And then more tar barrels. There was a group of drop-dead gorgeous lady pirates, and a contingent of Benedictine monks holding up a banner commemorating 'The Landing of Prince William of Orange', and a smuggler holding up two burning torches with a sleeping baby strapped to his chest.

There was a group dressed as Myrmidons pushing a large Trojan horse covered in firecrackers, clearly waiting for the moment to spark them off. There was a troupe of morris dancers, with bells on their knees.

'Boo!' I shouted down from the window. 'Burn them!'

'You're supposed to shout that at the Pope,' said Catherine.

'Yes, I know, but I thought I'd make a special exception for morris dancers.'

And then the Red Indians, with flamboyant feathered head-dresses, as high as their wearers. They carried a huge totem pole, covered in firecrackers. The parade stopped with them right outside the flat, so that the totem pole could be ignited, crackling and exploding in a million snapping sparks, some of which came through the flat window and fell onto the carpet. We stamped on the embers.

And then the Zulus, of blessed childhood memory, with a band playing 'Who Do You Think You Are Kidding Mr Hitler?', the implication being, I suppose, that if we'd had a few more Zulu warriors in blackface, Adolf wouldn't have thought about invading for one moment.

And then an effigy of Gordon Brown and Alistair Darling, as Laurel and Hardy, and an effigy of Guy Fawkes. 'Burn them!' shouted the crowd. And then a group dressed as clergy – archbishops, bishops, vicars – and behind them, carried by more monks, the effigy of the Pope.

Burn him burn him shouted the crowd.

Burn him burn him shouted everybody in the flat, including Monique. I looked at her. She shrugged.

'Eh, he's no John XXIII.'

'I think they still burnt John XXIII,' I said. 'I mean, I don't think they went, oh, Vatican 2 is great. We're all for the vernacular Mass; we'll not burn this particular Pope.'

'Shut up,' said Monique.

And that was that, except for some smugglers dragging carts and picking up spent torches; or it would have been, if they had not turned around and started the whole thing over again. And then again. The whole mad scary pagan pageant came past the window three times in all, by which time it was half-nine, and Catherine declared that we should go and look at some fireworks.

'We'll go to the South Street Bonfire, because it's free.'

So we left the flat, and fought our way through the throngs of people making their way to the bonfires, all seven of them. The various societies split off from the Grand Parade, and processed to their various bonfires. We took a short cut down by the river, and arrived at the site of the massive South Street Bonfire just as the South Street Bonfire Society march did.

'It's only a small one, this,' said Catherine. 'The really big ones are the Cliffe, or Waterloo Square.' But still the South Street Bonfire was huge, like a three-storied building, with a massive Guy on top, and when it was lit we could feel its heat from 200 metres away.

And then, all over Lewes, the pyrotechnics started to bloom. The sky was alight with far from standard fireworks; and, as we left the huge bonfire and walked back up through the town, they continued to flare. We would stop and look down a narrow street, or peer through a gap in the houses, to watch as another batch of fireworks was launched from the various bonfire sites on the flood plains that surround Lewes.

We stopped at a pub for a last drink (a concept that Catherine finds hard to grasp: 'Don't worry,' she said, 'we can have another bottle when we get back to mine'). When we came out of the pub it was gone eleven, and we were just in time to see the last parade of the night, consisting of the archbishop, the bishops and the various clergy marching through the back streets by torchlight. The effigy of the Pope they had carried earlier had now been burnt.

'What do you think, Mon?' I asked. 'Of all this?'

'Well, it's still scary. It's still sectarian; but it's also quite funny.'

'I think my neighbours would be upset if they thought they'd really scared any Catholics,' said Catherine. As we arrived in Catherine's street, her neighbour, dressed in full Red Indian kit, was opening his gate.

'Hello, Dave,' said Catherine. 'Had a good night?'

'Yes thanks, Cath,' said the chief Dave. 'Best night of the year, as always.'

I write these final words a year to the day after I was in Lewes. It is November the 5th, and I'm in Holywood, just outside Belfast. Here, sectarianism isn't any kind of joke. You couldn't cheerfully call for the burning of the Pope without sparking off a lot of very real burning in return. So, Guy Fawkes Night is silent. There are next to no fireworks, no bonfires. The Troubles which came to Brighton have largely gone from here. It is quiet, and peaceful, albeit at times a guarded peace.

And for this night only, I wish I were in Lewes. I wish I was a smuggler, throwing firecrackers at the spectators' feet. I wish I could walk down the street, with a flaming torch, and shout 'Burn him! Burn him!' at an effigy of the Pope.

Just in fun, you understand.

SHE'S ABOUT A MOVER

I've put the kettle on, and have come outside Neil's place to play with Billy while the tea is making. I get a couple of CDs out of the car. I don't know what they are; the interior light broke months back. I hold them up to the light from the kitchen window, and I am no wiser, not really, because they are lovingly hand-crafted-by-me playlists, what we used to call mixtapes, with nothing written on them. They are damp with condensation. I take them through into the sitting room, where Neil is stuffing logs into the wood-burner.

'This is some stuff I had in the car,' I say. 'If I give it a bit of a wipe, do you fancy seeing what it is?'

'Don't you know?' says Neil.

'No. It's just a few things I burnt off my computer. I've no idea at all what's on 'em . . .'

'Alright. Give it here.'

I rub the first CD on my fleece, and hand it to Neil, who slots it into his laptop. I don't know what's coming. Neil presses PLAY.

'Oh wow,' I say to the first track.

'What's this?' says Neil.

'You don't know this? This is "She's About a Mover", by The Sir Douglas Quintet.'

'Never heard of them,' says Neil.

'I'm shocked. It's what they call "Tex–Mex". From Texas. And, er, Mexico. The borders, anyway . . .'

'It rocks.' Neil is right; it certainly does.

'My brother lives in Texas,' says Neil.

'Oh yeah?'

'Right out in the sticks.'

'Further out than here? Than Presteigne?'

'Much further. Funny place, America.'

'The States is odd,' I agree.

'I mean, great music,' says Neil.

'Brilliant. Better even than you expect. But . . .' I shrug.

'This is brilliant. Who is this again?'

'Sir Douglas Quintet. From 1965, the year it was illegal to make a bad record.'

I'm in a very good mood. This is the first spliff I've had for about six weeks. And any compilation CD that kicks off with The Sir Douglas Quintet is surely going to be a good thing. This is made clearer still as the second song starts. I cackle with joy.

'What's this?' asks Neil.

'You don't know this?' Neil is winding me up.

'No.' No, I don't think he is.

This is 'I'm So Proud' by The Impressions. Not knowing this shows the terrible damage that playing 'The Fields of Athenry' your whole life can do to a man. I stare at Neil, unable quite to understand that somebody could have lived to the age of fifty-three and not heard 'I'm So Proud' by The Impressions.

'Perhaps you know the Todd Rundgren version . . .' I suggest, trying to be helpful.

'I don't really know his stuff either.'

'Oh, for goodness' sake . . .'

And then track three.

'Oh, I know this . . .' says Neil.

'Go on then,' I say. We are now playing 'Guess The Intro'.

'Bryan Ferry?' says Neil.

'Well, yes. Roxy Music. This is the second single. It's called "Pyjamarama".'

'Naah. Not so sure about this. Little girls' commercial pop music.'

I am blinded with rage.

'This? This was about the most exciting British band of its time.'

'Yeah? Doesn't do it for me. I never did like pop music, especially all stuff like this. Girls' music.'

'Of course it was girls' music in 1973. All great music is girls' music. Pop music is designed for teenage girls; that's why they're usually the best judges of what's interesting.'

'It's commercial. Manufactured. Not authentic.'

'What? Are you nuts?'

Neil pops another tinnie, while I am left to reflect. I know I'm right; that everything that is ultimately great about pop music has its heart in the hearts of teenage girls. I thought of the girls at my school, from my class: Lesley playing *A Thousand Volts of Holt* at the Youth Club; Mary making me listen to

Transformer in her bedroom; Jackie Sinclair carrying *The Slider* under her arm, Marc nestling against her tits where I should be; and Janet and Julie playing us the first Roxy album, over and over, until we got it. And how my mates were listening to Zep, Purple, Heep, Quo, Floyd etc. And how time has proved that the girls were spot on. And that pop music (and teenage girls) are about dancing, parties, laughter, fun, playfulness and joy; and angst, misery, loneliness and uncertainty: and that pop music is therefore a thing of the night.

It was always about the night. There is only one great day band that I can think of, and that's The Beach Boys. You might well argue that since The Beach Boys are probably the greatest pop band ever, their day-nature disproves my theory. Au contraire. I would argue that The Beach Boys, in this as in so much else, are the exception that proves the rule. You might also argue that The Beatles made their name at those lunchtime Cavern sessions. But they learned their chops playing all-nighters in Hamburg, pumped up on purple hearts and belting out 'The Sheik of Araby'. It's about the night.*

At my great age, you begin to wonder if and when pop music will ever leave you. I've tried to make it go away. Every so often I buy classical music CDs, feeling that it's the right thing to do, but I find them deathly dull, the music you listen to while you are waiting in a phone queue. A great-aunt of Charley's once interrogated me about my music taste; I would

---

* 'The ear, the organ of fear, could have evolved as greatly as it has only in the night and twilight of obscure caves and woods, in accordance with the mode of life of the age of timidity, that is to say the longest human age there has ever been: in bright daylight the ear is less necessary. That is how music acquired the character of an art of night and twilight.' Friedrich Nietzsche, *Dawn*.

have been twenty-one or so, and I tried to come up with a useful list.

'Oh . . . The Clash. Elvis Costello. Marvin Gaye . . .'

She blew through pursed lips with undisguised contempt.

'Poof. One day you will like real music. Like Webern. Alban Berg. Schoenberg.'

I felt deeply ashamed, but I am still waiting for the day.

Perhaps it's the power of those teenage nights when music first started to speak to me. I remember Boxing Day 1967, when I was allowed to put on my pyjamas to stay up and watch *Magical Mystery Tour*. I was too young to understand that it was a car-crash of a film; I just loved the music. And I loved The Beatles' faces as they sat in the dark of a nightclub and watched the stripper. One day, I resolved, I too will grow my hair, maybe even a beard, and watch strippers. I saved my pocket money and went to Noise, the little record shop in Newhaven which I was to haunt for years to come, and bought the double EP, the first record I ever bought for myself.

Or, in pyjamas again, allowed to sit up as late as I liked by candlelight during the pristine unspoiled darkness of the Three Day Week, listening to John Peel on a battery-operated radio as he advocated Iggy and Captain Beefheart and the New York Dolls, nursing a mug of Ovaltine, looking out over the darkened town and dreaming of escape and nights bright with adventure.

Or wobbling on platform heels on a spring night with my mates down to Newhaven Fair, and hearing 'Starman' belting out from the tinny speakers of the bumper cars, and thinking that was the best, the only way to hear it; that hi-fi might be great for your Beethovens and Weberns, but that you couldn't beat a few shit old speakers on the side of a bumper-car ride if you wanted to hear Bowie at his truest. I still think this; although I hate going on rides, I love wandering about fairgrounds at night because I love the way the music sounds.

Or teenage parties somewhere in the mean suburban streets of Peacehaven, parents persuaded into Brighton for the night, so that we could dance to 'Hi Hi Hi' and 'Suffragette City' and 'Voulez-Vous Coucher Avec Moi', longing for the moment when I would get a snog from Jackie Sinclair, her breath Dubonnet and Consulate and cheese and onion crisps (not that it would mean anything, because Jackie was kind, and made sure that all the boys at the party got a bit of action, which meant that the wait was an agony of expectation and jealousy).

Or night after night after night, up in my room, having told my parents that I was doing my homework, standing in front of my mirror with an upturned golf club for a mike stand, singing along to Tim Buckley or Van Morrison, trying to learn how to be a rock star, and watching myself as I did so, and dreaming of all the bands I would front, and of Jackie Sinclair's eyes shining with pride and desire, waiting for me in the wings as I ran off stage at the end of the gig.

I have played in bands, in a pretty much unbroken line, since I was fourteen. Hundreds, maybe thousands, of my nights have been spent onstage, in pubs and bars or inside tents at festivals.

I started in my bedroom, with my pal Dave on guitar, and another pal pounding the doors of my wardrobe in approximate time to Dave's three chords; we sacked him after the door fell off, and recruited our other pal Dave, whose dad had died, and whose mum spoiled him, and had bought him a bass.

Back in the day, when you started learning to play guitar, you started by playing 'Wild Thing'. Perhaps you still do. 'Wild Thing' is the only thing of any kind I can play on the guitar. This doesn't really matter, because I'm a singer.

'Wild Thing' goes like this:

Ay Dee, Ee Dee, Ay Dee, Eee Dee, Ay Dee, Ee Dee, Ay Dee Ee Dee . . .

Gee Ay Gee Ay! (stop)

Gee Ay Gee Ay! (stop)

Ay Dee, Ee Dee . . . (etc.)

It's very easy. It's based on 'Louie Louie', the Ur-riff of rock and roll, which is even simpler, because it uses Ee Minor instead of the more complicated Ee Major, and which dispenses with the Gee Ay middle bit. Everyone in the mid-60s was rewriting 'Louie Louie', but 'Wild Thing' is still the best-known 'Louie Louie' clone. It's by an American songwriter called Chip Taylor, who also wrote a song called 'Angel of the Morning'. My occasional alt-country band, Little Dolly Daydream, still plays 'Angel of the Morning', so I've been singing Chip Taylor songs for thirty-five years, because my bedroom band played 'Wild Thing'.*

That band was called Ruby Crystal and the Diamonds. I was Ruby Crystal, because I was the singer. My two mates Dave were on guitar and bass respectively. We found a drummer called Glen, and went electric, and moved our rehearsals to a

---

* The odd thing is, I didn't know this till just now when I looked it up. I thought 'Wild Thing' was written by Reg Presley of The Troggs. The Troggs had the first hit with 'Wild Thing', and theirs is still the definitive version. Lucky I checked my facts.

room in the Youth Club. Glen was the lead drummer in the Air Cadets band, so although he wasn't a bad drummer, he looked like a twat. He had a short back and sides, and wore straight trousers. We were cool; our hair was long, and our flares were wide. In July 1974 we were allowed to play at the Fifth Form Leaving Disco. It was our first gig. Bass Dave's mum collected our stuff from the Youth Club, and drove it up to the school. We set up on the stage next to the Stardust Mobile Disco, who had crushed velvet flares, and looked a lot like Jesus, as men did in those days.

'Alright, lads? Whaddya called?'

'Ruby Crystal and the Diamonds.'

'How long you playing for?'

'About ten minutes . . .'

Stardust Mobile Disco had a new sound-to-light box. We stood outside in the darkness, watching the lights flash behind the ill-fitting blackout curtains of the school hall in time to 'Rock the Boat' by The Hues Corporation, and such like. We were pumped up with nerves; 250 of our contemporaries and lots of our teachers were bopping round the hall, hoping we might forget to come on.

Nobody was much looking forward to our set, except us. We were looking forward to it because a) we'd been practising for two years and b) we felt that we were pretty much guaranteed a tit-rub, since the girls would see us as, if not exactly rock stars, then at least rock stars manqué, and therefore of relatively high status within the school. There was a girl called Mandy whose bra I considered that I had a moderate to high chance of exploring. She was no Jackie Sinclair, but what the hey.

Deciding on our set had been easy even though we all liked different things. Dave the guitarist liked Steely Dan. Dave the bass player liked Free. I liked Van Morrison. Glen the drummer liked the theme from *The Battle of Britain* played by the Band of The Royal Air Force. But it didn't much matter what we liked, because after two years all we could play was a 12-bar blues jam and 'Wild Thing'.

So our set list looked like this:

1) 'Blues Jam'

2) 'Wild Thing'

In 'Blues Jam' the Diamonds played a crude 12-bar structure while I sang humorous lyrics about our teachers over the top. In 'Wild Thing', when the Gee Ay Gee Ay bit came in, and the lyrics go 'Wild Thing, I think I love you', I would sing the words and pretend to bum Dave the bass player. It was hilarious, though I guess you had to be there.

The gig went gratifyingly well, somewhat anti-climactically for the purposes of this story. I liked the sound of my voice through the Stardust Mobile Disco's speakers. The Daves were mostly in tune. Glen had been coaxed into a pair of flared jeans for the evening. The girls all pretended to go crazy. Mandy smiled at me as I screamed at the end of 'Wild Thing'. My heart sang, and everythang looked groovy. The tit-rub was a cert.

Afterwards, I took Mandy outside the school hall. It was a warm night, and we sat together on a wall by the playground. And there, for an hour, perhaps more, I explained to Mandy why I was a Communist. I wasn't a Communist; I wanted to be a rock star, and therefore obscenely rich. But for some unknown reason, I told her that I was a Communist, and I explained my reasons at great length. I was nervous, I guess. Perhaps I hoped she'd make some connection between 'red' and 'bed'. She was much too polite to stop listening to my crap. I cannot remember her opening her mouth once, certainly not for the snog which should have gone before any putative tit-rub. The next day, she told Glen our twat drummer that I was really boring, and that pretending to bum your friend during 'Wild Thing' was childish and stupid.

And you can't argue with that.

But I found out an important thing about my life as a performer. After a show, I'm really dull. I wouldn't throw the TV out of the hotel bedroom, because I'd want to watch it; ideally something along the lines of *A Touch of Frost* or *Midsomer Murders*. I'd like to drink a nice pot of tea, and smoke a couple of spliffs. Then I'd like to sleep.

As the years spun by, and the line-ups and the fashion and the bands all changed, this remained constant. As soon as we came off stage, I turned into a 53-year-old who liked to drink hot chocolate and read *The Spectator*, which is fine now, because I am, and I do. But it was annoying when I was twenty-two and full of vim the rest of the time.

Now I still do gigs, mostly with top light-entertainment duo Your Dad. We played at Netty and Jim's wedding as the fireworks turned the Radnorshire night polychromatic, if you remember. My partner is called Chas, and he is twelve years older than me. This means, at the time of writing, that he is sixty-five. After a gig, it is as though he were still seventeen. He wants a party. He wants booze. He wants drugs, and not just a bit of spliff. He wants MDMA, designer psychedelics, anything he can get to burn off his post-gig energy. He wants to dance! He wants to talk to girls!

But I don't. We have a deal; he can have fun for half an hour, before we go home, while I deal with earnest men who like to talk about the songs of Burt Bacharach; men very like me, at least the me that takes over after a gig. By far my favourite part of playing gigs these days is the journey home, banged up in an Astra Estate from before the dawn of time with Chas, him pissed yet voluble, skinning up in the passenger seat, me driving through silent streets with him nattering on about long-lost 70s anarchist groups and his first spliff after a gig with Engelbert Humperdinck's backing band, and how he had a curry with astrologer Jonathan Cainer. And, if we're lucky, stopping at a van for a bacon bun, before levering myself into bed as dawn pinks the sky.

This means that, for much of my life, nights out have often been quite dull for me. I've been a daddy since I was twenty-one, and never successful enough to employ a nanny to look after the kids. If I went out at night, mostly it was to sing. And, although I loved the gigs themselves, afterwards I was Mr Anti-Climax. So, although I did have wild nights, it was when I wasn't playing. And I played lots of nights.

I have missed out.

I can dance. Trust me; I dance real good. I dance so good that I don't embarrass my daughters if we are at a family wedding or something, when I get up to shake my not-inconsiderable thang. And if I get lucky, and the DJ plays a few disco classics, I love to get out on the dancefloor, and express myself. It's just that I feel there haven't been enough of these dancing nights.

And I blame my daughters Charley and Minnie and my post-feminist baby mothers, who wouldn't let me go out, given that I'd already been out three nights that week and only earned thirty quid.

So, it seemed only appropriate that I make my daughters take me out to a nightclub. After all, the last time I could really just go out whenever I wanted without wanting to drink hot chocolate and read *The Spectator* was before Charley was born, in 1979, when I was at Lampeter, and could show off my moves to the sound of The Bee Gees at the Student Union Disco. This is what I want to recapture, thirty years later.

I told Minnie and Charley of my wishes when they were both visiting me for Easter. Charley pointed out that since she was no longer a student, she would be unable to accommodate me, but that Minnie was very much a student, and one who likes to partay, at that. It's not often that my younger daughter Minnie gets down on her knees and begs me not to do something, but my announcement that she had to take me to a Student Disco at her university sparked just this thing.

'Please, Dad. I'll do anything. Anything. But just please don't make me do this.'

Charley, my elder daughter, thought it was a very funny idea, and told Minnie not to be a wuss.

'Daddy needs to do it. I'll come too.'

'But why me? Why am I being picked on like this?'

'Because you're the only student I know who owes me big time . . .'

And so it was arranged that Charley and I should visit Min towards the end of the summer term of her first year, so that we could both go to a Student Disco.

'And stop calling it that,' said a defeated Min. 'It's called Club Night.'

Even before I set off, I faced a massive dilemma. What to wear? It was no part of my intention to actively embarrass Min. I didn't mind if that was a by-product of the evening, but I didn't mean to set out to cause as much embarrassment as possible. Luckily, a well-judged visit to the Boden website a few years back had seen me acquire two identical shirts in a bold yet slimming vertical stripe. I rather fancy myself in these shirts; they make me look stylish, and yet at the same time fifty-ish. They have, in my view, become something of a trademark; I've lost count of the number of gigs I've done over the last six years wearing them. One of my signature shirts, then, with a pair of comfy-fit jeans and a casual jacket, which although it smells a bit of cat piss despite several trips to the dry cleaners, should enable me to hold my own in the scrum of the Lower Common Room. I packed my bag and hit the road, with some carefully selected CDs for company; the very CDs, I now realise, sitting in Neil's front room, that we are listening to tonight.

Because Charley was staying in Minnie's room, I'd booked myself into a hotel in the centre of the city; the campus, where Minnie shared a flat with five other students, is a little way out, on the edge of the suburbs. I was due to arrive in Minnie's flat at eight. The long drive from Presteigne had taken it out of me; I slept a disco sleep, showered, and climbed into my disco outfit. I thought I looked rather well, under the circumstances. I drove out to the campus. It was a beautiful summer evening.

'Oh dear God no . . .' said Min when I arrived in her flat.

'What?'

'You can't wear that.'

'What?'

'That fucking shirt. It looks like you're wearing pyjamas.'

Minnie took me into the kitchen.

'Hello, Mr Marchant,' said one of Minnie's flatmates. 'Are you coming out with us tonight?'

'Yes I am.'

'In your pyjamas?'

I had no answer. It seems that the young people, identikit creatures that they are, have lost all sense of style. Charley came through from Min's room, and gave me a kiss.

'Hello, Daddy.'

'Hello, darling.'

'I see you're wearing your trademark shirt.'

'Well . . . yes. I thought it might keep me cool when I'm dancing.'

Minnie groaned.

'You're not dancing?'

'Of course. I'm good at dancing. I like dancing.'

'Yes, Daddy,' said Charley. 'You're good at disco dancing. But they won't be playing any disco tonight . . .'

'Won't they?'

'No, of course not. It'll be house, and techno, and dubstep, and things like that.'

'No ABBA?'

'Have you ever been to a rave?' asked Minnie.

'Yes, once, sort of. A rave night in a club, anyway.'

'Did you enjoy it?' asked Charley.

'Well, yes, in a way. I went with my friend Saleel, and we found that if we got right at the back of the hall, we could talk if we shouted into one another's ears. We had a fascinating chat about the possible pitfalls of Church disestablishment.'

'O . . . K . . .' said Minnie.

'Well, I don't like house and techno and . . . what was it?'

'Dubstep.'

'I like reggae. I like dub. Bit of Augustus Pablo.'

'No, Daddy. Dubstep isn't reggae.'

'Isn't it?'

'No, Dad,' said Minnie, the note of exasperation in her voice rising to a pitch. 'Dubstep goes wob wob wob, like that . . .'

'Really?'

'Yes, really. It's for people who've been taking ketamine. It mimics the way ketheads walk.'

'Oh. I don't want to take ketamine.'

'And techno only really makes sense if you take MDMA,' said Charley.

'I knew that. The music is so dull that you need drugs to enjoy it.'

'Says Mister No Drugs Ever,' said Minnie.

'I don't get it at all. I can't tell the difference between any of that stuff. It always sounds like a set of directions: you go past Handbag House, turn left at Old Skool, and you'll find us right next to UK Garage.'

'That's sad, Daddy,' said Charley. 'You are turning into an old get.'

'Turning?' said Minnie. 'When was he not?'

The friends who shared the little campus flat were in and out of the kitchen, in various states of readiness; borrowing make-up, and taking glasses of cider from the four bottles of Strongbow on the kitchen table. Their weapon of choice was the mobile phone, on which they txted endlessly; often, so far as I could tell, to people who were actually in the same room. One mobile phone was plugged into a pair of speakers, and the kitchen echoed to the sound of Handbag House. Or Old Skool. Or UK Garage. Or something.

Charley was looking after me (as she has for thirty years now), making me cups of tea, and trying to keep my spirits up. Minnie came back into the kitchen and said, 'It's going to be packed tonight.'

'How can you tell?' I asked.

'Well, it's an event on Facebook. You can see how many people are going. If there are, like, five hundred people going, then you know it's going to be a shit night. But tonight there are like twelve hundred people signed up.'

'Oh.' I was starting to feel really uncomfortable. I'd long been resigned to being the oldest person there, but the thought of 1200 post-teens off their heads on ketamine and cider and . . .

'Ooh, what's that?' I said. 'Is it cocaine? How can you afford cocaine?'

Two of Minnie's male flatmates were chopping up lines of powder on the kitchen table.

'No, Mr Marchant . . .' I am touched by the show of respect.

'This is mephedrone . . .'

'No it isn't! Good lord, I know methadone when I see it. It's shit, and you shouldn't touch it. And do try and pronounce

71

your th's properly. No wonder we're all going to hell in a hand basket . . .'

'No, Mr Marchant. Mephedrone. It's a legal high.'

This was the first time I'd heard of 'meow meow',* which was to so incense the *Daily Mail* over the winter of 2009–10.

'Would you like to try some, Mr Marchant?'

Such polite boys.

'No thanks, lads . . .'

And so the time came. Charley and Minnie were dressed and ready for the off, and were both merry in a way that I didn't wish to enquire too closely into. I smoked a spliff as we crossed the campus.

The LCR at Minnie's university hosts Club Nights every Tuesday, Friday and Saturday, and is a short stroll away from the iconic block of flats where Minnie was living. The pretty things who skipped and fluttered across the campus on their way to the Club Night reminded me of the Eloi in the film version of H.G. Wells' *The Time Machine*. The Eloi are the beautiful and feckless denizens of the far future, who spend their time frolicking by day before the Morlocks emerge at night to gobble them up. Yes, I know that this is how the Middle Aged have always perceived the young. And if you are knowing enough to realise this, then you know that everybody thinks it was better in their day. The awareness of participating in middle-aged disapproval does not, however, stop me from feeling the disapproval. Things really were better in our day.

I seem to have said this out loud.

---

* I think you'll find I'm still down with the kids! I know the talk!

'Oh no, Dad. Not punk rock and freak politics again . . .' said Minnie.

'Yes, punk rock and freak politics. We had both, and they were great . . .'

'This is great, too,' said Charley as we arrived at the LCR. 'Just differently great.'

I'd been here before. By day this place is a café; Minnie brought me here on my first visit for a coffee and a croissant. Now it was heaving with the Eloi. Handbag House, or Old Skool, or UK Garage, or Grime or Jungle or Drum 'n' Bass were belting out of huge speakers. The Eloi all faced the front, and stood with their hands raised in supplication to the gods of binge drinking, swaying back and forth, looking miserable as sin. It was my idea of hell. I've been suffering from a touch of deafness these last few years; I couldn't hear a thing that people were saying.

The crush at the bar was ten deep.

'What do you want?' I bellowed.

'Coors Lite,' shouted Minnie into my good ear.

'Dear God, what's that?'

'Piss,' said Minnie.

'I'll have VK!' shouted Charley.

'That's tropical piss,' said Minnie.

And so I stood for twenty minutes, using my bulk and seniority to force my way to the front. The boys all stunk of Lynx. The girls all had their mobile phones tattooed on their eyes, and were txting while they queued. And when I got to the front, a vacant-eyed youth served me the various kinds of piss, and I fought my way back to where I'd left Charley and Minnie.

The music thump thump thump thumped. I thought: how can you dance to this? This isn't dance music! It isn't funky! It doesn't swing. The Eloi waved and txted and shouted. And Minnie and Charley had gone. I stood holding their glasses of piss, surrounded by creatures from an old science fiction movie, my trademark shirt covered in sweat. I must have looked . . . dear God, I suddenly realised how I looked. I remembered old Welsh hill farmers who occasionally came into our student discos in the 70s, dressed in what they thought was the mode. I must have looked like them: red-faced with heat and embarrass-ment, an object of derision, as out of place as Tony Blair at the Al Qaeda AGM and Family Picnic.

One of the Eloi from Minnie's flat came up to me and said, 'They're out in the smoking area. Smoking.'

So I went out to the smoking area, and found my lovely daughters smoking, and I gave them their plastic glasses of piss.

'Didn't you get anything, Daddy?' said Charley.

'No, darling. They didn't serve proper drink.'

Minnie sighed.

'No, Dad. It's a student bar. We come here to get ridiculously drunk, not to weigh up the merits of various kinds of real ale . . .'

'I know.'

'Poor Daddy,' said Charley.

'Why do all the dancers look so miserable? I mean, I know the music is shit, but presumably they like it . . .'

'Oh, you can't smile any more, Daddy . . .' said Charley.

'Smiling went out years ago,' said Minnie. 'They all have bass face.'

'Bass face?'

74

'Bass face. Like this.' Minnie screwed up her pretty face into a disagreeable scowl, and wobb-ed about.

'I think I might go,' I said.

'Oh dear,' said Minnie. 'We will miss you.'

'Poor Daddy,' said Charley, again.

'I'll call you in the morning,' I said, kissed them both, and headed back to my car. I had lasted just twenty-five minutes, most of it spent queuing for the bar.

Driving back into the city centre, I felt much too old to want to go back and sit all alone in my Travelodge room. It was getting on towards mid-summer, and there was still some light in the sky, even at 10.30. I drove out of the city, and saw a sign that made my heart sing. It was for a lake, a lake that I had read about, but never seen. I turned down lane after lane, and found myself beside a quiet staithe. I rolled myself a spliff, and got out of the car. Boats were moored by the staithe, and anchored out in the middle of the lake. The lights from their cabins were reflected in the still waters. A couple of swans came up to where I stood, wondering perhaps if I was going to give them a late-night snack of some kind. Here was silence, and peace, and solitude, and everything that could make a middle-aged man happy. The last of the sun faded in a dim west.

Since I can remember, I've always loved the Swallows and Amazons novels of Arthur Ransome. One of the things I liked about the books was that they were always set in real places. This lake is where Dick and Dorothea learned to sail, while they sheltered Tom Dudgeon from the Hullaballoos.* In the still dark

* *Coot Club*, by Arthur Ransome, published by Jonathan Cape in 1934.

night, I could almost see the white sail of *Titmouse*, her wake wavering a little as Dick takes the tiller from Tom. Of all the kids in the books, it was speccy Dick that I most identified with. Tonight, I wish I was out on the little lake, sailing with an imaginary friend into the faintest of sunsets, signalling to Mars with a paraffin lamp, leaving the Eloi to their pleasures; pleasures which, it is now quite clear, I will never share again.

NIGHT RALLY

Last night I dreamt I went to Wembley again.

It was 1973. It was 14 November, and England were playing Italy in a friendly. I was sitting with my Old Feller, and my Uncle Frank, who was a proper man, and who had secured us the seats. The floodlights were on, and England were doing badly.

England had drawn 1–1 with Poland a month before, which meant we weren't going to the World Cup. I'd sat with my Old Feller in our lounge, watching Poland's goalkeeper Tomaszewski enjoy the game of his life, while Brian Clough castigated him for being a clown. He wasn't a clown; he was a fucking genius. I was coming to suspect that it was England who were the clowns. I've suspected it ever since.

The first football game I can remember watching all the way through took place in bright sunshine, though we were watching on a little black-and-white telly in my great-aunt's house in Newhaven, with the curtains drawn. It was England versus West Germany. It was 1966. Geoff Hurst scored a hat trick, and

Martin Peters knocked one in for good measure. West Germany only scored two. Aged eight, I became convinced that football was top, and that England were the greatest football team in the world; which, in fairness, we were, at least that afternoon. There has been precious little evidence of it since then, but the damage was done; I am Eng-er-land till I die.

My relationship with live football began in the same way as Nick Hornby's; my mum and dad had been divorced, and my dad had to do something with me on his monthly visits. Before my parents split up, we had lived in Northamptonshire, and my dad had followed Northampton Town on their remarkable rise through the leagues. During their only season in Division One, he went to most of the home games.*

My dad didn't take me to see Northampton Town when they were in the top flight, for which, as in so little else, I'm eternally grateful, or I would have been a Northampton fan, which is one of the handful of things which is worse than supporting Brighton.

After the divorce, my mother had taken me and my brother to Newhaven – to stay with her great-aunt in the first instance, but soon to settle and eventually to marry my beloved step-father, The Old Feller. When my dad came to take me out, he had to take me somewhere, so, one Saturday in December 1968, he took me to the Goldstone Ground to see the second-round FA Cup clash between those titans of the game, Brighton and Hove Albion and Northampton Town. The Cobblers won,

---

* Note to young people: Division One is now the Premier League. Division Two is the Championship, Division Three is League One, and Division Four is League Two. It's like how you went from being passengers on a train or patients in a hospital to being customers; meaningless shit which is supposed to make you feel better about yourself. Or, in the case of football, your team.

1– 2, but by the end I was a Brighton supporter. Hornby's dad took him to see Arsenal for his first game; I didn't get so lucky.

My dad started taking me to see the football on most of his visits. Mostly, I wanted to go and see Brighton, but sometimes he'd take me up to London to see Chelsea, who were his team, but who didn't impress me at all. One of the teams we saw Chelsea play were Manchester United, with Best and Charlton in the line-up. Didn't do it for me, I'm afraid. I care nothing for the beautiful game. I supported, and still support, Brighton and England; the supporting is the thing, the shouting, the swearing, the abject sense of personal worthlessness – and I just want to see my teams win, however crudely. But I came to realise that if you support a lower-division side, and you're a kid, you do need a proper team to support, in order to hold your own in the playground. And my team, and I still don't really know why, were Liverpool. And I loved Liverpool, in a way I didn't even love Brighton, at least when I was twelve. Brighton were like my mum, or something, a love that would never go away, but Liverpool were like a first girlfriend: an intense, painful love, that time will cure, though you don't believe anyone when they tell you so.

I never cried when Brighton lost, because if I had I would have been severely dehydrated (not that there was such a thing as dehydration in the early 70s). But I can remember howling my eyes out when Liverpool lost. And I didn't really know why. My favourite player was Emlyn Hughes. I still think Emlyn is the nearest I've ever had to a gay crush. Age twelve I had posters of Emlyn Hughes and Gandalf on my bedroom wall, and Emlyn had much better legs.

I'd never seen Liverpool play. My dad had started taking me all over London and the Midlands in order to see various teams: Birmingham, Coventry, Spurs, Norwich even. But never Liverpool; never my lovely Emlyn with his ball-winning ability, and his crazy runs and his funny squeaky voice. And I'd never seen a floodlit game. So when my Uncle Frank told us that he'd got tickets for the England vs. Italy friendly at Wembley, I was crazed with excitement.

I can't remember how we got there, but I remember walking up the Wembley Way, clicking through the turnstiles, walking up through the belly of the great stadium, and emerging into the arena. The pitch was as bright as day; brighter, greener, the bright green of a Subbuteo pitch, the only pitch I'd previously seen floodlit; though, it has to be faced, Subbuteo floodlights are rubbish, and hadn't been any kind of preparation for the real thing. We were sitting high up on the right-hand side. We bought a programme, which sadly I no longer have, since I sold my really rather fantastic programme collection in the 80s; but I remember that two of the World Cup winners were playing, Bobby Moore and Martin Peters; I remember England as they ran out onto the pitch in their white shirts, and how excited I was to see my beloved Emlyn.

After that, it becomes a good deal vaguer. I remember how dull the game was, as anyone who has sat through a lot of Italy games will surely attest. I can't remember the Italy goal (scored by Fabio Capello, of course); just the groan and the feeling of dull resignation which has become so familiar over the years.

It was not, in short, the greatest game that I can remember being at, but it's still the only time I've seen England live as opposed to in bars, or in front rooms, or, on one particularly gloomy occasion, standing with Perry Venus and 35,000 other people in front of the main stage at Glastonbury on the Thursday night, watching England lose on penalties to Portugal in the quarter-finals of the European Championship. The Pilton site fell silent for the first time in living memory, and Perry Venus and I slunk back to the Tiny Tea Tent to despair and get mongered. An atmosphere of mourning hung over the vast site.

No, England vs. Italy, November 1973, was not the best game I've ever seen. In fact, it was one of the worst. But it was, as I've said, the first floodlit game I ever saw. These days, the floodlights of a football ground are one of those markers that show you've come to a place that deserves to be taken seriously, a place that comes alive at night, and where you'd better be home before 6.30, or else you're going to be stuck in traffic as thousands of fans overflow the pavements. I used to think it had always been so. But these great pylons rising from town centres are relatively new, at least in their modern state.

There had been experiments with electric floodlighting from the earliest days of the professional game. Sheffield United were first, in 1878, but the lights were held up on wooden gantries, rather than the pylons that dominate the Blades end of Sheffield now. Mike Jackman, in his history of Blackburn Rovers, gives an account of an early game held under floodlights:

The visitors were Accrington and the ground was illuminated by the Gramme light – one being situated at the east end of the Meadows and the other at the west end. Each light was attached to a scaffold that rose some 30 to 40ft from the ground. An 8hp portable engine was required to work the battery and it was said that the system provided the equivalent of some 6,000 candle power. However, it was felt necessary to paint the ball white to aid both players and spectators.

As is hardly surprising, these somewhat Heath Robinson-ish arrangements could on occasion be unreliable. When professional League football started in 1888, the League decreed that the sport was much too important to risk a game not coming to a conclusion; and so floodlights were banned from the professional game. However, Sabbath observance laws meant that football couldn't be played on Sundays, and promoters of the game were reluctant to give up the opportunities that floodlighting afforded for games to be played on weekdays. In the late 1890s Arnold Hills, who owned the Thames Ironworks Shipbuilding Company, decided to set up a works team, called, wittily, Thames Ironworks. Hills said that he wanted to help those 'who are prevented through their daily avocation from attending afternoon matches by carrying out those by the aid of electric light on the ground at Canning Town'. Since the Thames Ironworks team weren't in any league, they were permitted to play two floodlit friendlies against League opposition in a week; Arsenal on the Monday, and West Bromwich Albion on Friday. They lost both games, and when they were admitted to the Southern League in 1900 (and changed their name to West Ham United), the experiments with floodlighting came to an end.

The next period of floodlit football seems the most unlikely. During the First World War the men's game effectively came to a halt, and the women's game became hugely popular. They played for what became known as The Munitioneers Cup, since most of the women who played worked in munitions factories. In 1920 a charity match was arranged at Preston North End's Deepdale ground between the winners of The Munitioneers Cup, the confusingly named Dick, Kerr Ladies* and a team representing the rest of England. Winston Churchill arranged for two floodlights to be loaned to the teams for the occasion, and a crowd of 12,000 watched the Dick, Kerr Ladies team win 4–0. The Football League didn't approve of the growing popularity of the women's game, and in 1923 they prevented women's football matches from taking place on League grounds, because they felt it was unseemly. This not only condemned the women's game to sixty years of obscurity, but also meant yet another end to floodlit football. Although the great Herbert Chapman, manager of the Huddersfield Town and Arsenal teams who swept all before them in the late 1920s and early 1930s, asked for permission to play some games under floodlights, permission was refused, except for a handful of friendlies, and it wasn't until well into the 1950s that the Football Association and the League finally relented. So the first official League game played under floodlights was between Portsmouth and Newcastle United, in 1956. Those icons of modernity only became a fixture of the urban landscape two years before I was born. I am a member of the first generation of football fans who grew up taking the floodlit game for granted.

'Do you follow the Beautiful Game?' I ask Neil.

'Not really. I guess I always look out for how Norwich are doing. Why?'

---

* Sic. Not Dick Kerr. Dick, Kerr.

'Did your dad ever take you to a game?'

'No. I wouldn't have been that interested. Did you ever take your girls?'

'Once. I took Minnie to see Plymouth vs. Brighton at Home Park. Two-all draw.'

'Did she like it?'

'I had hopes, but I don't think she did really. But I took Olly to a game last year.'

'Mac's wee brother?'

'Yes.'

'He's a smashing lad.' Neil looks sad, and shifts in his armchair. Mac is his boy; Olly is Mac's half-brother.

I never wanted boys. I love having daughters. But there was one thing I'd always wanted to do, and that was to take a lad to the football. Silly really, but there it is. It seems such a daddish thing to do. So when my pal Pittsy called me up to say that he had four tickets for Liverpool vs. Aston Villa, a Monday-night game, and he was taking his boy, and would I like to come, I thought at once of Olly. Olly's mum is a friend of mine, and I knew that Olly was a fanatical Liverpool fan, but that he'd never actually seen them play. My ambition to take a lad to his first game looked like it might come true; and then there was my very slight desire to go to Anfield. Over the years, that teenage longing for the Reds had worn away to nothing, like a first love grown stale. In fact, Villa have become the Premiership side I follow, for several very good reasons. One is that I liked Martin O'Neill and the teams he put together. I liked it that in going to see Villa you got a chance to see some contenders for the England side; that O'Neill seemed to have a marked preference for the best of British, rather than buying in talent. I also liked Villa because this was Gareth Barry's last season with them, and Brighton had sold Gareth to Villa after he graduated from our Academy. So really, that makes him a Brighton player. And, importantly, I work in Birmingham, and from my office I have a corking view of Villa Park.* But Pittsy is Red through and through, and so is his lad, and so is Olly. So I knew that I would be sitting with the Liverpool fans, and would need to revert for one night to that teenage boy who cried when Liverpool lost.

Olly's mum agreed that I could borrow him for the night. He was twelve, a proper age to go and see your first game. But he'd grown up in the West Country, and he's a very talented rugby player; so although his dad had taken him to see plenty of top-grade rugby, he'd never had a chance to see football, unless he'd gone to see Exeter, or Plymouth, which would be enough to put anybody off for life.

Once again, I had clothing decisions to make. I wanted something that was 'dad taking his boy to the match', and of course a sheepskin coat would have been ideal. But I didn't have such a thing. I opted for a roll-neck sweater under a trench coat, which made me look respectable, I thought; a minor company director, perhaps, or a senior middle manager. You can't take a boy to the match looking like a Bohemian, in my view, not unless you support Queen's Park Rangers. When my Uncle Frank and my Old Feller took me to Wembley, they looked like what they were: working men wrapped up against the cold. When my dad

---

* And Perry Barr greyhound stadium. And a glue factory.

took me, he looked like a successful businessman. These were the two looks I was trying to combine.

I picked Olly up from his mum's house. He'd just finished school, but it was winter, and the light was already leaching from the sky. Pittsy and his boy picked us up from outside Elda's Colombian Coffee House, High Street, Presteigne, and we drove to Liverpool.

Pittsy had allowed four hours for the drive, in case we got stuck in traffic, and so we could get some chips on the way. Four hours is a long time for two twelve-year-olds to sit in the back of a Honda Civic while their dad and pseudo-dad for the night talk about football. They bickered, it has to be said. There was, after all, very little to be seen out of the window, until we hit the M53, which is my favourite night-time motorway because of the chemical factories along the banks of the Mersey. Thousands of tiny lights sparkle across the pipes and chimneys and retorts, and although I've no idea why chemical factories need all these lights, I'm glad that they do, because they are beautiful. Even the boys were quiet for a minute or two, as they tried to work out what the lights might signify.

Pittsy comes up to Anfield a couple of times a year, so when we came through the Mersey tunnel and into Liverpool proper, he already had an idea where he was going: a private match-day car park on a bit of waste ground behind a social club. And although I'd never been there before, I knew which way to go from the car park to the ground. It was obvious.

'We just follow the glow in the sky,' said Pittsy.

Anfield sat glowing like a UFO landed in a particularly grim part of Liverpool. Like any major football ground at night, it's a cathedral of light.

'A cathedral of light,' I said to Pittsy as we walked from the car towards the glow in the sky.

'Don't say that,' said Pittsy.

'Why?'

'Albert Speer used hundreds of spotlights for the Nuremberg rallies. He called it his "Cathedral of Light".'

And so he did. Speer lit up the sky with 150 searchlights borrowed from the Luftwaffe. Leni Riefenstahl filmed it, and a mad spectacle it makes, watching the film now.

'Football at night is like a night rally, I guess,' I said. 'I can't really think of any other occasion these days when people gather in floodlit auditoria . . .'

'Sometimes quite drunk and aggressive people . . .'

'To see a spectacle. To shout slogans, and chant things . . .'

'Speer was on to something, no doubt,' said Pittsy.

We approached closer to the glow in the sky. The streets around Anfield have been abandoned. Most of the houses are boarded up with metal grilles. We stopped to have a slash on a pile of old mattresses down a back alley. Olly was getting a bit agitated.

'Come ON, Ian!'

Olly is a West Country hippy boy. Not only had he never been to the football before, he'd never seen urban decay either. He didn't seem to like it much, and I can't say I'm a huge fan myself.

Olly's face was glowing with excitement, as Enid Blyton might have said if she'd taken boys to the match, instead of constantly shoving them down secret passageways and leaving them in locked rooms with the key still on the outside. We turned down the last of the abandoned streets and the bowl of light loomed out of the mist. We were approaching from the Kop end, and the stream of spectators with whom we had been walking through the darkened streets joined a river of red. It was almost as though Liverpool FC had bought up the adjoining streets, to make the contrast between dark and light more stark, and more of a relief.

And so we entered Anfield. For Olly and me it was the first time. For him, it was a thrilling pilgrimage; for me, like a date thirty years too late with a girl you had loved at school, and had re-met through Friends Reunited, and which you could only be disappointed by, no matter how well preserved she was, or how louche you had grown.

But that moment when you come up through the belly of the stadium for a night game, and first see the electric green of the pitch! There is no green like the green of a football pitch lit up by floodlights. It's green's green, the essence of green, a Platonic green. Even the red of the scarves of 40,000 Liverpool fans seemed to pale to a faint pink against that illuminated green. Even when Stevie Gerrard came out onto the pitch to give a prize to some schoolboy players, even the red of his shirt was overpowered by that green, green like the leaves of a beech tree in May.

And then, of course, Anfield sings. Timed so that it reaches the chorus as the teams come on, they sing 'You'll Never Walk Alone'. And even though I no longer love Liverpool, and was secretly rooting for Villa, I was deeply moved. All around us, the fans stood with their arms in the air, singing their anthem. And I sang too, with tears running down my cheeks. Pittsy was a bit tearful too, but then Liverpool is his club. My reaction surprised me.

'It really is like a night rally,' I said. 'You can feel the power of it. No wonder the Fascists exploited it.'

'No wonder people went along with it,' said Pittsy. 'You'd need to be strong not to get swept up . . .'

And what must it be like for the thousand or so Villa fans below us in the adjacent Anfield stand? We were high up in the Main Stand, and there they were below us, a puddle of claret and blue, trying to sing something as Anfield sang their great anthem. And what must it be like to be an opposing player, to come out of the tunnel, and see that green, and hear that singing? Might some of them cry too? Might some of them be childhood Liverpool fans, moved to tears by 'Walk On . . . Walk On . . . With Hope in Your Hearts . . .'? My heart would be filled with despair before a ball had been kicked.

And then the game itself. I found it a bit . . . polite. I'm used to watching Brighton play in the lower leagues. I'm used to hulking great big farmers' boys knocking lumps out of one another. This was the first live Premiership* game I'd ever seen, and it reminded me a little of a visit to Sadler's Wells. I mean, it's lovely to see those silky skills, as opposed to watching Brighton vs. Hartlepool on a wet night in February at the Withdean, but the game didn't do it for me in the same way. The crowd were funny, though, especially in their hatred of Dirk Kuyt, who was, after all, a Liverpool player.

---

* Though I'd seen plenty of First Division games. See earlier note.

'Fuck off back to Eindhoven, you twat,' said an unappreciative fan behind us.

The game was polite, but the fans weren't. Liverpool scored first, and I stood up and punched the air, coward that I am. At half-time, we queued for pies. Olly likes a pie, and so do I.

'What do you think, boy?'

'Yeah, it's great. I like all the swearing.' I made a note to myself that I should remind him on the way home not to emphasise this point to his mum.

We sat high above the Liverpool goal for the second half, so we got a great view of one of the best goals I've ever seen, an overhead jobbie, scored by Villa's Marlon Harewood. O'Neill, who had been pacing the technical area, leapt into the air with joy, and I just remembered not to. The Villa fans started chanting 'Who are you?' which goaded the Liverpool fans around us to new heights of sweary-ness, to Olly's evident delight.

When Liverpool scored an own goal, the travelling Villa fans went ape. 'Who's laughing now?' they sang, and I looked forward to admitting my mild thing for Villa on the drive home; until Peter Crouch came on, and scored a last-minute equaliser. I rose and shouted my false appreciation, feeling a bit like St Peter must have done while the cocks were crowing.

And then it was all over; a trip to the Liverpool shop to buy the boys some souvenirs, and then the walk back through the darkened streets to the car. The boys slept on the way home, while Pittsy and I talked about whether or not it would be possible to use wind and sun power to get the floodlights going.

'It's more of a spectacle at night, the football,' said Pittsy. 'More exciting.'

'I agree. Don't you think that if they used alternative sources of power to light the thing, you might lose a bit of the candle-power? Isn't the intensity of the light in contrast to all these darkened streets a great deal of the point? Of the spectacle?'

'Maybe.'

Maybe it's the light that makes it so exciting, that intensity of colour. Maybe it was the light that made Nuremberg possible. Certainly these night-time spectacles are really a twentieth-century phenomenon, firework displays excepted. And there is one sport which has traditionally always been held at night, under electric lighting, a sport which relies entirely on flood-lighting and electricity in order to function, and is actually one of the first products of electrification as spectacle, making it, I might wish to argue, a perfect exemplar of modernity. This sport is, of course, dog racing.

If there's one thing that the English love, it's their dogs. And their bears, and their bulls, and, of course, their lovely cocks. There is a fine old English tradition of bear, bull, and horse baiting, which was stopped by bleeding-heart liberals in the 1830s. Before these health and safety fanatics put a halt to everyone's fun, bull terriers and huge mastiffs would bait bears, bulls etc. which were tied to posts; and although the bears, bulls etc. often gave a good account of themselves, the dogs always won. These hugely popular entertainments took place by day. You might imagine that they would be ideally suited to night-time, but they almost always took place in the afternoon; often on Mondays, which was a day when nobody really bothered too much going to work in the pre-industrial age. Before the advent of electric lighting, sports and games were either held indoors, or during the day; that's why animal baiting always took place in the afternoon. By the time efficient electrical floodlighting arrived, which is to say roughly the 1920s, you couldn't kill animals for fun any more. But you could race them.

Greyhound racing was devised in Florida in the 1920s, coinciding exactly with the advent of floodlighting. Greyhound racing arrived in Britain in 1926. There were 1600 people at the first meeting at Manchester Belle Vue. At the second meeting, there were 16,000. Dog tracks mushroomed all over Britain. By the end of 1927, 5.5 million people were going to the dogs every year; by the end of 1928, it was 13.5 million; and by 1945, 50 million people clicked through the turnstiles. Whilst it's certainly true that many of those people were dog nutters who went twice a week, that's a very impressive growth rate; one might almost say an electric growth rate, since dog racing needs electricity to light the lights and to make the hare run.

Dog racing is what you might call the family sport. My dad and my Uncle Frank liked football, but their true passion was for the dogs. On many of the nights when my mum sat alone looking after me, my dad was off at the dogs, usually at White City, and often in the company of my mum's brother, my Uncle Frank. When my parents divorced, my dad and Uncle Frank stopped going together, but their obsession continued. My dad moved into David Cameron Country, that slice of territory between the M4 and M40 motorways, but he worked in Slough, and it was to Slough dogs that he devoted much of his attention and a large part of his salary.

His problem was that he was utterly convinced that he had devised a system for picking winners. He took no notice of their names, which is how most sane people choose their dogs. He was obsessed with form, which makes some sense with the horses, but really very little with the dogs.

Here's why: dog racing is not quite as straight as one might hope.* When I started working in bookmakers' shops in the 1970s, we would occasionally come into work to find the doors of our shops done up with SuperGlue, which was fun, because it meant we got the morning off work while people came and replaced the doors. This was due to the action of 'The Glue Gang', who had been involved in a doping scandal at Rochester dog track, in Kent, the details of which escape me as they were arcane in the extreme. The guys who were involved had been tried for conning a million quid out of the bookies, but had been found not guilty. Now they wanted paying out, and were holding the bookies to ransom until they got their winnings. Doping and the substitution of one dog for another (so called 'ringing') are still quite commonplace in the world of dogs*. It's a small world; all the trainers know one another, and are usually based at one track, so there can be few surprises. A trainer will run a bitch when she's on heat, so that she loses, thus guaranteeing much longer odds for what might be a top-class bitch when she runs under less testing circumstances. Owners give their dogs cocaine to make them go faster, or doped chocolate to slow them down. As a betting medium, dog racing leaves quite a bit to be desired. As a night out, however, it's hard to beat.

None of this deterred my dad, who became known at Slough dogs as 'Mr Computer'. This was because he would stand with

* Allegedly.

a clipboard covered in reams of paper and a pocket calculator, working on his hopeless 'system'. Several times he explained to me how it worked. If I remember rightly, it was to do with speed in the last race as a relationship to the recorded weights of the dogs, and the differences therein. He even made the Slough papers from time to time. The headlines would read things like 'Slough's *Mr Computer* presents the trophy to the winning owner'. He claimed that this was because his firm had sponsored the odd race, but I'm convinced that it was simply because he had lost more money there than any other punter in the whole of recorded time. However his 'system' was supposed to function, it quite clearly failed to live up to its promise.

Meanwhile, his erstwhile comrade in caninity, my Uncle Frank, had taken up dog owning. If you want to find a great way to throw money away, owning a racing dog is a very good way to go about it. And at least my dad threw his cash away at Slough dogs, which is regulated by the National Greyhound Racing Association, and is therefore as clean as possible. Uncle Frank ran his dogs on unregulated tracks, the so-called 'flappers'. He took me a couple of times: once to Portsmouth, and once to Reading. The tracks were much less posh than Slough or Hove, which was the track I used to go to with my pals in the 1980s. At Slough and Hove, you could sit in the restaurant and order a meal, and a girl would come round from the Tote and take your cash while you ate. I can't remember that they had the Tote at the flappers; certainly Uncle Frank would give his money to shady bookies, and we would stand leaning on wooden rails in the driving rain, which hissed off the floodlights, and watch his dogs fail to live up to expectations, despite the fact that he had been assured that his dog, or dogs, could not conceivably lose that night.

I love going to the dogs myself. This is why my office is so fabulous, with its view of Villa Park and Perry Barr dogs, since football and dog racing are the only two outdoor sports in which I've ever taken much of an interest. In the 80s, my pals and I used to go regularly to Hove dogs, where I had the enormous pleasure of seeing Ballyregan Bob run, the greatest dog since Mick the Miller in the 1920s. You couldn't back Bob. If I remember rightly, the odds were 1 to 5 the night I saw him. It was maybe three quarters of the way through his world-record run of 31 races unbeaten consecutively. Bob was a four-corner dog, a sprinter; he'd usually take under 30 seconds to cover 650 metres or so. The trick was to find the dog who was going to come second to Ballyregan Bob, and I didn't. But because I worked in bookies for so many years, and because I'd seen my dad and my uncle lose so much money, I'm a naturally cautious punter. I had a fiver forecast (that's where you try to predict who is going to come first and second in a race). And I lost. Ballyregan Bob won, of course, and my dog was third or fourth. But it was worth it to see one of the world's best. I've seen George Best and Bobby Charlton play football, but Ballyregan Bob is by far the greatest athlete I've ever seen live, and under floodlights.

Years pass, and time has conspired to keep me away from the dogs. My uncle is dead, my dad has been living in the States putting dimes into the slots on Indian reservations, and I've never been back; not, in fact, I now realise, writing this, since the night I saw Ballyregan Bob. But when I conceived of this book, I was determined to go dog racing. The obvious place would be Perry Barr, since the track is actually owned by the university where I teach. So far as I know, we're the only British university which owns a dog track. Rubbish Oxbridge colleges own woodlands and fishing rights. Not us. We've got Perry Barr dog track. I couldn't be more proud.

But in fact, my return to the dogs was at Drumbo Park, just outside Belfast. My new wife, an upstanding member of the Unionist community, had never been to the dogs; much to my surprise, she had never even considered it as a possible night out.

'It's great,' I said. 'You eat burgers, and drink lager, and bet, and watch dogs race. What could be more fun?' She wasn't convinced, until I promised her that we'd forgo the pleasure of the Drumbo Park burger bar, and go out for something to eat after we'd lost all our money.

'All your money,' she pointed out, since I'd promised to pay for the whole thing.

Drumbo Park takes a bit of finding. Although the address on the posters says Drumbo Park, Belfast, that's a bit of optimistic re-addressing on behalf of the track operators, as it is right out in the flat country towards Lough Neagh.

Northern Ireland is like a bowl. Around its edges you have the Mountains of Mourne, the Antrim Hills, the Holywood Hills and the Sperrins. In the middle there is Lough Neagh, surrounded by flat country. Drumbo Park is out there some-where, though I'm not sure I could find it again. The map on the website was vague. I was vague. They advertise themselves as Northern Ireland's new night out, which might be true, but only if you like driving around featureless countryside in pitch darkness.

When we found Drumbo Park, it was mysterious. As well as dog racing, it is home to Lisburn Distillery FC, but the whole thing is surrounded by an elliptical concrete wall. If you are a visitor to Northern Ireland, you never quite get used to concrete walls in the way the residents do. There are 'peace lines' that bisect Belfast, separating the communities. The police stations are surrounded by high concrete fortifications (and the police have guns, which never fails to frighten me). So the fact that Drumbo Park is surrounded by high concrete walls just made me feel uneasy. We couldn't find the way in. There were no signposts. Perhaps it is just a perfect concrete ellipse, I thought, like something from a South American postmodernist short story, an arena with no visible entrance, where sport is endlessly performed behind permanently sealed doors. There was light inside the ellipse; once again, I was reminded of *Close Encounters*, the light from the stadium illuminating the sky, another UFO landed in another pool of darkness. We realised that we had turned the wrong way – we were going widdershins – and that if we went the other way round we might find a car park, and the entrance, and so it proved.

There were to be ten races, and I'd budgeted for two quid each per race. That's £40. And it was a tenner each to get in. That's £60. And then a few drinks, call it £80 all in. Going to the dogs isn't necessarily cheap. A couple of girls with inch-thick make-up paid us in. Drumbo Park was on two levels. Up above, there was the swish restaurant area, which was packed with hundreds of people who all looked as though they should be singing for Girls Aloud, even the men. They were dressed and coiffed up to the nines. The restaurant at Drumbo Park is award winning, and it really could be Northern Ireland's best night out. You sit with all the Girls Aloud people, eating award-winning food, while between races girls from the Tote come round and take your money. My wife might have fancied the posh restaurant, but she was to be sadly disappointed. Because we were going on the lower level, where there was a bar, a burger place, a few old ladies in expandable-waisted slacks sitting at the tables drinking Harp, a couple of Tote outlets, and fifty or so shady-looking guys watching the dogs from Harold's Cross in Dublin screened on large TVs. We walked out to the track. It was cold and pouring with rain. The brightness of the flood-lights lit up the smooth sandy track, like an elliptical Japanese Garden, raked to perfection. Half a dozen or so bookmakers had set up their stalls, but had yet to display any prices.

It was clear that there was a two-tier class system in operation: the Girls Aloud people, isolated in the restaurant from the noise and dirt of the track, and the keen punters, hanging around the bars. Never the twain would meet. We looked at our race card. I told my wife about my dad and my Uncle Frank, and how it seemed to be alright to pick dogs just because of their names.

'Don't patronise me . . .' She is not a woman easily fobbed off with names. She has a mathematical bent, and so she began to pore over the columns of figures next to each dog's name, while I went back outside in the rain, ostensibly to keep an eye on the bookies, but also to smoke, which is now an outdoor sport, like kayaking. There were a couple of guys, serious-faced guys, in jeans and leather jackets, who looked like they might know what they were doing. Still, so did my dad and my Uncle Frank, and they lost a fortune. I watched as one of the serious-faced men sidled up to the bookie, muttered something, and passed him a roll of cash. The bookie reached up, wiped off the prices on his board, and re-made his book. What had previously been out at 5 to 1 was now a short-priced favourite. I hurried back into the saturated-fat and lager haze of the bar.

'It's Trap five,' I announced.

'Hmm,' said my wife. 'But Trap four finished two lengths ahead of Trap five on its last outing, and has lost two pounds since. With the going a little sticky, which it seems to like, I think it could be worth a tickle.'

'I thought you said you'd never been to the dogs before?'

'I haven't.'

So we backed them both in a reversed forecast, and went out into the rain to watch. Greyhound racing doesn't last long, but it is exciting. Greyhounds are idle beasts for nine tenths of the time, but for the other tenth they get the light of battle in their eyes, and like nothing more than to belt after a floppy bunny on a little trolley. So we shouted; and our dogs came first and second. My wife's choice was first, and she was triumphant.

'Ha ha ha! Call yourself a dog expert? Well you're not. I chose the winner, and yours only came second.'

This didn't seem the moment to explain the principle of fore-casts, or that it was a good thing that her dog had won, because it had a longer price. I just went and picked up our winnings. It didn't seem worth explaining after the second race, either, where her dog also won, and where I'd also picked the second dog, and had thus the forecast up again. She hugged herself with glee.

After the third race she was less triumphant, because my dog had won and hers had only come second. She was inconsolable. I finally bit the bullet and tried explaining the forecast thing.

'No, you see, my dog won, yes, but it was the favourite. But your dog coming second, at odds of 16 to 1, means that we've won loads of money . . .'

'Really?'

'Really. You seem to have the knack of this . . .'

The fourth race was the clincher for me. Once again, we'd picked the first two dogs, me by watching what people did at the bookies, and my wife by close study of the form. And after four races, we had got our entry money back, paid for our drinks and our bets, and had made a clear profit of eighty quid.

'Eighty quid!' I said. 'Eighty fucking quid! Clear!'

I remembered my dad, and my Uncle Frank, and I knew what we had to do.

'Let's go,' I said.

'What?' said my wife, tearing her eyes away from the tiny columns of figures over which she had such natural mastery.

'Let's bet on race five. And if we lose, we go. I'll take you out for dinner on the winnings . . .'

And that's what we did. Race five, we were nowhere. And even though we were only betting very small amounts, and could have afforded to keep doing it all night and still come out on top, it wasn't what I wanted. I wanted, just for once in the sorry history of my family and the dogs, to come out with a wodge of folding money. So we left the lit-up bowl of Drumbo Park. We left the serious-faced men muttering to the bookies, and the ladies drinking Harp in expandable-waistline pants, and a large restaurant full of Girls Aloud people, who were quarantined in any case from the real action; and we took our winnings and slipped away into the dark, ending up at Deane's Deli in Belfast, where a three-course meal for two and a bottle of wine came to exactly the sum of money we'd managed to escape with from Drumbo Park.

'I enjoyed that,' said my wife. 'We should go again.'

'No, you're alright,' I said. 'Quit while you're ahead. Next time I'll take you to the football . . .'

AUTHENTICITY

Neil and I are still arguing about music, pop music in particular. Like most musos of our generation, we can keep it up all night, if need be. Outside in the darkness, Billy is whining at the door. I'm not sure if he's meant to be a guard dog, protecting the farmyard from unwanted visitors, but if he is he's a particularly shit one, because all he would do anyway is lick the hands of any intruders.

'Just because something's manufactured, that doesn't mean it's bad,' I contend, as I've contended in countless pubs, bars, and recording studios over the years.

'How do you mean?'

'Well, cars, medicines, computers, they're all manufactured, but that doesn't mean they're no good.'

'But it doesn't mean they've got soul,' said Neil.

'Er . . . well, no. But it doesn't mean they haven't. Like Tamla Motown, or Phil Spector.'

'You've lost me,' said Neil, who at this level of intoxication would probably be lost by Delia Smith explaining how to boil an egg.

'Well, Phil Spector didn't make "Be My Baby" in order for it to tower over our culture as a beacon of artistic excellence. He made it to make money from the best pop music record he could produce.'

'But it doesn't tower over our culture,' says Neil, clearly puzzled.

'But it does,' I reply, equally bemused. It is clear that the place where our musical Venn diagrams overlap is increasingly slim. I try again.

'OK, Motown.'

'Yes?'

'Well, Motown was an attempt to reproduce some of the techniques of motor manufacturing in the recording studio. You know, they design models, like, say, The Four Tops, and then they churn out records on a production line. But the fact that they are churned out on a production line doesn't stop them being brilliant.'

'Thing is, Ian,' says Neil, 'I don't really know much about pop music at all. I'm a traditional Irish musician.'

'That's not your fault,' I say. 'I can help you, if you'll let me . . .'

'Everything She Says' by T.A.T.U. is coming towards its end on the CD. Clearly not Neil's cup of tea, though if anyone knows a better record by a fake lesbian Russian girl band, I'd like to know about it.

'I haven't heard all that much rock music either, to be honest,' says Neil, apparently unrepentant. 'I like the Stones, and stuff like that. I love New Orleans stuff . . .'

'What about Little Feat?' I ask, spotting a light at the end of Neil's dark traditional tunnel.

Neil starts to sing 'Willin'':

(*The first line of 'Willin'', the one concerning the effect of rain on the narrator.*)

I join in with:

(*The second line of 'Willin'', in which the narrator sings of what the snow did to him.*)

We sing together:

(*The third line of Willin'', in which the narrator explains that, despite his poor personal hygiene and state of intoxication, he is, none-theless, still willin' . . .*)[*]

And by an extraordinary coincidence that sort of spooks us both out, at this exact moment Little Feat's 'Willin'' starts playing on my mixtape. We smile all over our big red pissed and stoned faces, and start to sing the whole thing together. At the end of the song, we hold out our hands to one another, and clasp them in a hippy handshake, thumbs interlocked, fingers grasped around each other's wrists.

'Mate,' I say, and he says it back to me, and we were mates anyway, but we have bonded over one of the few songs in the world that we have in common, bonded good and proper. It doesn't matter what inauthentic production-pop surprises the rest of the mixtape might have in store; we are buddies. It is

---

[*] Sadly, I'm not allowed to quote the actual lyrics without paying Lowell George's estate a vast sum of money. Ridiculous given that you can look the lyrics up online for free. I realise that some readers will be less familiar with popular music than others. I have therefore made a playlist of all the songs mentioned in the book, which you should be able to link to via your Spotify account; although I also realise that this class of readers (i.e., those readers not particularly familiar with popular music) are the least likely to have Spotify accounts.

time for Neil to crack a tinnie, and for me to roll a spliff and make another cup of tea. Once again, I stand outside and play with Billy and watch the stars. The tune of 'Willin'' runs through my head.

Had my head stoved in but I'm still on my feet.

WILLIN'

I was driving south from Penrith on the M6, steering with my knees so that I could roll a fag, and listening to 'Willin'' on the radio. 'Willin'' is still the greatest ever driving song, even if you're not driving every kind of rig that's ever been made, from Tucson to Tucumcari, Tehachapi to Tonopah, but merely bimbling along in a Hyundai Accent from Cockermouth to Presteigne. I was following the tail-lights of a Norbert Dentressangle wagon through rain that was turning to sleet as we climbed up into the mountains. It was eleven o'clock at night, and I still had a long way to go.

I'd been spending the day filming a car rally in a forest outside Cockermouth, and I was cold and damp and seething with age-related ill-temper.* For the film, I'd had to 'navigate' one of the rally cars round a forest section. I say 'navigate'; in fact, all I had done was cling to the roll-over bar and weep bitter tears of self-pity. I was supposed to be talking; there was a tiny camera

---

* In my very occasional role as a presenter of regional television programmes.

clipped to the sun visor, and I was wired for sound, but nothing came out except 'Please slow down', which made the driver laugh. I hated him more than I'd ever hated anything or anybody. Later, in the evening, I'd had to stand in the middle of Cockermouth, in darkness and freezing rain, attempting to fake some small enthusiasm for whoever the hell it was that had won the stupid rally. Climbing Shap on the M6, in darkness, through sleet, tail-gating a wagon, rolling cigarettes, and listening to Radio Two, one thing was very clear to me. Whatever fate might have in store, I was not going to be presenting *Top Gear.*

'Willin'' faded in a blur of static. I jabbed at the search button, but I'd passed beyond all transmission range. I kept the volume up to listen to the white noise; it suited the sleet and the spray, and the tchick tchick tchick of the windscreen wipers. It suited my mood. I thought about how much I hated rally car drivers.

Past the sign that shows you've crossed Shap Fell, the radio started to crackle back into life. I pressed the search button again. The music had gone; now it was either Radio Three or, most likely, Radio Four. I turned up the volume. The programme was about a series of tapes recorded by Philip Larkin, which had been found in a lock-up garage in Hull. The tapes had been forgotten for years, and just recently rescued from the lock-up; this was their first airing.

Poetry reading has for years been trying to escape from under the impersonal nose of T.S. Eliot, to whom we can fairly attribute the introduction of that up and down poetry voice, a dangerous voice when you are driving at night and trying to stay awake. Larkin doesn't sound like that. Larkin sounds like he's reading his mother the editorial of the *Sunday Express* after a particularly dull lunch one dreary afternoon in Loughborough, with a cork stuffed up one of his nostrils.

'Toads,' said Larkin.

Excellent, I thought.

> Why should I let the toad work
> Squat on my life?

Why indeed, I thought.

> Six days of the week it soils
> With its sickening poison –
> Just for paying a few bills!
> That's out of proportion.

Yes, I thought. That's just right that is. Well said.

> Lots of folk live on their wits:

Oh, hang on: I live on my wits. I mean, I may have hated being flung round a forest in a specced-up Subaru Impreza, but I had just been paid three hundred and fifty quid by way of compensation.

> Lecturers, lispers
> Losels, loblolly-men, louts -
> They don't end as paupers;

I lecture. I don't lisp, but I've been a lout, and a losel, and a loblolly-man, come to that, and am still not quite a pauper. A sickening realisation dawns. I am the opposition in 'Toads'.

> Lots of folk live up lanes

I lived up a lane! In a caravan! With a chicken called Ginger!

> With fires in a bucket,

I've lost count of the fires in buckets I've sat round.

> Eat windfalls and tinned sardines –
> They seem to like it.

I did like it!

> Their unspeakable wives . . .

I've had unspeakable wives, more than one. Will I always have to have unspeakable wives, just because I once dealt a little loblolly and sat around the odd fire in a bucket? Must I cease to live by my wits, and yield to the toad, if I am to have a wife of whom I can cheerfully speak?

> Ah, were I courageous enough
> To shout, Stuff your pension!
> But I know, all too well, that's the stuff
> That dreams are made on . . .

I haven't got a pension. Should I have a pension? I'm a writer, aren't I? You just keep writing till you stop, don't you? You get 'late style'. If the dream is not to have a pension, then I'm living the dream, aren't I? I felt a panic attack coming on. If Larkin doesn't make you think about your imminent death, or your woeful lack of pension, what does? Killington Lake Services, the signs told me. Strong coffee would be a mistake, because my heart was rocking like Gepetto's workshop due to rally rage and Larkin-induced anxiety, but I needed to stay awake, so strong coffee it had to be. As I pulled off onto the slip road, Larkin started to read another poem:

This was Mr Bleaney's room . . .

I clicked off the radio before the panic became uncontrollable, before Mr Bleaney's fate brought home further the dire consequences of a pension-less old age. Though I reckon I could live with the summers in Frinton, if not the Christmases in Stoke.

Killington Lake motorway service station is one of the quietest service stations you'll ever visit. There are several reasons for this. One is that it's on a stretch of motorway which is mostly for passing through. It's just south of the Lake District proper, and well north of Preston, where several motorways meet. Also, it only has south-bound facilities, so you don't get cross-motorway action: north-bound travellers coming over on the footbridge to sample the forbidden delights of the other side. But the main reason it's quiet, it seems to me, is that anybody with any sense would have stopped at the service station before, the thrice-blessed Tebay.

Tebay is so good that it annoys me. The food is excellent, the service is friendly, there is a superb farm shop, and even the gift shop is the best of its kind. If you were racing north to see your gran in Motherwell, and it was late on Christmas Eve, and you suddenly realised that you hadn't got the old love a present, you could get her something half-decent at Tebay Services. People go out of their way to stop at Tebay. A few weeks previously, after another bout of filming in Cumbria, I'd stopped there round midnight, and got chatting to a couple from Hertfordshire who'd been to visit their daughter and their new grandson in Glasgow.

'We always like driving through the night,' said the husband. 'Why?'

'Much less traffic,' said his wife. 'We stay on till our grandson is in bed, and head off about nine.'

'Get here for midnight, have something to eat, and then have a couple of hours' kip, wake up, come in here for another coffee, and set off again at about three. Get home just as the rush hour starts.'

'It means we get more time with our grandson.'

Tebay is civilised, clean, stylish, a good place to stop. It doesn't get many truckers, because it can be a bit pricy, but private drivers expect motorway service stations to be pricy. The priciness of the thing is part of the experience. And the food there is a bit special, anyway, and good value for the motorway. No, it's not because Tebay is pricy that it annoys me. It annoys me because it really is great. So why can't all service stations be this good? A visit to Tebay just fuels your resentment at all other motorway service stations. I mean, it's halfway up a mountain. If they can do it, why can't anybody else?

But it doesn't annoy me so much that I don't stop there. That would be perverse. I would have stopped, but tonight it's Killington Lake, just because I thought I could keep going to Charnock Richard before stopping. Sadly, I was wrong. Larkin had driven me off the road.

Killington Lake was deserted. It was as though somebody had exploded the neutron bomb, the one that kills humans and leaves buildings and games machines intact. There was a smiling Thomas the Tank Engine ride for kiddies, and no kiddies to ride it. The gambling machines flashed their gaudy come-ons to no one. There was a Costa, and a Wimpy concession, neither of which were open. The only bit that was open was the generic caff, the one that has to stay open 24 hours a day by law. And there was no one there, either. I called, and a smiling lady came through from the back.

'Oh, hello, love. You been waiting long? What can I do yer?'

'Coffee, please. And a doughnut.'

Her name was June. She hadn't been there long, 'about three month'.

'Do you do shifts?'

'No, love. I'm on permanent nights. Hang on, I'll tek me break wi yer.'

Why not? There was no one else there. She felt sorry for me, I expect, since I had a book under my arm, which is, to many people, a sure sign that one is seeking company.

She came over to my table with a coffee of her own.

'Do you like working nights?'

112

'It's alright, aye. I'm getting used to it, anyway.'

'Didn't you like it at first?'

'No, I felt that ill. My friend said to me, you look ashen. And I did. I looked at meself in the mirror, and she were right. I did look ashen.'

'What happened?'

'You get used to it, don't yer? Your body tunes itself. Now I don't mind it.'

'What do you do when you get in? I mean, do you have breakfast?'

'I have it here. I knock off at seven, eat me breakfast, go 'ome, and go ter bed.'

'Don't you watch the news, or anything?'

'No, love. The secret is, get 'ome, and then go straight ter bed.'

'What time do you get up?'

'Between three and four. Then I do me bits of shopping, and cook and watch telly, then I get 'ere fer eleven.'

'How many of you are there?'

'There's two of us in 'ere, me and Pauline. Then there's Graham in the garage.'

'Do you ever get scared?'

''Ow do yer mean, love?'

'You know. Does it ever kick off? Do you ever get weirdos?'

'No, nothing like that. There's a bloke from Liverpool who comes in most weeks who's a bit doolally.'

'What's he like?'

'Oh, he's alright really. He gets his tea, and then he brings it to the till, and then he talks for about ten minutes, non-stop.

You can't get a word in edgeways. If anything did worry us, Graham from the garage would be over 'ere like a shot.'

'And what about ghosts? I mean, do you ever get spooked?'

'Not 'ere, love. I've seen ghosts. I believe in 'em. But not 'ere.'

'You've seen ghosts?'

'Aye, love. Before I was divorced. My ex-husband and me used to tek our dog fer a walk over this little bridge int' Lake District where someone had been killed on their bike, and he didn't like it at all.'

'Your ex-husband?'

'No. The dog. Dogs are sensitive.'

'And you've seen a ghost?'

'Oh aye. Me and me ex-husband used to run hotel int' Lake District, and that were haunted bad.'

'What happened?'

'Oh, I used to get a feeling. I 'eard footsteps. And once I'll swear I saw a hooded figure go past the serving hatch.'

I finished my coffee, and said goodbye to June and her spine-tingling tales. I walked across the deserted site to the garage, which stood blank, blazing with light, waiting for something/ anything to happen. The guy behind the counter seemed surprised to see anyone walking over his forecourt, and certainly much more worried about safety than June had been. The automatic doors failed to open at my approach. He spoke through the security hatch.

'Yas?'

'Packet of Gold Leaf and some silver papers, please.'

'Is that the big papers or the little ones?' He spoke into a mike, and his voice crackled out of tiny speakers. He sounded like Davros on forty a day. He must have been in his late fifties, unless the bandit screen flatters those who sit behind it. This was Graham, as his name badge confirmed.

'Little ones, please. You need a secret ingredient for the big ones, which I don't have.'

He smiled at my little lie through his scratched-up Perspex window. I did have some spliff, and I was thinking of popping one together in the deserted car park before heading south, but I find the little papers more than adequate for my modest cannabis needs these days. Besides, I disapprove of king skins. If young people haven't got the gumption to stick a couple of Rizlas together, then we really are all doomed.

'Five-twenty please,' he crackled.

'You're not from round here?' I said.

'No, mate. I'm from Devon.'

'Whereabouts?'

'I come from Okehampton. Do you know it?'

'I used to live near Hatherleigh. Used to go shopping in Okehampton Waitrose.'

'Has it got a Waitrose, now, Okehampton? Years since I've been back.'

'No family left down there?'

'A brother I don't see, if he's still alive.'

'What brought you up here?'

'Followed a lady.'

I laughed. 'Does she mind you working nights?'

'Split up years ago, we did.'

'Sorry to hear that.'

'I just loved it up here. The mountains, and the lakes and the people. So I stayed.'

'Do you get to see much of the lakes, though, if you work nights?'

'No! Best time to work, nights. All the best people work nights. Go home, walk the dog, go to bed till about two. Then the rest of the day's mine.'

'But don't you get lonely?'

'No, mate. The wagon drivers come and chat. There's always something happening.'

Nothing had happened for at least three-quarters of an hour, since I'd pulled off the motorway.

'You're not very busy, though?'

'Not this time of year. You should see this place in summer.'

'Busier?'

'It can be heaving some nights.'

'And does it ever get scary?'

'Not behind a bandit screen, it doesn't.'

'But if something happened over at the café? Would you go and sort it out?'

'Can't leave the cabin, mate. I'd call the police.'

Graham, I had begun to suspect, was less of a White Knight in waiting than June had been led to believe.

I used to work shifts in an all-night garage, and I loved it. The garage was down on the West Quay in my home town of Newhaven. Our next-door neighbour fixed me up with the gig; he was site manager of the ferry terminal, and his name was Mr Cartwright. My brother was at war with his kids; my brother and his mates would scrap with the Cartwright brothers and their mates, with fists and boots and nuts. Once, my brother stuffed lit newspaper through their letterbox, and got whupped by our Old Feller. It was in the Cartwrights' garden, too, that the band of the Newhaven Air Cadets would rehearse for Newhaven Bonfire Night. The band of Newhaven ATC was most unusual at that time, because they only used glockenspiels and drums. Oddly, it's a combination that never really caught on.

Far and away the best thing about the Cartwrights' back garden, though, was the fact that Mrs Cartwright would sunbathe topless in it, and if you got a chair, and balanced it on the step where the stairs turned, and peered out of the landing window, you could get to see her tits. They weren't great tits, I now realise. I think I half-realised it at the time, when I hadn't seen any tits other than Mrs Cartwright's, because she was odd-looking. She was tall, and thin, and bottle blonde, and she walked funny, with her back very straight. She never spoke to anybody; never looked at you or smiled. My mum said she was mutton dressed as lamb. She wore mini-skirts, which didn't suit her; not because she didn't have good legs, but because her good legs looked like an autobahn map of West Germany. Still, what thirteen-year-old boy cares about varicose veins? The tits were reward enough. Given our family's chequered past with the Cartwrights, I was pleased when Mr C gave me the job at the filling station when I left school, though I suppose he didn't know about me, my brother and our friends taking it in turns to balance on the chair on the step where the stairs turned to crack one off while we looked at his wife's tits.

There were only two busy periods at the filling station. The first busy period was just after half past midnight when the ferry from France came in, and the other was at six in the morning, as wagons started to arrive for the first ferry of the day over to Dieppe. And it wasn't self-service, and we didn't sell Golden Virginia or Mars Bars for stoners, as they do in all-nighters these days. A large part of an all-night garage's business in towns is with people buying sweeties and Rizlas. No, it was a proper filling station; petrol, diesel and oil, that's what we sold.

In between the two boats, there was nothing much to do but listen to Radio Luxembourg[*] and read. In August 1977, I tuned in on my arrival at midnight to hear Tony Prince announce the death of Elvis. So unthinkable was it that Elvis was dead, that I thought for at least ten minutes that it was a bad-taste joke, perpetrated in the holy name of punk rock. I thought Tony was saying that Elvis was metaphorically dead, a sentiment which I heartily endorsed. By the time the ferry came in, however, I was convinced that it was true. Usually newly returned holiday-makers wanted to know the cricket scores; this time I could fill 'em up, and break the news that The King Was Dead. I knew Mr Cartwright would be upset, as he'd told me he was an Elvis fan.

There was an old mattress tucked behind the till. Mr Cartwright didn't mind too much if you had a bit of kip between the two boats, so long as you shut down the pumps and locked the cabin door. He knew that it was very rare to get

[*] Radio Luxembourg was the only all-night radio station in those days, unless the weather was right and you could pick up the faint sound of Radio Caroline.

any traffic between the boats. He was a good bloke, I always thought. There wasn't much to him; I was about a third taller than him, and I was only nineteen. He wore horn-rimmed specs, and liked to chat about music. So long as you turned up on time, and were awake when needed, he didn't much mind what went on. You could make tea. Mates might drop by. Sometimes my friend Andy came down with a bit of blow, and we'd have a smoke in the cabin. This went horribly wrong one night when a Customs Officer stopped by at 2 a.m., when nobody ever stopped at my pumps. The cabin was full of fragrant smoke; he pulled away from the garage, pulled up outside the dock security office, and went inside. Andy and I popped his bit of gear into the lavatory cistern, and opened the door of the tiny glass cabin to let the smoke out. Five minutes later, the policeman on the dock gate strolled over to 'chat' with us. He suspected something was up, I think, since he stayed for about an hour, with me and Andy like paranoid bunnies trapped in the headlights. Then he went back into his hut, and Andy went home. In the morning, when I finished my shift, I hoiked Andy's spliff out of the cistern, and went to his in the afternoon after I'd had a sleep to see if the hash had survived its night in the damp.

One night, I came home off my shift to find police cars parked up the Brighton Road, lights flashing. My mum was very upset as she cooked my breakfast.

'Cartwright's murdered his wife.'

Which he had. We found out later that he'd strangled her on their couch, because he'd said something to her, and she hadn't answered. That was the story around the town, anyway. There was a lot of talk. A few weeks later, I left the filling station to go to Lampeter.

When I came back at Christmas, I met Mrs Stevens in the High Street. She was the Cartwrights' neighbour on the other side.

'It was our thirtieth wedding anniversary that night,' she told me. 'And all night we had the police in and out. Ruined the party. Bloody typical Cartwrights.'

But he was a good boss.

I left Graham in his cabin at Killington, got into the car, decided against the spliff, checked the radio. The Larkin show had finished; now it was the World Service as I headed south. I looked at my trip odometer, and estimated a time I'd get home. About four-ish, if I was lucky. Shouldn't be too much trouble. The coffee would keep me going. By the time I'd gone another fifteen miles, the car was veering between lanes, and even though I had the window wide open and freezing rain was stinging my face, I knew I couldn't stay awake. I stopped off at the next service station, which is the excellent Truck Haven, outside Carnforth, wrapped myself in a blanket I keep in the boot, and fell into a light sleep.

When I came to, it was still dark, and still raining, but when I turned on the radio it was *Farming Today*. I rolled a fag, and stepped out into the rain. Truck Haven is, quite literally, a haven for trucks. The truck park holds hundreds of wagons; and 5.50 is wake-up time for many of the drivers, who were starting to emerge from their cabs to take breakfast in the excellent café. You don't have to sleep in your cab at Truck Haven; it has fifty or so rooms. I've stayed there on occasion, and it's cheap and clean.

I went in for my breakfast. Already the place was a third full and filling. The ladies who cook at Truck Haven are lovely, but they were busy in the kitchen, too busy to chat. The day was due; had started for some people. Tebay might be a rather lovely spot to stop if you want a home-cured ham and whole-grain mustard sandwich with a bit of wild rocket on the side, but for a proper cooked breakfast, Truck Haven is hard to beat anywhere on the British motorway system. I had extra black pudding. BBC News 24 was playing on a huge TV screen. They were interviewing a man from the European Broadcasting Union who was threatening to move the venue for that year's Eurovision, as an unforeseen consequence of Kosovan independence. Seems I had woken up to a world of trouble.

After breakfast, I stood outside with a couple of fellow smokers in the rain. One of them was called George, and he was the night manager. I told him that I used to work in an all-night garage.

'Not from round 'ere, are yer?' he pointed out.

'No. Not exactly. But I lived in Lancaster for eleven years.'

'I regard Lancaster as the backwoods.'

'Do you?'

'Aye. Shithole. Do you know, I've not been shopping in Lancaster for twenty-odd years?'

'Where do you live? In Carnforth?'

'No! Morecambe. Great place, Morecambe. I get 'ome, take the dog for a walk along the prom, and I always think 'ow lucky I am to live in Morecambe.'

'Do you always take the dog for a walk before you sleep?'

'Aye. Then I sleep for a few hours, then do a few bits and bats, have a kip in the afternoon, then I walk the dog again before I come in to work.'

'How long have you worked nights?'

''Ere, about six month. But all me life, really. I were night foreman at Reeboks before they closed it down. I couldn't work days, now.'

'Because your body clock is tuned to the night?'

'No, not really. When I go on 'oliday, it only teks about a day to change back. No, I like the people you meet on nights.'

'Why?'

'They're friendlier, aren't they? People aren't so much on their guard at nights. Besides . . .'

He lit another cigarette.

'Besides,' he said, 'it needs doing, dunt it?'

'What does?'

'Night working. All this.' He nodded towards the motorway. The roar of the traffic was starting to pick up volume.

'Yes.'

'If it wasn't for night workers, nothing would work. The transport network would break down. The roads would be jammed up all the time, if everyone lay in bed all night.'

Back in the car, radio on, fag on, I pulled out onto the motorway. John Humphrys was interviewing a man from the European Broadcasting Union about political upheaval in the Balkans. I couldn't help wondering if Kosovo would have been so cavalier in declaring its independence if they'd known it might call the Eurovision Song Contest into question. I pressed the search button. On Radio Two, Sarah Kennedy was playing something by Elaine Paige. I searched again, and found Heart. They were playing something by Simply Red. I tuned back to 'Today'. The dawn was trying to break through the rain. 'Willin'', and Larkin, seemed a long way away.

DAVID!

I have pushed Neil too far.

'Please tell me you don't like this?' He is close to tears, old memories of early-70s rockist opposition to pop clearly overwhelming his emotions.

'Man, I LOVE this! This is fucking brilliant.' I smile at him.

'No . . . you can't mean it.' His hands are shaking as he grasps his tinnie.

'I can. I do. This was the first song I bought off iTunes.'

'Now I know you're fucking mental. You bought *this*? You paid money for *this*?'

'Yep.'

'This' is 'How Can I Be Sure?' by David Cassidy. It really is the first song I bought off iTunes, which does give me pause for thought occasionally, but about which I am largely unrepentant. I'd always moaned at my daughter Minnie and her friends for the illegal downloading of music, telling her that it might lead to people illegally downloading e-books, e-books written by me, which might cause Daddy a huge loss of income, which in

turn might affect her ability to buy meow meow and white cider.

'Yeah, about 85p a year,' said Minnie. 'I mean, you're not exactly Madonna, are you? One shit CD and four shit books, that's what you've had out . . .'

'Six, actually.'

'Six shit books, then. People still aren't going to be downloading you, are they?'

Perhaps not, but that's not the point; I am against illegal downloading, because artists, even if they are Madonna and not exactly hard up, need and deserve protection. So I was an early adopter of iTunes, keen to start buying singles again seriously, for the first time since the late 80s.

The night came where I'd downloaded all the software, and uploaded all my payment details, so that, at about 2.30 in the morning, I was ready to go. I selected Cassidy's mawkish ballad, and clicked to download. 'How Can I Be Sure?' is now mine forever.*

'But why?' moans Neil.

'Why not? It's a great song.'

'But it's not. I mean, it's really really not.'

And here, dear reader, Neil and I embark on a long and, to me at least, fascinating conversation on the subject of taste, with which I am obsessed. So fascinating is this discussion that when Neil drops off after ten minutes or so, I make a few notes, which, in my stoned state, suggest to me very strongly that I must devote what remains of my life to the question of taste, and what it is,

---

* Obviously, I had it on 7" already.

and why I have got it in spades, especially when it comes to music.

I nip out to my car for another couple of unlabelled CD mixtapes, and bring them back in. Neil is snoring a bit. I don't want to wake the poor old fucker up, so I roll myself a spliff and take my book out of my bag. I'm reading Roberto Bolano's *2666*, and I'm bogged down in the middle bit, the bit about the murders.

Reading, and reading at night in particular, is something I've been at since before I can remember. Like eating, it's just something I've always done by night. Many of the Mass Observers also talk about reading in bed; one forty-year-old man from Stockton-on-Tees remembered how he rigged up a dressing-gown cord to his wall light so he could switch it off if his parents caught him reading after lights out. As a kid, I read under the covers with a torch; first Enid Blyton, then Malcolm Saville and Arthur Ransome and Anthony Buckeridge, then, at twelve, *The Lord of the Rings*. It took me about three months to get through the single-volume paperback. I was struck by the sheer scale of the thing on my bedside table, by the delicacy of the paper, by the beauty of the Pauline Baynes cover. By the time I was twelve, my mum had given up the struggle to stop me reading all night. So that's what I did: I read all night, night after night. Having broken the back of *Lord of the Rings*, I felt invincible as a reader.

Sad to say, reading is beyond doubt the thing that I've done second most in bed, after sleeping. Sexual intercourse probably comes sixth, after sleeping, reading, drinking tea while reading, smoking fags while reading, and wanking, which in terms of sheer volume still probably just beats actual sex. Some nights I still don't sleep at all due to reading. Sleeping is what the day is for, after all. One of the worst cases I remember was reading Charles Palliser's mad Dickensian homage, *The Quincunx*. I got to the end of the twelve hundred-odd pages at 3.30 a.m., after three nights glued to the thing, only to realise that in order to understand the ending, I had to go back and start the bastard over again. So I did.

Tonight I am struggling with Bolano's swampy middle, Neil is snoring like a buffalo, and it's getting cold.

I open the wood-burner and pop in a new log, and while I'm rustling around Neil comes to.

'Do you read in bed?' I ask him.

'Put the kettle on,' he says. 'I'll have a coffee before I have another tin.'

Neil gets up for a stretch; he walks through into the kitchen where I am pouring hot water onto instant coffee granules.

'No, I don't really read that much at all. I mean, I loved *The Longest Mile*,* but other than that, not really. I'm usually too pissed to read in bed . . .'

That's alright, Neil. Apparently, 80 per cent of people have less than ten books in their homes. I'm glad to be one of your ten. Anyhoo, as anyone who writes knows, lots of people don't give a toss about books, never mind in bed. Perhaps we make too much of it. Reading is supposed to improve us. But Hitler read extensively in bed, whilst it seems to be about all Mao ever did. His bed was always covered in books. There's a famous

---

* It's *The Longest Crawl*, Neil. I've told you this already.

painting of the Chairman, called 'Searching The Truth', where he sits in bed reading some good old-fashioned Marxist-Leninist bodice rippers. Handily, of course, he is already wearing his pyjamas. They might have been readers, Mao and Hitler, but it didn't turn them into great guys, did it? Hitler was also a vegetarian, which says it all.

Plato was reading in bed the night he died, and he was a great guy, but you can't say for sure it was the reading in bed that made for the greatness. Pepys loved to read in bed, and even on occasion hired a student to come and read to him, which sounds like a good idea, but it would drive me mad, because they'd pronounce the words wrong, and say, 'This is boring. Got any white cider?' all the time. Robert Burton in *The Anatomy of Melancholy* writes that reading a favourite author is a good way to get to sleep, but I can disprove this by pointing out that when I first read his astounding book I was on an eight-hour flight to the States, and I couldn't sleep a wink.

Until the advent of gas and subsequently electric lighting, reading in bed wasn't entirely safe. There are many stories of straw mattresses catching fire from readers' candles; most disastrously in Albemarle Street in London where, in 1734, several houses were burnt to the ground after a gentleman fell asleep reading. Even the advent of gas lighting wouldn't have helped straight away. At first it was regarded as good only for the servants, because it was vulgar and polluting. Sadly, though, when gas lighting first started to arrive in Britain in the 1840s, female literacy was only around 50 per cent, so lots of the servants who benefited from improved lighting wouldn't have been able to read in bed anyway.

The servants would, however, have delivered trays of food to their employers' beds, always assuming that their employers' mattresses hadn't caught fire from all the reading. Eating in bed is a luxury, but, like so many other luxuries, one shot through with peril. For example, several of the Mass Observers mentioned the discomfort of toast crumbs in bed. As I may have hinted earlier, I seem to do a great deal of reading in bed, and few things help the reader along more than a few McVitie's Plain Chocolate Digestive biscuits. I find skilful dunking helps the crumb problem.

As a hypochondriac schoolboy, I used to love being brought lunch in bed on a tray; my favourite was oxtail soup and unbuttered bread soldiers. I was ill a lot when I was a kid, but no one cared. My parents thought I was just an idle little shit, but now we know I have health anxiety disorder, thanks to them. Still, even if they were sometimes sceptical about the exact nature of my ailments, I always knew when my mum believed me, because she brought me the soup on a tray.

Probably the worst meal you ever have in bed is on Mother's or Father's Day, when the kiddies get it into their pointy little heads that it would be a treat for you if they brought you breakfast in bed at 7.30 a.m. You have to get it all ready yourself the night before. I have two favourite breakfasts: the special one, which features crispy bacon, a perfectly fried egg with a slightly burnt white and a just barely cooked yolk, creamy black pudding, juicy fried bread, a pot of proper tea and two hand-crafted cigarettes – and the ordinary everyday breakfast, which is just the tea and fags. On Parents' Days, instead of your favourite breakfast you get muesli and orange juice, because they can't operate a frying pan or a kettle, as they are seven, and they haven't yet learned to roll your fags for you either. And I reckon muesli is a great breakfast if you are an actual bird; but if you are an actual bird, and you get breakfast brought to you in bed, then it's not muesli but a mouthful of macerated worms, which I honestly think I'd prefer to muesli, which is only kept in the house for the occasional health-conscious visitor, for Mother's/Father's Day festivities and for feeding birds in winter.

And the best meal eaten in bed is not one that is brought to you at all, but one which you prepare yourself (perhaps an omelette, a peach, and a glass of something sparkling) and bring to your lover, who is propped up on pillows and is happy to see you back. The joy in this act of bringing things to your lover in bed is one that never seems to go away; a large number of the male Mass Observers take pride in the fact that they still bring their wife tea in bed every morning. This usually started as the menfolk were leaving for work, but seems to continue right through into retirement.

Pillows are the commonest complaint amongst the Mass Observers about bed. It's a bugger to find one that is comfortable. The great pleasure that one takes from reading in bed, or eating with a lover in bed, and the openness and frankness of the subsequent pillow talk, relies on a supply of comfortable pillows. And they are hard to find. Comfort, which is the main thing we look for in beds, isn't always easy to come by. We are our own worst enemies. The British used to have great bed linen, which was made from actual linen. In the 60s, we thought it would be good to get rid of those linens which we'd inherited from our grandparents, and go to Brentford Nylons instead. Nylon sheets were much more modern; all you had to do was pop them in the twin tub, and you could have fresh, clean, easy-to-look-after, wrinkle-free sheets every week, sheets which just happened to make your skin crawl. To younger readers, who have never experienced sleeping on proper nylon sheets, all I can say is I envy you.

Where do you go now if you're looking for comfort? I would suggest that Northern Ireland is the place. There is still a functioning Irish linen industry, even if it only hangs on by the skin of its feeble old teeth. And linen is still the top stuff for a good night's sleep. Linen soaks up moisture, which makes it ideal for hot climates, which admittedly is not the UK, and most certainly is not Northern Ireland. But linen is cool; and although it takes more looking after than Brentford Nylons, the care repays the sleeper, the idler and the lover, as there are few greater treats than sliding into bed between crisp linen sheets.

I found a factory in Banbridge, not far north of the Irish border. Northern Ireland place names put equal emphasis on each of the syllables; perhaps, if you are a Sussex man like me, you'd prefer it if I wrote it like this: Bann Bridge. Ferguson's Irish Linen took some finding, not so much geographically as online; I knocked about for a good few days before I found a linen factory that was still weaving.

I booked a ticket on the night boat from Birkenhead to Belfast (Bell Fast); and, standing smoking a fag on the deck of the ferry, I decided that the view from Birkenhead across to Liverpool is the finest night view in Britain, finer even than a lit-up Blackpool during the Illuminations, which is, I admit, something to see. When I came up to Anfield to watch Liverpool play, I was struck by how the stadium looked under lights; now I could see what a thing of beauty the whole city is by night. The Liver Building, the cathedrals, the Radio City tower, all look OK by day; but by night they are remarkable, and I added Liverpool by night to my list of places to take aliens who were only in the UK for a few days, and wanted to see something worth seeing.*

Sadly, you'd have to take them to Birkenhead to see it.

Night boats, like sleeper trains, are potential theatres of great romance, of course, and, as always when travelling alone, I hoped to meet the femme fatale who would break my balls and my heart, though not necessarily in that order. Instead, I met a loony. As the ship slipped its moorings, and we sailed down the night-time Mersey towards New Brighton, a lady came and started saying something to me, I couldn't tell what; but it was clear that she was very upset, crying and panicking.

'Can I help you?' I asked, but she ran off down the deck, so I went in for dinner (which is still provided by Norfolk Lines on the night crossing).

After dinner I went back on deck, and the lady came out to join me, still visibly upset, and tending increasingly towards the psychotic. She stared at me (lots of people do this, because they mistake me for Boris Karloff in *The Body Snatcher*), but she was

* This idea of finding somewhere to take aliens if they are on a short break is a long-term project of mine. My other contenders are: 1) taking them by narrow-boat from Oxford to Leeds, 2) catching the miniature railway from Ravenglass to Eskdale, then climbing Scafell Pike, assuming they are non-smokers, 3) walking through the City of London from Farringdon tube station to Brick Lane, at night, and then having a chicken tikka, 4) cycling from Jaywick Sands to Southwold, via Clacton and Aldeburgh, and 5) walking along the River Itchen from Winchester Cathedral to the Hospital of St Cross. Your suggestions, please, to ian@ianmarchant.com.

becoming more agitated by the minute. I walked into the bar, and she followed; once again I asked if I could help; once again she ran off. As I sat in the bar drinking a last Guinness before bed, she came up again; she was desperate, desperate for what I couldn't tell, but desperate. The waitress came across, and asked if she'd 'like to see the boss'. Again, I asked if I could help. This time she managed a reply: 'No, it's OK.'

She had what you might call a Middle European accent. But the waitress didn't believe her; she took her by the arm and led her off; to where? The brig? The infirmary? What do they do with agitated passengers on the *Lagan Viking* from Birkenhead to Belfast?

I like sleeping on boats. I was rocked to sleep in the comfortable cabin by the choppy seas, but woken at 5 a.m. by the ship-wide alarm that calls the passengers down to breakfast. It was still dark, but the lights of Bangor and Carrickfergus were twinkling at the entrance of Belfast Lough as I gloomily scraped at some underdone bacon and a sickly egg. Smoking is more my thing; I stood on deck as the *Lagan Viking* sailed towards the illuminated cranes of the Harland and Wolff shipyard. The sun was starting to colour the sky behind the hills; I didn't see the agitated lady as we disembarked.

Six a.m. is not my time of day; I drove towards Banbridge in a fug of sleep deprivation, and got there just after seven. It's a nice-looking place, with a wide High Street, but no cafés were open, so I pushed back the seat of my car and dozed until nine, before drinking a latte in a coffee place and heading off to look for Ferguson's Irish Linen.

Banbridge is a town that was built on linen and its associated trades, such as bleaching and spinning. The atmosphere is right, because linen manufacture demands high humidity, and if high humidity is not to be had in Northern Ireland, then it is not to be had anywhere. The River Bann was regarded as 'the most economised river' in the British Isles in the late eighteenth century. There is a fall of 441 feet from source to sea, which made it perfect for operating mills, all of which were associated with linen manufacture. In addition, the water of the Bann was seen as perfect for bleaching. A list of the weirs across the river in 1874 lists the function of the mills: scutching, beetling, spinning, bleaching, weaving; all the way down the river, the process of linen manufacture.

The finest linen, damasks and lawns came from the Linen Triangle, drawn between Belfast, Armagh and Dungannon. In 1780 the agricultural writer Arthur Young wrote of Ulster: '. . . you see a whole province peopled by weavers; it is they who cultivate the soil, work the looms . . .'

It was a monoculture; linen was the only industry of Northern Ireland worth speaking of. In the late eighteenth century, five to six yards of linen were consumed by everyone in Great Britain every year, made mostly from flax, but occasionally from hemp. Northern Ireland was rich. The great buildings of nineteenth-century Belfast were all built on the wealth created by linen, at least until shipbuilding came to prominence towards the end of the century. You can still visit the excellent Linen Hall Library, opposite Belfast City Hall. The growth of the industry in the late seventeenth century was linked to the arrival of Quaker and Huguenot weavers; the first Huguenots were recorded in Lisburn in 1698. Since Marchant is supposed to be a Huguenot name, I like to imagine that one of my ancestors was a highly skilled weaver, involved in the start of Northern Ireland's prosperity. I like to imagine it, but there is no evidence of it whatsoever; we all seem to have been farm workers in Sussex, which is a bit anti-climactic; like life, I guess.

The Irish linen trade had dropped off by the 1840s, in the face of competition from French linen and cheap Lancashire cotton, but it stayed strong in Banbridge, where it was given a boost by the American Civil War and the consequent hike in the price of cotton. And now it is the last place left in all of Ireland where damask is woven; and Thomas Ferguson's is the last factory, the relict of a province-wide industry.

This historical remnant is now housed in a drab 50s factory on the outskirts of town. They are happy to show people round, and if you've never been up close to a loom, I can't recommend it highly enough as a fascinating morning for boys AND girls. The gift shop manager Nigel showed me round the plant.

'Not many people know it still exists,' he said.

Nigel had worked for Ferguson's for twenty-nine years, starting on the looms and moving over to the gift shop a few years back. The highlight of his career was spending two weeks working in the Smithsonian Institute, showing Irish linen as part of a world trade exhibition.

I could tell that Nigel loved this place, and loved the skill which went into the beautiful fabrics he sold in his gift shop. He took me into the factory itself, which hummed with industry, but was largely devoid of people. Almost all the processes are automated now; there are perhaps a dozen people working in the factory, including hand-workers.

'I have people coming in the shop and telling me they've still got linen they inherited from their great-grandparents,' Nigel said. 'It's not a cheap thing, linen. It's a thing that will last for lifetimes. So you should make yourself afford it. It seems expensive, but it's much better value than cheap stuff.'

To illustrate his point, he introduced me to Mary. Mary was sitting at an old-fashioned sewing machine, making pillowcases. I asked her how long she'd been making them.

'Forty-five years. Since I was fifteen.'

The pillowcases were beautiful. There are eight separate processes that go into making a pillowcase, and Mary makes about twenty a day, all by hand. She is alone; when Mary retires, any day now, there will be no one left making these special things. Mary is a survivor. I asked Nigel how much they go for.

'Each one sells out the factory door for fifty quid. They mostly go to Harrods, where they sell 'em for I don't know how much.'

I'd happily pay a couple of hundred quid for a pair of pillowcases made by Mary, if I didn't have children with an ongoing and seemingly irrepressible desire for food and drink. It would be worth it; soon Mary will have retired, and all our pillowcases will be made by slave labour in China. And they will be cheap, in every sense.

Moisture is sprayed out from pipes in the ceiling of the factory to mimic the humidity of a normal summer's day in Northern Ireland. You need 85 per cent humidity to spin and weave linen. A large vacuum cleaning system is piped around the factory to suck away the fluff that linen manufacture produces. The factory was hot and moist, a bit like putting your hand into a launderette tumble-dryer to see how many more 20ps you need. The looms, fantastic in their complexity, chattered away, and different kinds of linens – lawns, damasks – came off the looms at different rates, according to their quality. The fastest one is the loom producing tea-towels.

'These are the best tea-towels in the world,' said Nigel, and anyone who has worked in a bar will agree. They were those white ones, with a coloured stripe down the side, with 'Glass' woven into them. Nothing soaks up moisture like linen; so nothing makes your glasses shinier. The towels are woven together on a big roll; I watched it coming off the loom, at a rate of about an inch a minute. That's sixty inches an hour; 600 inches in a ten-hour day. If a tea-towel is about eighteen inches long, that means Ferguson's makes about thirty-five tea-towels a day. No wonder they are so expensive; no wonder the linen industry has moved further and further away from places which have actual labour costs. But for all that, your Irish linen tea-towel is a top-of-the-range piece of kit.

Nigel talked me through the linen production process. The flax is mostly grown in France these days.

'It has to be pulled up, not cut,' said Nigel, 'because the fibres run right through the plant.'

'Really? That must call for complicated harvesting machines.'

'It does. In the old days, it just broke backs.'

Nigel showed me some unprocessed flax. It looked like brown hair, a little coarser than human hair; perhaps dog or donkey hair would be nearest the mark.

'It's a complicated process all round,' Nigel said. 'First the flax gets rippled; that removes the seeds. Then it has to be retted.'

'I've read about retting dams. It's rotting, isn't it?'

'Fermentation, really. You can find old retting dams all over County Down. The flax gets gathered into bundles and placed roots down in ponds or dams four to five feet deep, through which flow soft lime-free water. Fermentation takes ten to fourteen days. And it stinks. Stinks to high heaven.'

'And is it ready to use then?'

'No. After retting comes scutching, which is done in scutching mills, and removes the outer layers. Then you hackle it; hackling is combing. Then spinning and bleaching. We can do the spinning here now.'

He pointed to two vast spindles which dominated either end of the factory. The spinning machine is so huge that I had hardly noticed it. It is so large that it essentially fills the plant.

But it was the looms that fascinated me. Hundreds of threads were guided by hooks from spools into the modern German-made looms. If a thread breaks, an alarm sounds, and an operator appears to rethread it. Other than this rethreading process, the looms tick on unattended; this is why there are so few people who still work here. The threads of linen are so fine that it is almost as though the beautiful cloth that emerges onto the bed of the loom is made from nothing. This is an illusion, of course. The main ingredient at Ferguson's is love. The process is largely automated, but the bulk of the handful of employees have been working here all their lives. They care about Thomas Ferguson's, and they care about the stuff they make. If you want to sleep on Irish linen sheets, under an Irish damask duvet cover, and rest your head on Mary's hand-made pillowcases, it will cost you. But, looked after properly, they will last forever, and your grandchildren could still be sleeping on them in fifty years' time.

Back in the gift shop, Nigel showed me some cards from a Jacquard loom which had, until very recently, controlled the weaving process at Ferguson's, and hence the design on the fabric. The looms were invented by a Frenchman called Joseph Marie Jacquard in 1801, and if you read pretty much any history of computing, Jacquard looms are there at the start of Chapter Two. The presence or absence of a hole in one of the cards allows a thread to pass through. Essentially, using these cards, Jacquard could program his looms to produce any fabric design he wished. There is a famous portrait of Jacquard, woven from silk, which was produced on one of his looms using over 10,000 punch cards to control the process.

These punch cards became essential to the development of computers. The first person to recognise that any kind of information could be stored on punched cards was Charles Babbage. His Analytic Engine, which was supposed to be an improvement on his better-known Difference Engine, was designed to be both programmable and to use conditional statements. Both of these essential steps towards the 'Universal Computer' were to be achieved using punch-card technology borrowed from Jacquard looms. In homage to Jacquard, Babbage called the information-storage cards the 'Store' (what we now call the memory) and the programmable card-handling unit the 'Mill' (now the Central Processing Unit). Both the 'Store' and the 'Mill' are terms derived from Jacquard; it seems a shame that we no longer use them. Modern looms have just taken the obvious step of using digital computers to control the weave, but essentially they are doing the same job that punched cards did almost 200 years ago.

Perhaps you are lying in bed, on Irish linen sheets, reading this on your laptop or iPad (and I hope you've paid your couple of quid for the privilege; remember that I have Minnie's thirst to slake). It may seem unlikely, but there is a direct link between the weaving of the sheets and the development of the computer. And remember that one will keep you awake all night, but the other will take you by the hand and lead you gently, softly into the Land of Nod. And remember that the sheets will probably cost much more than the computer to replace. They are much more valuable – because they have been made with love.

I'M AGAINST THE EIGHTIES

Taste is still very much on my mind. The spliff-fuelled decision that I would devote the rest of my life to thinking about it is firming up.

Neil says, 'You're very quiet, mate. What you thinking?'

I say, 'I'm thinking that "I'm Against The Eighties" by Denim* is currently playing on the mixtape. I'm thinking about how much I love Denim, and how I would much rather listen to Denim than Beethoven, and how this probably says more about me than it does about Beethoven's immortal music. I'm

---

* OK, even I don't really expect Neil to have heard of Denim. They were an early-90s outfit fronted by a bloke called Lawrence, who had once fronted another excellent band in the 80s called Felt. If ever I get on *Desert Island Discs*, the Denim song 'The Osmonds' is one of my definites. In case of an oversight on the producer's part, which might deprive you of the full list, the other seven are 'The Way Young Lovers Do' by Van Morrison, 'She's Gone' by Hall and Oates, 'For a Dancer' by Jackson Browne, 'New York's a Lonely Town' by The Tradewinds, 'This Woman's Work' by Maxwell, 'She Bangs The Drums' by The Stone Roses, and 'I Love Your Smile' by Shanice. And 'If Looks Could Kill' by Camera Obscura. Hang on. That's nine. Oh well; by the time I do get on, I'll probably be ninety, and end up choosing something by Webern, or Alban Berg.

thinking about the girl I dated who loved Denim almost as much as I do, and how we'd play the CD over and over again in my little two-up two-down house in Lancaster while Charley slept upstairs. You might imagine that a girl who loved Denim almost as much as me might be worth hanging on to, but I'm thinking about how mad she was, and about how one night coming back to mine from the pub on the towpath next to the Lancaster Canal, she asked me at what stage in a duck's life-cycle it turned into a swan; and how offended she'd been when I laughed, and how she told me she knew it was true because of "The Ugly Duckling"; and how she'd called me patronising when I explained that "The Ugly Duckling" was a fairy story, and that anyway the whole point of the story was that it wasn't a fecking duckling at all, but a swan all along, and I'm thinking about how our listening to the Denim album had been slightly less enjoy-able that night, and how she decided to go home instead of staying over.

'And I'm thinking about the souvenir mug I won from the old Mark Radcliffe show on Radio Two. It was 11.15 at night and I was alone in the house, enjoying a soak in the bath while listening to Radcliffe's show. And I'm thinking about how there had been some fuck-awful Queen tribute thing on earlier, so when Radcliffe started playing his spot-the-intro game, and it went "BOOM BOOM BAFF! BOOM BOOM BAFF BAFF!" you were supposed to think it was "We Will Rock You" by Queen, but how I knew that it was "Back in Denim", by Denim, and how I leapt naked from the bath, and ran, for the first time in almost twenty-five years, into my study, and emailed the title of the song and my phone number to the show; and about how ten minutes later Radcliffe called me back, and I got on late-night Radio Two, where I managed to plug *The Longest Crawl*,* then nearing completion, make a sheep-shagging joke about the Devon village where I was living at the time, and pour scorn on Queen's entire recorded output before getting to listen to "Back in Denim", by Denim, on Radio Two in my hot bath. And then get a souvenir mug too. That's what I'm thinking.'

'I think you're stoned,' says Neil.

'I think you're right, my friend. I'll get some fresh air.'

Outside, Billy is still waiting to lick my hand.

The rain has cleared away from the west, blown on a sea-scented wind that will see tomorrow beautifully clear for the drive back to Belfast, and which has now opened up the stars. It's a long way from anywhere out here, so the stars are the brightest I've seen them since I left Devon, living as I now do in the centre of a town, albeit an ill-lit Radnorshire one.

And now I'm thinking about the night when I saw the stars for the first time.

---

* My last book. *Longest Crawl*, Neil.

BIG STAR

It had been snowing all evening, that much was evident as we emerged from the window-less bar. It lay a foot or more thick over the car park as we slid and snowballed our way back to Nik's decrepit Ford Escort van under the brightness of the streetlights.

We were drunk and stoned, and we were high up in the Cambrians, and it was late January. It had been Baltic cold for a couple of weeks. Our shared house, six miles out of town, stood on the scarp of a hill overlooking the River Teifi and the village of Llanddewi Brefi, famous now as a comedy Welsh village, but infamous then as the site of Operation Julie, the acid bust to end all acid busts.

In the freezing fogs and rains one wall of our house had become covered in a sheet of inch-thick ice. In order to micturate*, we had to break the ice in the lavatory bowl. There was no heating other than a feeble fire in the sitting room, which none of the six

* piss

of us were really man enough to get going; it burnt a faint pink, and gave off as much heat as an EU-accredited low-energy light bulb at the UKIP national conference. For several nights now, none of us had bothered to get as far as our rooms to sleep, but had all brought our sleeping bags into the front room, to cluster round the little fire, and to take whatever warmth could be had from sleeping in the same room as one another.

And now the snow which had been threatening had finally come, and four of us were stuck in Lampeter, while two of the lads shivered in the house. Our choice seemed simple; either we could kip in Lampeter on friends' floors, and stay warm and safe, or we could attempt the six-mile drive through snow-choked lanes in Nik's disgusting van. It was for Nik to call, because he was the only one of us who could drive, and when Nik was merry on beer and buzzing with drugs, nothing as soft as a blizzard was going to stop him getting in his van; so off we set. I sat in the front next to Nik, because I was the tallest. You had to keep your feet up on the dashboard, because the floor on the passenger's side had rusted away long ago. We scythed through the snow, which was coming in through the hole in the floor. Although it had now stopped falling, it was much too late at night for the snow-ploughs to be out, especially on the back road to Llanddewi Brefi, which Nik had decided to take because he was much much too drunk to face the A road out of town, on which Dyfed Powys police could sometimes be found sitting waiting to nab hippies on their way back into the hills after a night in the fleshpots of Lampeter.

We got about two miles before Nik's van decided that it had had enough of trying to get through the snow. With a little judicious wheel-spinning from Nik, and some half-assed pushing from the passengers, we managed to get the van into a field gateway, where we abandoned the thing, and started the four-mile walk back to the freezing ice-covered house.

It's difficult for people who have only ever lived in towns to imagine what night is really like, because we burn the darkness away. And now even the tiniest village is lit bright orange at night. But in the 70s, street lighting had yet to spread to the heart of the countryside, and it was still dark. And up in the mountains, even in snow, there was not enough light to see our hands in front of our faces. None of us had a torch; that would have been much too sensible. Nik and I had lighters, which we would flick so that we could pick our way through the snow in the unyielding Welsh night.

But help was at hand; the clouds started to part and drift away, and after maybe half an hour and perhaps half a mile, the stars came crashing out in all their glory.

In total darkness, we are alone with ourselves. As often as not, we send ourselves to sleep. Consciousness seems barely possible in a blackout, stuck with only our egos for company. During the day, our sense of wonder can be diminished. It is clear that we are not then in the same sense alone as we are in the night, because we can see other people, or at least the familiar stuff of nature, even out in the middle of a wilderness. On the odd day when the clouds break, the blue of the sky serves as a reassuring ceiling which lets us focus on our lives, and on the lives of others. On a starlit night, we are confronted with the infinite nature of the universe, as countless billions of stars mock us with our insignificance. It is the stars that remind us of our microscopic size. The night sky can confront us with the sheer pointlessness of our existence; the things that seem to matter so much in the sun hardly matter at all by starlight.

The four of us were struck dumb by the vastness of the sky, by that infinitude of stardust. The Milky Way revolved around our heads. Where the road had been invisible, it now shone with empyreal light. In awed silence, we marched home through the snow, aware as certainly I had never been before both of our insignificance in the cosmos, made clear by the opening up of the starlit sky, and by a new-found ability to appreciate that insignificance. It was funny how close to zero we all were.

Emerson said that 'the universe protects itself by pitiless publicity'. At night, we can truly see. The sun, life giver though it might be, is too bright for our tired eyes. Our earliest calendars are based on the moon, at least in part because the moon is easier to observe accurately than the sun. Our ancestors, learning to navigate, would have been lost by day. We followed in their footsteps, a line of lanky punky hippy boys wearing ex-RAF greatcoats in file ahead. We stared at the sky in silence, and navigated our way down snow-stuffed lanes to the stone bridge across the Teifi, a last ribbon of blackness in a landscape of glittering crystal.

At least one of my pals from that night has become an enthusiastic amateur astronomer as a consequence of that star-struck walk through the snow. I like enthusiasts. I'm enthusiastic about all kinds of things, but sometimes enthusiasm is inimical to wonder. I tried to stay with the wonder after that night, and never really bothered to get into the nitty-gritty of star-gazing. Nature, innit? Living in an area with low back-lighting, I get to see the stars a lot; I crane my neck, and still think about the beautifully appropriate nature of my insignificance, and go 'Wow', but I don't know the names of many of the stars. Perry Venus has an 'app' on his phone whereby you can hold it up to the sky, and it will come up with a map of the bit of sky you are looking at, so that you can identify what you are seeing, but there is so much that it hardly seems worthwhile. It's like putting a name to every blade of grass on earth, and those are not infinite, not exactly, and could theoretically be counted. Of heavenly bodies, there is no end.

The only things we really need to identify, now that we navigate by satellite and no longer take notice of astrology, are asteroids and comets. They're the ones that we need to be thinking about. And they're the ones that we ignore. Stars might be infinite and beautiful, vast nuclear furnaces in which all matter is made and sprayed around the place, but they are not going to blow up in our atmosphere and sterilise life on earth. Asteroids could. One day, asteroids probably will. Asteroids hurt. We need to know where they are and what they're doing. And we are especially aware of this in Radnorshire, because there is not much to do with the kids on school holidays. So every summer, on any wet August afternoon, all the parents of Radnorshire in turn pop their kids in their cars, and drive up Stonewall Hill to pay a visit to our oddest visitor attraction, the Spaceguard Centre.

There is very little light pollution on top of Stonewall Hill; that's why they built the Spaceguard Centre there. There are a couple of farmsteads up towards the high summit; six miles off in the south you might just see the faint glow of the streetlights of Presteigne, and deep below in the valley of the Teme the slightly brighter glow of Knighton, though neither of them are exactly Times Square at New Year. It's dark at night, and you could argue that cuts are good for astronomy, because the turning out of the streetlights in Powys makes an already dark place even darker.

You can see the Spaceguard Centre for miles, which is, I suppose, the whole point of an observatory. It was built in the early 90s, and it looks it; it was a tough call, I guess, to design something which is both a house and an observatory. It has a hint of postmodernism, a pinch of brutalism, and a bloody great big observatory dome sticking out of the top. It was built by a somewhat mysterious couple, who managed to get it adopted as the Powys County Observatory. Why Powys wanted an observatory, nobody can now say. Perhaps it was to spot unpaid parking tickets and streetlights left on as far afield as Ystradgynlais and Llanrhaeadr-Ym-Mochnant. Who can tell? The point is, Powys saw the need for an observatory, and this was it. In about 2000, Powys presumably having obviated the need for an observatory by the launch of their first spy satellite, the building was bought by a benefactor who allows the Spaceguard Centre to operate in this unique place.

I love taking the kids up to the Spaceguard Centre. It's run by a man called Jay Tate. His mission is simple: to save the earth from certain doom. **CERTAIN FUCKING DOOM, MAN!**

It is also one of the tiny handful of British visitor attractions that can't offer you a latte and a bit of lemon drizzle cake. The tours are strictly timed: ten-thirty, two and four. They only run if you book ahead. You arrive on time. The lady who takes your money is strict. She might have made an excellent school nurse. Before the tour, she emphasises the seriousness of what you are about to undergo. She tells you to ask Mr Tate questions as you think of them, and not store them up till the end. She tells you that there is no water available on the tour, and that it will take an hour and a half. She tells you to go through the double doors, and wait in the foyer till the tour starts. You do as you are told.

In the foyer, there are copies of letters that Mr Tate has sent to various politicians and ministers, demanding that his work be taken seriously. There are lists of Parliamentary questions asked by Lembit Opik,[*] who is a confirmed supporter of Spaceguarding. Inevitably, the minister's replies only serve to highlight the woeful inadequacy of asteroid protection in government provision.

The tour is timed to start on the hour; and by God, it does. Like Kant walking through Königsberg, you could set your watch by Mr Tate's appearance through the door from the observatory area into the foyer where the punters wait. Astronomers probably have those radio-controlled watches that are accurate to one nanosecond in a billion years. You would probably do quite well to set your watch by astronomers, now I come to think of it.

As he comes through from the observatory, Mr Tate's entrance is stagey, and commands our obedience. He doesn't speak. If there are children in the group, he sighs, and pretends to draw a zip across his mouth. And then he begins his tour with

[*] 'We'll have to find someone new,' Mr Tate said to me of Lemby's defeat at the 2010 election.

an attack on Political Correctness, which he describes as 'asinine nonsense', and by reassuring us that there will be no sexism on the tour, as he treats everyone as a 'proper male'. No 80s Feminist Boy, he. His wife never sat around writing essays on Luce Irigaray and Hannah Arendt, did she, while he cooked lunch and entertained the children?

His jokes aren't funny. They do, however, make you feel uneasy. Tate isn't an evangelist, he's a prophet. Over the next hour and a half, he builds a devastating argument in favour of asteroid protection. He begins by showing pictures of nearby planets, pocked with craters. He takes particular notice of the moon, pointing out that there must be a lot of asteroids in our part of space, since the moon is being hit pretty much all the time. This is demonstrated by showing us how many asteroids hit the moon in an average year; dozens, rather than the odd one or two. He takes you into a small planetarium, and shows you the process of planetary formation. It is as you might expect; over time, due to the action of gravity, small lumps of stuff join together. But not all the lumps in a solar system so cohere. In particular, in our solar system, we have the millions of fragments of debris that we call the asteroid belt, between Mars and Jupiter. These fragments were prevented from forming a planet because of the gravitational pull of Jupiter. And they are dangerous. Tate takes you on to show you, first, a cabinet full of meteorites (which are the bits that hit the earth), and then evidence of the number of times the earth itself has been hit, which really is a fair old few. He explains why the craters are hard to find; essentially, because we've only recently learned how to look for them; but also because lots of the meteorites fall into the sea. He shows what happens if they are not big enough actually to hit the ground, but merely explode in the atmosphere. Tunguska is what happens: hundreds of miles of devastated landscape, the potential death of millions of people, the destruction of our communications systems and a concomitant return to the Dark Ages; maybe, even, if the asteroid or comet that hits us is large enough, the sterilisation of life on the planet.

And then, having persuaded you utterly of his case, Tate outlines what it is necessary to do. There need to be, globally, four dedicated telescopes, whose cost would amount to half of the cost of building the media centre for the London Olympics (this is how, in 2012, people in science and the arts measure the cost of anything). But, having found the things, what then? Mr Tate points out that a decent detection system would give us about a hundred years' worth of warning. He points out that the thing wouldn't need blowing to bits, but would only need a bit of a nudge to change its course, and that since we've already intercepted a comet, we already know how to intercept any other fast small object (and they are fast; a half-decent asteroid would hit the earth at about 40,000 mph). We would have time to work out what to do.

Then Mr Tate takes you to the gift shop, and you buy a rubber, maybe even a pencil. And you are released back onto the wind-blasted summit of Stonewall Hill.

Few Radnorshire people can fail to be convinced by Mr Tate's case. It isn't so much a tour as a highly developed and convincing argument. The schoolchildren of Radnorshire, inevitably taken by their parents every wet summer up to the

Spaceguard Centre, look to the skies with dread. He's right, though, I reckon, because the system Spaceguard UK proposes would be cheap and easy, and it's just the sort of thing governments and international bodies should be doing. Mr Tate is after funding to set up a new telescope, which would then make Spaceguard the main asteroid-detection observatory in Europe. He already has the telescope, a huge Schmidt, built in 1947; it was donated to him by Cambridge University, through the good offices of the Astronomer Royal, Sir Martin Rees, who is a long-time supporter of Spaceguard. All he needs now is the cash to get it going. Mr Tate deserves to take his argument to a much wider audience than the good people of Radnorshire, so that we can be sure that one night we are not all blasted to bits by a spare bit of unused planet.

I drove up Stonewall Hill to talk to Mr Tate, outside of one of the tours. There was a full moon, with flying clouds reflecting light over the landscape. From the Skirrid in the south to the Stiperstones in the north, from the Radnor Forest in the west to the Malverns in the east, the country was the colour of the moon. Mr Tate was waiting outside the Spaceguard Centre, and he was smoking a pipe.

He was very friendly. He led me into a semi-circular kitchen area built around the base of the telescope, and made me a brew. I don't think it was used as a kitchen much, because apart from tea and coffee, the only things being prepared in there were bits of old telescope. He relit his pipe, I relit a fag from behind my ear, and we chatted, smoked, and drank tea. I told him I'd been a couple of times on the tour, and was already sold on the big idea.

What I wanted to know was this: 'Why do we think we are safe?'

If you ask a philosopher a question like that, you can expect a pause, lasting anywhere from a few seconds to fifteen minutes. Pipes are the ideal accoutrement for bridging these gaps. But Mr Tate didn't need his pipe to cover up thinking time. Mr Tate was ready at once. He clamped his pipe between his teeth.

'It's because of the replacement of the catastrophic with the gradualist world view.'

'I see,' I replied, wishing I had a pipe of my own to chaw down on.

'Yes. Because of Lyell and his work on geology, and of course Darwin and evolution, we've come to believe that the world largely changes gradually, rather than all at once. Which, largely, it does. But that doesn't mean catastrophes don't happen. They do. We know they do.'

'What is the likelihood of the earth being hit by an asteroid large enough to do catastrophic damage?'

'Oh, one hundred per cent. We know it has been in the past, and we know it will be again in the future. What we don't know is when. All we can go on is probability.'

'And that's what you're trying to work out? The probability?'

'Exactly. We're trying to find as many of the jokers as possible to declare them safe, so that we can make smaller the statistical likelihood of us being hit by something we hadn't seen coming.'

'What is the statistical likelihood? Current estimate.'

'Well . . . we used to say one Tunguska-type event every thousand years, but that was when it was thought that Tunguska was about fifty metres across. We now know it was about half that. So, one Tunguska every five hundred years.'

A meteorite (or comet fragment) exploded about 5 km over the remote forested area of Tunguska in Siberia in 1908. Thirty million trees were levelled over an area of 2000 km^2, with the power of 1000 Hiroshimas. There were no people there, by chance. Next time, there might be lots of people.

'A joker about a kilometre in diameter, which would be enough to end civilisation, about ten in a million years. That doesn't mean they all come evenly. You might get all ten in a hundred years, and then nothing for the next million, if you were unlucky. A C/T boundary event, like the one that killed the dinosaurs, about one every fifty to sixty million years.'

'Why aren't we looking seriously?'

'Astronomy isn't really a practical subject, not for 250 years, since we cracked navigation. Astronomers don't do anything but look at the sky.'

'What about things like the moonshot? Don't they help with that?'

'No! It's just there, look.' Mr Tate pointed from the window at the full moon behind the scudding clouds.

'You just point the rocket and press GO. You don't need an astronomer for that. No, what we are doing here is practical; there's no theory involved at all. If academics want to study asteroids, they need a sample to look at. We don't need a sample. We need them all.'

He relit his pipe.

'So the academics control where the research money goes, and this isn't research?' I asked.

'Exactly. And we're not academics. We get no funding at all. The only money we get comes through the till.'

I've put money through Mr Tate's till. Last time I came on the tour, I bought myself a novelty Spaceguard key-ring for £3.50. Nobody can say I haven't done my bit.

'Is there no money about for this at all?'

Mr Tate smiled.

'Oh, there was. A tiny drop. The government set up a National Information Centre for Near Earth Objects at the Space Centre in Leicester. Sadly for them, a week before, the International Astronomical Union had made us their International Information Centre for NEOs. Which we still are. They've stopped the national one, of course.'

'Now it's just you?'

'Correct.'

'It must be an awesome responsibility, to be the sole guardian of earth from the dangers of space.'

Mr Tate laughed.

'If you're the only person who knows anything about a subject, then you become the expert by default.'

'Were you a star-gazer as a kid?' I asked.

'No. I was a career officer. Twenty-six years in the army. One night, 14 June 1977, as it happens, I was carrying out surveillance operations in South Armagh with my number two and my signaller. We'd been there for four days and were getting a little bored. My signaller was scanning the sky with his night-vision goggles when he pointed at a star and asked, "What's that, sir?" As an officer you're supposed to know everything, but I couldn't answer his question. So I went out and bought a basic book on astronomy.'

'What was it?'

'A planet.'

'That got you interested?'

'Yes, but I didn't get involved in NEOs till the 90s. I was seconded to the Canadians, and down on holiday in Wyoming I watched when Shoemaker-Levy hit Jupiter. I thought I'd put together a staff paper about what we'd do if a large meteorite hit Britain. What I found out was that there was no plan, and that nobody knows anything. That's when I started Spaceguard UK. That's why I'm the expert.'

It's a defence issue, you see. The US Department of Defense gives NASA money to scan the skies for NEOs. The rest of us just don't bother to look, trusting in Captain America. It's good that retired British army officers, their jaws a little less square but their eyes just as steely as ever, with their pipes clamped firmly between their teeth, are still trying to look after the rest of us, even if we force them to sell novelty key-rings to do it.

Now Mr Tate is trying to raise money to get his massive Schmidt telescope operational, the one he got from Cambridge. He calls it Project Drax.

'What does it stand for?' I asked.

'Nothing. Acronyms are for wimps,' he said. 'We just name our projects after Bond villains.'

He only needs to raise about 50k, which is risible. But still: 'We'll get there. The tough bit is going to be aligning the base to within a few arc seconds of true north . . .' He clamped his pipe between his teeth, and waved me away down the hill. I've slept a little sounder ever since I talked with him.*

* In July 2011, asteroid 2000 DZ12 was renamed 'Jaytate' by U.S. Spacewatch in recognition of Mr. Tate's work.

The idea that people sleep soundly in their beds as a consequence of gradualism is one I can't help but love. Evolution is supposed to cause us angst, as we are now one of a series of random events in a Godless universe, but it turns out that it makes us complacent.

'Oh, we've been here a quarter of a million years or so. No, nothing really happens roundabouts . . . no, hang on, there was that Ice Age a few millennia back. But even that crept up on us.'

We don't need to take money away from academic astronomy to fund Mr Tate's big idea, because we need them both. The practical stuff would never work if we didn't have the theory. After all, the way we see the world, the way we see the sky, the way that Mr Tate can work out the positions of incoming meteorites, all have their root in the work of one man, in one short period of time, and in one particular place. And he was an academic; THE academic, really. And, in his way, the Father of Gradualism, because he posited a perfect and unchanging universe. He was a deeply unpleasant man who had no friends and, so far as anyone is aware, never took a lover. His name was Isaac Newton.

My wife has MA (Cantab) after her name, which never fails to impress me, and her college is Trinity, which makes me hop up and down with glee, or so it did the night she took me as her guest to dine at High Table. She's allowed one guest a year, and this year it was me. She was worried that I would be uncool, and she was probably right to worry. I was beside myself. Because Trinity was Newton's college, and we can say, without a shadow of a doubt, that everything we think about the world was changed, by Newton, in this place, in the years between 1684 and 1687.

In fact, I did say that very thing, as we came through the gatehouse into the court.

'Everything changed! Just think! One man! And right here! In your college!'

'Yes, dear. We're coming up to the Hall now, look . . .'.

The undergraduates were queuing to get in for their dinner. It was a cold night.

'I had chilblains for three years,' said my wife.

'Hey! It can get cold in Lampeter, let me tell you.'

'Don't get defensive, dear,' said my wife.

A college servant showed us the entrance to the Senior Common Room, where a butler took our coats. My wife was wearing her gown under her coat; you have to if you want to dine at High Table, and you're an MA. Which I'm not, but I really really did want to eat at High Table. Those of us without the classical education may mock our brothers and sisters who went to Oxbridge because they can't tell their Marx from their Marcuse, and know next to nothing of contemporary currents in social theory, but by God they eat well. We envy them, if we're really honest. No amount of occupying Senate Rooms or planning the revolution in the Nelson Mandela Bar can ever really compensate us for the fact that we never took crumpets with the Master, or warmed tinned steak and kidney pie over the fire in our studies.

We stood in the Senior Common Room (it's probably called something in Latin), and waited to be called in to dinner. My wife sat in an upholstered armchair, crossed her dancer's legs and cast her eye over that morning's *Times* crossword, while I bounced about gownless.

'Just think of them all! Just think who came here! Who stood about in here sipping dry sherry! Don't even think about the Drydens and Byrons! Or your Wittgensteins and Bertie Russells. Just think about the magicians. John Dee. Aleister Crowley. Even your wackos out-wacko everyone else.'

'I know, dear. I actually came here.'

The butler called us into the hall, and we climbed a flight of stairs, lined with portraits ('Macaulay! William Whewell!'), at the top of which was a low doorway which led through to High Table. Going through that door was like stepping into a blaze of light, like Michael Jackson coming onstage. This may be true, or it may be a false memory, but that is how I remember it feeling. The undergraduates in Lower Hall stood up as we came to the table, which, again in memory, was candlelit. Then the butler whacked a gong, and everyone shut up, and a professor from before the dawn of time intoned a Latin prayer, and then we all sat down to tuck in. I looked about me, at the vastness of that hall, and thought, 'Newton ate here.'

Newton ate here. The greatest of Englishmen, the man who changed the way we see the world forever, might have sat just here, and drunk these truly fine wines, and eaten something not dissimilar to this excellent carrot and coriander soup, or these deep dark venison steaks. His rooms were in the North Corner, near the Gatehouse. Edmund Halley came to visit him here, one day in 1684. Halley wanted Newton to clarify his views on certain matters regarding planetary motion.

Perhaps Newton brought him here into this hall, where I was now eating tropical fruit salad and sipping a fine dessert wine. Perhaps this was where he told Halley that he'd cracked all those problems years back, and had it all written down somewhere, back in his rooms. Halley asked that Newton write up those eighteen-year-old jottings, and present them to the Royal Society.

Newton went back to his rooms, failed to find the paper, and decided to write it up again. It took longer than he thought; three years, in fact. He would have lived in Halls while he wrote up his missing notes, and come here for all his meals . . . here!

Something was happening.

The butler had rewhacked the gong, and the old duck was saying another prayer in Latin, probably the opposite of the first one. We all filed out of the dining hall, to the bottom of another flight of stairs, where a college servant beckoned us upwards. She led the MAs and their guests into the combination room; there were dark panels, more portraits (Francis Bacon, the Father of Science! Adam Sedgwick, the reluctant gradualist!), and a huge polished table, shining under candlelight, this time for sure, and squeaking under the weight of enough silver to ransom Helen of Troy. Sitting at the head of this table sat a long-haired hippy with a braided beard and a Fellow's gown.

'Oroit?' he said in a Norfolk accent as I sat down next to him. 'I'm Sean. Machine Learning Fellow.'

I shook his hand. Port went round one way, claret the other. We dug at a vast Stilton, and smeared it on water biscuits. We chatted to our neighbours.

Newton might have sat just here while he was writing up his notes, and watched the candles flicker in the dark windows.

That's what I imagined. Here was where he showed that the world could be described in mathematics. On his lap in the statue of him that dominates the entrance to Trinity Chapel is the result of his writing up, *Principia Mathematica*, the most important book ever published in England. Here was where he made that book. Here was where he described the laws of motion and formulated universal gravitation. Here was where he worked out that the earth must be flattened at the poles, and that tides were caused by the gravitational pull of the moon. Here was where he invented the idea of 'force'. Here was where he banished magic forever, here where he showed that science doesn't need to know the cause of the world, only how it works. Here was where rationality sprang into life, banishing both occult and common-sense explanations of the system of the universe. Here's where. Just here. *Aufklärung*. Lights on.

> Nature and Nature's laws lay hid in night:
> God said, Let Newton be! and all was light.

Alexander Pope wrote that on Newton's death in 1727. His contemporaries knew the importance of what he'd done, and done right here, in this place.

I told Sean about how thrilled I was to be here. He looked pleased, and told me about how a working-class hippy had ended up a Fellow of Trinity College.

'Rich, this place. Think that wine was special at dinner?'

I nodded mutely. I'm vulgar enough to have Googled the wine when I got home. Twenty quid a bottle.

'Well, it wasn't. That's just the stuff we get on ordinary nights. They save the good stuff for the big occasions, and that's not you, mate. They say you can walk from Cambridge to London on Trinity land. And because the college is so rich, anybody can come here, and get scholarships. All you have to be is great at what you do, and you're in.'

'I wouldn't have thought they did computer science. I thought it was all Etruscan vases.'

'This was Babbage's college. Computers started here . . .'

It was all too much. When, at the end, after the cheese had done the circuit a couple of times, they brought out a silver snuffbox to pass round, I truly thought I was in heaven. Newton might have sneezed on it! Now life is but a pale shadow until next year, when my wife once again admits me to the privilege.

The stars are wonderful. Dangerous too. And we really are made from the same stuff.

20TH CENTURY BOY

'Marc!' shouts Neil.

The colossal opening chord of '20th Century Boy' echoes through Neil's house; and then again. And then that beautiful dumb riff. Neil is smiling all over his big ruined face.

'You like T. Rex?' I ask, somewhat bemused.

'Man, I love T. Rex!'

'I thought you didn't like girls' pop music?'

Neil stops smiling. 'Would you say this was girls' pop music?'

'Of course it is. Or it was. Loads of the girls at my school worshipped Marc.'

'I did too.'

'Most of my mates preferred Slade,' I say.

'I liked Slade too. But I loved Marc. This still sounds great.'

'It does, though, doesn't it? I told you, girls know best about pop music.'

Neil sighs.

'I love girls,' he says.

I sigh.

'I do too.'

'I haven't had a woman in years,' says Neil.

'Really?'

'Who'd have me?'

I guess that Neil's is not a conventional beauty; but, then, neither is mine. And he does go on these monthly benders. But he's a sweetie, really. There must be someone for Neil somewhere, I think.

'How do you cope?' I ask.

Neil nods towards his laptop.

'The Internet,' he says.

'Not the same, though, is it?'

'No.' It's 3 a.m., and Neil is feeling sad.

I think back to reading the Mass Observation letters about the night. However much we might associate sex with the night, it is a link that few of the respondents made. In fact, in all the letters I saw, there was only one that seemed to have anything to say on the subject, and that was from a seventy-year-old man, who said that he hated sleeping with people, and that 'sexual activities were best conducted on and not in a bed, if they had to be in a bedroom at all'.

The night isn't necessarily the best time for sex anyway. The circadian rhythm insists that 8 a.m. is the best time, which is a modern tragedy, because that's when lots of people are banged up in commuter trains, pissed off, bored and, apparently, horny as hell. If sex is worth taking seriously (and, in my experience, few things are worth taking more seriously), then afternoons are better; languid, long afternoons in bed with your lover always beat a desultory shag at half-eleven at night, when everyone's tired and the kids won't settle. If we lived the life of hunter-gatherers, for which we are so admirably suited, we'd shag all morning, bimble around collecting berries in the afternoons, and tell stories and sleep at night.

But night is what we have. It's when work is done, and we go out to play. There's a very good chance that you first made love with your partner at night, because that's when we're free to go on dates. And it's dark, and transgressive. Secretive. Furtive. No one can see what you're up to. Our bodies may prefer that we postpone lovemaking till the morning, but the darkness insists that now is the time.

Perhaps this is one of the reasons why we've drawn so much darkness around sex, why it has gone so very wrong, in lots of ways, and for lots of people. It went wrong for me, and I used the night to try to cover up just how wrong it had gone.

I lived for five years in a largely sexless relationship. Why this was so, I will leave to others to speculate. What I do know is that celibacy, or the closest thing to it, nearly sent me mad. Stark staring bonkers. Enforced celibacy has to be the cruellest part of being a prisoner, and the granting of 'conjugal rights' the most humane prison reform that society could make. Enforced celibacy is the obvious candidate if we are looking for something to blame for sex abuse in the Catholic Church. St Paul urges celibacy as the first choice for Christian sexuality, and only reluctantly allows marriage for those who are not as strong as he. In the highly unlikely event that I get to heaven, I look forward to debating this point with Paul, if I can get an appointment. The Christian Church's attitude to sexuality is highly damaging, dangerous and wicked, and St Paul the neuter lies behind it.

How wicked of the churches to condemn human sexual relations. How wicked. What do they get? Control, I guess, especially control over women, whose unboundaried sexuality has been seen as a threat to phallocentric male domination for thousands of years, if you'll excuse my late-80s Feminist Boy rhetoric. But what else? Deprivation has long been seen as engendering spirituality, but that seems like rubbish to me. Great loving sex is very close to prayer. How is sex wicked, in and of itself? It isn't. It can go wrong, of course it can. So can eating; people can eat themselves to death, or drink themselves to death, but that doesn't make eating and drinking sinful. Sex gone awry lies at the root of a great deal of abuse. But loving sex is a celebration of life and humanity. Yet our society has surrounded it with horror and guilt and smut; and why? For what ends?

Christian friends, here's something you need to know – Jesus had a penis and testes. If Jesus was fully human, as Christians claim,* then he got hard-ons. Great big hard-ons. If Jesus was a human male, then a couple of times a week he cracked one off, from the age of thirteen onwards. More like a couple of times a day to start with.

Until he got married. Which, of course, he did. *The Da Vinci Code* might be the biggest pile of shit you've ever read, but that doesn't alter the fact that Christ was married to the Magdalene. Of course he was. He loved her, and he loved her physically. Why not? What am I supposed to learn from Christ's supposed virginity? What does it teach us? If he was fully human, his

* And I still count myself one; I'm not out to shock or horrify. I believe in Jesus, in both his humanity and his divinity; I write not as a post-Dawkins denier, but as a post-scientific Christian.

testicles were producing millions of sperm a day. They need letting go. If he could control his sperm production, then he wasn't fully human. I feel confident that he could remain faithful to one woman, but if he wasn't struggling with the demands of his sexuality then, I repeat, he wasn't human. And the whole point of Christianity is that he was one of us. And if he didn't love sex, then he wasn't God.

Other religions have coped much better, especially Hinduism. Krishna (also God become human, and come to earth to teach the fact that the universe is made from love) had thousands of wives. *The Kama Sutra* is a book of prayer as much as it is a technical manual, and Indian temples, especially in South India, are full of erotic imagery. Judaism insists that its rabbis are married with children.* Islam had *The Perfumed Garden*. Christianity stands largely alone in seeing sex as filthy, the agency by which original sin is transmitted. You didn't know that, non-Christian friends? Well, this is hardly going to convert you, but here goes. This is why Christian theology insists on the Virgin Birth. Original sin comes down to us from Adam, because we are born out of sin. Sex is sinful. Not just gay sex, or even unmarried sex: sex. Imagine that you are a sixty-year-old, and that both your parents are still living. Imagine that they've been married sixty-five years, and have never so much as looked at anyone else in all that time. What do you imagine has been the secret of their togetherness? How have they stayed happy and together into their nineties? Chances are, it's because they've had a cracking sex life. But you were born in sin. Your happy childhood, in the

* And Jesus was a rabbi, of course.

care of two loving parents, your own subsequent mental good health, are sinful. Because your filthy disgusting mum and dad had sex, even after their marriage. Sex is the root of all evil. And if you have followed their example, my sixty-year-old happily married reader, then you too have probably perpetrated this sin. Your children are born from your sinful desire to hold your husband in your arms; your grandchildren are a sinful consequence of the love that your son bears for your lovely daughter-in-law. Sinners all! May ye burn forever in the fires of hell!

Sin, according to those pillars of Catholic and Protestant theology, Aquinas and Luther, is a sexually transmitted condition. A few Christians have fully understood this. The Shakers, famous now for the loveliness of their freestanding kitchen units, were celibate. That's why their furniture might remain, but they died out long ago. I hope for their sake that they did get to heaven, where they now get to do up kitchens in paradise. I hope that living in hell on earth was worth it. Perhaps the guarantee of eternal bliss is enough for some people to postpone bliss here on earth, but it doesn't work for me. I don't believe you.

We do know why we are here, quite apart from religious considerations. We are here because life is made from a two-stranded spiral, which exists to replicate itself. It seeks to recombine with DNA from other members of our species, so that it can continue to reproduce itself. Creativity is at the heart of the universe. Existence is not circular, or straight; it is spiral. The galaxy in which we live is spiral. We don't circle the sun; we spiral it. The sun is spiralling through the Milky Way. We are spiralling through space. Space itself is the shape of life, of creativity, of continuance and reproduction. And, er, since I'm ranting, and still angry, I quite clearly didn't get on very well living without sex for those five years.

Sorry. Perhaps I'll calm down one day.

At first, soon after we started seeing one another, I thought, oh well. It's such a small thing. I'll manage. It's worth it, because I love my girlfriend. We moved to London together, where we had a high old time throwing parties and meeting people. It was great. Who needs sex, I asked myself. I have so much going for me. My second novel was due for publication, and I'd found my dream job managing a large second-hand bookshop on the Charing Cross Road. Life was good.

Except, of course, it wasn't. My balls kept producing those pesky sperms, and they needed dealing with. I tried a lavatorial approach to masturbation. They just needed flushing out. But it didn't work. More and more of my time was given over to fantasy. At night I was gripped by horrible erotic dreams. I felt as though I was losing control of everything that was truest in me. At night, after work, I started to walk home through Soho. I started to understand the true nature of temptation, which I pray not to be led into again, not like that. The signs of the sex shops, lurid and sleazy, seemed to become warm and inviting. I started visiting them, just to look through the magazines, never to buy. If I'd had a dirty mac, I should have worn it.

I remembered something of the Soho of my teens. Once, in 1974, I'd come up to Soho with one of my mates, determined to visit a strip joint. Soho was darker then than it is now; that is to say, there was less light. I suspect that metaphorically it has gotten darker since the 70s. I can't now remember if Nick and

I were in town for anything else; to see a film, or perhaps a band. I suspect not. I suspect, in fact, that amongst our group of friends we were the ones who didn't have girlfriends as such. I suspect that we just wanted very much to see some naked ladies. And in that limited sense, we weren't disappointed. We did see some naked ladies.

I can't remember how we found the club, or what the conditions of entry were. I can't remember if we had to buy a drink, or if the doorman asked our ages (we were both sixteen). What I can remember is sitting in a grubby room with half a dozen or so men, all of whom were on their own. On a dimly lit stage sat a lass in knickers and a bra smoking a fag. Thin curtains pulled to across the stage. When they opened, the lass had taken off her bra. She sat with her arms folded in front of her tits. Nick and I giggled. What we didn't know was that it was illegal for the girls to actually move, and that we had stumbled into 'an artist's modelling studio'. The scabby curtains drew again. This time, when they opened, the lass put out her fag, and unfolded her arms. We could see her tits, which was the whole point of coming. The next time, she was standing; and the time after, she had taken off her knickers, and had lit another fag. Pubes! Actual pubes! Hooray! Finally, at the last opening of the curtains, she had turned her back on the audience, and was bent over the chair and showing us her arse.

We applauded, and she walked off the stage. Another lass walked down through the grubby auditorium, climbed onto the stage, sat down in the chair, and lit a fag. The curtains closed. And so on. I remember the delicious combination of complete boredom and utter contempt on her face. I think we sat through her performance, and, when a third equally bored girl turned up, Nick and I left, laughing with equal parts embarrassment and bravado. So that was that.

Then, in my student days, in the Christmas holidays of my second year at Lampeter, I went round Soho with my pals Bob and Julian. I told them that the strip clubs weren't worth it, so we went to a peepshow. For those of you who have never been unfortunate enough to undergo this humiliating experience, here's what happens. A room is lined with booths. Each of the booths has a mechanical flap at eye level, about the size of a letterbox. If you insert money into a slot, this flap opens into an inner room, where a naked woman is dancing on a raised floor. If you hold up money, the woman will come and masturbate in front of you. After five minutes, the slot closes. You can see the eyes of the other men who are watching and presumably wanking from the other booths. None of us did this,* but Bob and Julian both left before their time was up, while I hung on for the whole five minutes. I had, after all, paid my money, and at least the girl was moving. It was horrible; not just the experience of watching, but also, I guess, our laddish poor behaviour in going along to gawp. In our defence, we were lads.

And now, twenty-five years later, I was back in Soho, and starved of sexual attention. Starved. Famished. One night, unable to go on, unable to go back home to my cheerful lovely funny and, so I thought, sexually uninterested girlfriend, I went back to the peepshow place. The format had changed. Now, you gave five pounds to a doorman, who admitted you to an

* Well, I didn't. Can't speak for m'pals, clearly.

inner room, where a plump blonde Russian lass danced for you, danced for you alone. She was in her early twenties, I guessed, and I remembered the look of boredom and contempt from my visit to the strip show with Nick in the 70s. She danced in a way which one might call languid, but which one might equally call exhausted. She played a Madonna track, I think; I can't really remember. I was embarrassed more than anything, embarrassed and deeply ashamed. How much was this girl getting paid? What was I doing to my dear, nice, convent-educated girlfriend, who loved me, but who just happened not to be keen on having sex with me? I sat on a sofa, red-faced, but unable to stop staring at the girl. After the song finished, I found out how the girl earned her money.

'Is there anything else you want?' she asked. There certainly was.

'Oh, gosh, no, thank you,' I said, standing up. I really did make my excuses and leave. The girl looked angry; the doorman looked startled to see me reappear so quickly. Clearly the normal state of affairs was to stay, and have a massage, or a fuck. I slunk home, and tried to put the experience from my mind. Which I did very badly. After another fortnight of sexless existence, I found myself going back. After all, I thought, the girl wanted me to fuck her; or, at least, she wanted my money. By NOT fucking her, I reasoned to myself, I had exploited her in a worse way than if I had. Clearly, the establishment got the money for the dance, while the girls got to keep all, or at least some, of the money from the extras. What kind of a monster was I, not to fuck this poor exploited girl? I must put it right at once. One night, after work, I went back to the place, and paid my five pounds again. This time there was another, prettier, livelier, dark-haired Russian girl, who actually smiled at me as she gyrated frenetically to the Madonna track. I looked forward to the end of the dance. I sat on the sofa, transfixed by her small tits, and what I could see of her cunt. She danced much faster; she wasn't exhausted, or, at least, she was up on something. At the end of the dance, she said, 'Do you want to stay with me?'

'Oh . . .' I paused. She really was lovely. 'Thank you . . .' She wanted me to stay, because she needed the money. I wanted to stay, I really did. But I said, 'I'd better not . . .'

And I left again; this time the girl looked sad, rather than angry. I had failed to pick up a prostitute, a nice pretty one, who clearly expected me to do the decent thing and pay for her services. Failed, because I knew it was wrong.

Why was it wrong? For two reasons, I think. Firstly because I was in a loving relationship, which just happened to be sexless, but where fidelity was nonetheless expected. Perhaps if I'd had the courage to talk about it with my girlfriend, perhaps if I'd had permission . . . And then it was wrong because I didn't know anything about the girl's true condition. Why did she need the money? To pay pimps? To buy crack? Had she been trafficked? Was she truly doing this thing of her own volition? I had no way of telling, and just enough shreds of conscience to stop myself from using her further.

But imagine a case where a man had no ties, and he found a woman who he could be 100 per cent sure was not paying a pimp, was not trafficked, and had chosen prostitution as a way of making money rather than being, say, a temp. Would sleeping with her and paying her money be morally repugnant? Of course, sex is a gift, and ideally it shouldn't be for sale. Of course, we don't want our daughters to do it. Of course, there are health issues, including mental-health issues for both parties. And, of course, late-period capitalism is a pile of shit. But would this ideal case be morally wrong? I'm not sure. And what if (say it quietly) the woman enjoyed her work?

I have a friend who uses prostitutes from time to time, especially when she's on tour. I'll call her Dee. It keeps her faithful to her husband, she says, and satisfies her bi side. She goes on tour quite a bit, because she's very nearly a pop star. She's had at least one Number One hit, has appeared on both *Top of the Pops* and the 'Where Are They Now?' identity parade on *Never Mind the Buzzcocks*. She's not a household name, because she sings with dance outfits, though these days she gets 'DJ Thingy Whatsit featuring Dee' billing. You'll have heard the records, and maybe even seen Dee singing them on MTV, without quite realising how well known she is in the world of dance music. She has paid her dues, has Dee. In her early days back in the 80s, she worked as a prostitute herself. It kept her from having to have a day job, so that she could find gigs and hang around in recording studios at night.

She was living with another musician friend at the time; looked at on one level he was living off immoral earnings, but as the old joke has it, 'What do you call a musician without a girlfriend?' 'Homeless.'

One day, Dee said to me, 'Oh, I never come with my boyfriends. I only ever come if someone is paying.'

She did enjoy what she did, up to a point and for a time. And when she uses prostitutes, she feels no moral compunction. She won't let them kiss her ('I said, I know where your mouth has been, love. Get down there . . .') but, other than that, she enjoys the experience.

So, Dee might be vanishingly rare. But if an unattached client had used her services, both parties had enjoyed the experience, and Dee had used the money to fund a day in the studio . . . was that morally wrong? I thought of another case. Another friend of mine, a fine sax player, worked for a few years in a hostel for severely disabled young men.

'I often had to put on rubber gloves and get out the Vaseline and relieve them,' he told me.

'I wouldn't fancy that,' I said.

'You could see how unhappy they were, and these guys had no way of coping with it themselves. What would you do if you had no arms or legs? One of my clients suffered hell, and he begged me to find him a prostitute. Disabled people don't fancy other disabled people, you know. They fancy Marilyn Monroe like you and me.'

'So did you find him someone?'

'Yes. A really nice lady in her forties, who had dealt with disabled people before, and was more than happy to take him on.'

'Did he enjoy it?'

'I don't think I've ever made anyone happier.'

'And what a kind lady,' I said.

So, I asked myself over and over again, as I walked home through Soho, night after night, is paying for sex always morally repugnant? And doesn't one counter-argument destroy a case? As I had thought of cases where it would be difficult to argue for moral repugnance, at least one of which moreover demonstrated human compassion, didn't that make the problems political rather than moral?

I was in a state of permanent argument with myself. I couldn't have sex with my girlfriend; I couldn't be unfaithful to her; I was going mad, and was beginning not to trust myself. Something had to give.

On one of my creeps through Soho, I'd passed the doorway to a club where a wildly attractive Chinese girl in her late twenties stood guard.

'Do you want to come in, Joe?' she asked me one night. 'Do you want to spend some time with me?'

With every atom of my being, I did want to spend time with her. I smiled, and shook my head, and hated myself. A week later, I passed the doorway again. She was still there.

'When are you going to come and spend some time with me, Joe?'

'Soon,' I said. 'I can't tonight . . .'

'Come and see me soon, Joe.'

The next night, I went back. I hoped that she would still be standing guard over the door to Wonderland, to release, to peace and rest and a dreamless sleep. And she was.

'You've come back to see me, Joe!' she said.

'Yes,' I said.

'It's fifty pounds to come into the club,' she said. 'Then you'll get a two-girl show, and a full body massage.'

I smiled, and counted the notes into her hand. She was fantastic; beautiful and sexy with long slim legs under a tiny miniskirt. I didn't even ask if she was going to be one of the girls. I just assumed it. She led me down dingy stairs into a dingier room, painted white, with a coffee table and a sofa, and a menu pinned to the wall, which I didn't read. We sat on the sofa, her knees touching mine. My cock throbbed with fear and lust. The Chinese girl talked about the show: 'Two girls, and a full body massage. I'll take you upstairs. Starting soon.' To my surprise, we were joined in the room by another woman, English, older, but very attractive; dark-haired, in a white blouse and black skirt. Clearly the other girl for the two-girl show, I thought.

'Have you seen the menu?' she asked.

She put down another copy of the menu in front of me. Coke, £5, it said. I decided not to bother reading on.

'Nothing for me, thank you,' I said, ever the polite boy.

She left the menu on the small table next to me. I chatted to the Chinese girl. I was puzzled as to when the action might start, but in these matters the girl was clearly much more experienced than I. I asked her about herself; she told me she was a student at University College, which impressed me.

Then the other woman came back into the room, and presented me with a bill. For £500. It was a bit tatty; in retrospect, I realised that it had been given to lots of punters before.

'What's this?' I said. 'I can't pay this!'

'I gave you the menu. It says £500 for half an hour, or part thereof, with one of our girls.'

I looked properly at the menu. It did say that very thing.

'But . . . we haven't done anything, have we?' I looked at the Chinese girl, who sat silent, staring at me with hard eyes.

'That doesn't matter. It says on the menu £500. You've spent time with one of the girls. That's how much you owe.'

'But I haven't got it . . .'

The woman looked serious.

'Oh dear. Have you got a credit card?'

'No.'

'If you'll wait here, please . . .'

I sat in the dingy room, detumescent, cowed into horrified obedience, and with my life ruined. I tried to appeal to the Chinese girl again.

'But you said it was fifty quid. I paid you fifty quid . . .'

'That was to get into the club,' she said.

The woman came back into the room with a large black man.

'Ramon will come with you to the cash machine,' said the woman.

Which was a huge relief, quite frankly, because as I knew perfectly well, the nearest cash machine was in Leicester Square, blazing with light and crowded with tourists. Ramon and I climbed the stairs, and walked towards the cash machine. I've never been so pleased to see streetlights.

'I've been really fucking stupid, haven't I?'

'It says on the menu,' said Ramon.

'I haven't got five hundred quid,' I said. 'Come on, mate. I only wanted a shag . . .'

'You should have read the menu.'

So we came to the cash machine, and I put in my card, and tapped in the wrong PIN, twice in a row, and the machine swallowed my card. Ramon was not happy, but in Leicester Square at seven on a winter's evening, there really was nothing he could do. Except call me a wanker, which he did, before heading off to clip some other deluded fucknut.

Because that was what is known as a clip joint. And though I had only been clipped fifty quid, I had been clipped good and proper. After that, I didn't try again.

Because after that, I went back to my girlfriend, and we moved away from London, and three years later, three years of no sex that you'd notice, three years of trying and trying and trying to be faithful, I found the worst possible solution to my problem. I met a nice, pretty and highly intelligent woman who was also in a sexless marriage, and I embarked upon an affair with her, under cover of night – at Pilton festival, in the car parks of motorway service stations, in tawdry Travelodges. I thought I had found a fuck buddy, but life is never that simple. We wrote to one another, also at night, by email. Email is dangerous stuff. Not a theme that needs developing, really. It's never a good day to bury bad news by email.

We sent one another compilation CDs. I started liking her in the first place because she'd brought along Gram Parsons' *Grievous Angel* to the course where we met. Pop music casts enchantment. We were enchanted. She told her husband about the affair. I didn't tell my girlfriend. After six months, my love for my girlfriend snapped me out of the enchantment. I ended the affair, cruelly yet somehow appropriately, by email.

A year to the day later, my girlfriend got a package. The package contained a letter from the woman with whom I'd had the affair, along with copies of the intemperate emails which I had sent. The package to my girlfriend, in an old A4 envelope sellotaped tightly shut, recycled from a mail-order company that sells self-help books of a spiritual nature, and with a label stuck carefully over the address to which it had originally been sent, was addressed in disguised handwriting, presumably in case I intercepted it. They say that vengeance is a dish best served cold, and I'd have to go along with that. If revenge was the object of the exercise, it worked very well.

Although the emails were clearly edited, they were also quite clearly true. I had written and sent them. I had had an affair. What I was being accused of doing, I had done. This is not to say that I did not raise some feeble protest. I pointed out that I had ended the affair a year previously. I pointed out that I had never stopped loving my girlfriend, and had told the woman with whom I'd been having the affair that this was the case. You might well argue that shagging someone else behind your partner's back is a funny way to show someone that you love them; and I think you'd be right. Certainly my girlfriend was in no mood to hear feeble protests.

There was a scene. My girlfriend asked me to leave for a few nights. I left. I caught a train from Exeter to Carmarthen, changing at Bristol Parkway; a night train, a terrible journey, undertaken in a haze of unbearable misery. At Carmarthen, Perry Venus picked me up and took me back to his. I didn't know who else to ask. I sat in his spare bedroom, alternately crying in self-pity and self-loathing, and reading Butler's *Lives of the Saints*, which he had up on a shelf. Sleep was out of the question.

So I ended up betraying everyone. I betrayed my girlfriend. I betrayed the woman with whom I'd had the affair. I gave her the moral equivalence of a prostitute. Less, even. I could stop myself from paying a prostitute for sex, but I couldn't stop myself from becoming enchanted by a real person, who loved me, and wanted me for myself. I couldn't stop myself from breaking her heart, and my girlfriend's, and my own.

Three weeks later, my girlfriend said that I could come home. But when I got there, she had gone.

That's what enforced celibacy did for me. Thank you, God.

I can't say for sure that things would have been different if I had managed to pass under cover of the night and find a prostitute. Germaine Greer wrote in the *Guardian* that 'men are not brutes; prostitution would hardly be possible if men did not delude themselves that women enjoyed it.' I had brought myself to that point of delusion; that the commodification and sale of sexuality can be a good thing. Perhaps a two-girl show for fifty quid might have kept my girlfriend and me together, and perhaps I could have found a way to stay deluded in every possible sense.

Because I do know that my girlfriend and I should have spent five weeks together, not five years, because no matter how much you care for someone, if the sex isn't right, then nothing is right. The night hides nothing; except, perhaps, ourselves from ourselves.

'I hope you find someone soon,' I say to Neil.

Neil smiles sadly, and pops a tinnie.

'Billy shags my leg when I go out for a slash,' he says. 'At least somebody still wants me.'

WILD NIGHT

I look at my watch. Three-thirty a.m. Above me, eternity hangs in an infinite sky. Billy is gearing up to shag my leg. Quite clearly, his affections are not reserved solely for Neil, who needs them more than I. I guess Billy sleeps, but I'm not sure when. Most mammals, including humans, are diurnal; that is, they're awake in the day and asleep at night. Neil and I are currently ignoring the urges of our circadian rhythms, and staying up way too late to talk and listen to music. Dogs need sleep, so presumably Billy will catch up on it sometime. For now, he is awake, standing guard over us from the privations of a wild night.

It is remote up here, but it's not truly wild. If there is any wilderness left in the British Isles, it is now hard to come by. On Jura, maybe? In the flow country of Sutherland? Only very rarely do we come across true wildness in our tamed and civilised lives. It has been a long time since we needed to light our fires at night to keep bears and wolves away. Britain is a garden, on the whole, and the wild things are best left where they are; out there, away from the light.

Wild things need food and warmth and shelter. Only tame things like us need light as well. As a highly specialised and overdeveloped social creature, I cannot be sustained under anything other than artificial light. It drives away the darkness, and the fear of the wild, but mostly it increases our domestic dependency. With industrialisation, we have reached a pinnacle of domestication; a chronic lack of wildness. Where once we would have been unable to survive without cattle or salt, now we can't live without oil, engineering, agribusiness, the brightly lit chemical plants of the Mersey Delta, or the spotlights on a combine cropping the wheat for our bread by dead of night. That we can now work and live by night is due entirely to the increased efficiency of artificial lighting. Without it, we would be back in the aptly named Dark Ages.

Before the widespread use of artificial light, the sky would have been seen as portentous, because people could see the comets and meteorites and strange conjunctions of planets much better than we can. For the most part, humans lived according to their diurnal nature. The night was still dangerous, even if fire and hunting had seen off the bears, and even if court astronomers came to be able to predict the movements in the sky. One of the great medieval dangers of darkness was that people fell off and into things.

People fell into holes and caverns and potholes. People fell from bridges into rivers, and even into canals in Venice and Amsterdam. Before the late 1600s, the only source of street light was from households and from pedestrian lanterns. The by-laws of the fifteenth and sixteenth centuries which demanded that citizens carry lanterns or torches were not made to stop them falling into things; no, they were made so that the authorities could see who was wandering about after dark, since anyone who was wandering about was clearly up to no good; was, in fact, a little bit wild. Before 1100, it was illegal to show a light outdoors after curfew, the time after which the authorities decided that, if you were out, they wanted to see you. I live opposite a church where the curfew bell is still sounded, at eight every night. In 2004, the then mayor of Presteigne attempted and failed to enforce this curfew on the town's youth. Our handful of feral youths still sits outside the library drinking cider well after the curfew bell has rung, and not one of them carries a candle to show who they are. It was the curfew that was the signal for people to carry their lights once they left home. No one minded if they fell into things, so long as the authorities could see who was doing the falling.

From the beginning of the fifteenth century, London officials ordered households to hang one lantern outside their homes on designated evenings; for example, on saints' days or when Parliament was sitting. These privately maintained lights hanging outside private houses were the main source of street lighting until well into the early eighteenth century. A candle would be lit inside a metal cylinder with narrow slits; or else transparent sheets would be made from sawn horns which had been soaked, heated, flattened and sliced. That's why they're called 'lanthorns'.

Later in the fifteenth century, London homeowners were obliged to keep a candle lantern burning outside on every evening between 31 October and 2 February, and similar rules applied in Amsterdam and Paris. The idea spread quite slowly;

although York and Chester had similar ordinances by 1500, Bristol and Oxford did not light up their streets by these uncertain means until the 1600s. And even between the specified dates, no one would be obliged to light up on the night of the full moon. There are stories of cities full of life during times of full moon; revellers, theatre-goers, shoppers even. You could see your way around, after all, and be sure of not falling into any but the most shadowed chasms.

One problem with this policy was cost. Not everybody could afford candles. The poor side of town would be barely lit. A photograph of London taken from above in 1650 would have low-lit areas of poverty and wildness, much as the famous photograph of earth at night from space which shows North Korea still blacked out. John Aubrey, writing in the 1650s, records the case of the mathematician William Oughtread, whose wife was too parsimonious to allow promiscuous candle burning, and who demanded that Oughtread work in the dark. Furniture was routinely pushed to the side of rooms at night, so that people could save candlelight by being able to walk through dark rooms. People were not permitted to make their own candles, not like today, when your ex-sister-in-law and her new partner can set themselves up in a little candle-making enterprise in Totnes without anyone batting an eye.

There is no evidence that there was public lighting in major European cities before 1650; yet by 1700 it was widespread. The technological innovation that made it viable was part of the reason for its rapid growth, for example the use of reflectors to magnify the light of oil lamps. The growth of the state, aiming to provide more services for people with greater wealth and an increased appetite for nightly entertainment, and also to protect them against the parallel rise in night crime, forced authorities to use public funds to illuminate urban areas, both to light the way to theatres and pleasure gardens and to make it easier for the night watch to operate. These early attempts at street lighting would have followed the timings of the private lights and would, in any case, only have been found along major thoroughfares.

Gas lighting arrived as a serious source of public light in the early nineteenth century, again as a result of technological innovation and growing municipal pride. At first it was expensive and lighting was still reserved for main roads. And no one could afford to keep them on all the time, any more than Powys Council can today. In the 1820s, for example, Lancaster and Norwich kept street lighting 'for dark nights' only. Lighting was still mainly reserved for major roads. And plenty of places would still have been in darkness. Pudsey, in Yorkshire, was described in 1887 as having: 'No gas, no street lamps, and very little light shown from the dwellings.'

As gas fell in price, thus increasing the popularity of gas lighting, so, sadly, the pollution from the production of 'town gas' made from coal increased, meaning that the nights grew brighter as daytime streets became darker from soot and smoke. But it is from this lamp-lit smog that we take many of our images of late-night London – the Ripper, shrouded in mist, *Fanny by Gaslight*. By the end of the nineteenth century, it was becoming clear that electricity was the light at the end of the smoggy tunnel.

One of the first problems was that incandescent light bulbs grew very hot; too hot for practical outdoor use, night after night. Experiments were started with so-called 'discharge lamps' which, rather than heating up an electric filament, passed an electric charge through gas to make it glow. By 1930, it had been established that lamps containing sodium gas were the most efficient. The first of what we would now recognise as modern sodium lamps was installed on the Purley Way in Croydon, in 1932, outside the Phillips factory, which made the things. And so it was that the true colour of a suburban night spread from the Purley Way, deep in the heart of the suburbs, to bathe the whole nation, town and country, in a ghastly yellow light. Why is it yellow? Because incandescent lights cover the full spectrum, but gas discharge lamps can only light up one part of it. In the case of sodium, it just happens to be the yellow part of the spectrum which glows.

That's why you can stand pretty much anywhere in Britain, and see a yellow glow in the sky. You might be high up in the Yorkshire Dales, but you'll still be able to see the glow from Leeds. In the old poem by Macaulay, 'the burghers of Carlisle saw the red glow from Skiddaw', the last in a long line of beacons which warned England of the coming of the Armada. Now, of course, you can stand on Skiddaw and see the orange glow of Carlisle on the northern horizon.

The light has driven the wild away, so I'd like to find a place which is still dark enough to encounter a bit of what is left of the untamed. I'd like to see some wildlife at night, and for this I'm going to need a wildlife guy. Lots of my friends are wildlife guys, and I'm really not. It's nothing personal. I weep when I read about species falling extinct. I rage when I hear about vandals stealing eggs from ospreys' nests, or digging up wild orchids. I care, but only up to a point. I want there to be willow-warblers and pine-martens and dragonflies. I want there to be lots of them, and I want them to be thriving. I want the way we live and farm to give wildlife priority over cars and out-of-town carpet warehouses. But what I don't want is to have to identify things. I don't want to have to learn their names. I struggle to remember my children's names, so throwing flowers and birds etc. into the mix is not going to make life good, either for me or for the things that I am (not) identifying.

As a country boy, there are some things I can't help but identify, of course. I know a rabbit from a hare, a buzzard from a red kite; but that's probably as far as it goes. So to identify things by night, I'm in trouble. I need a wildlife guy; but which one? One of my oldest pals in the world, one of the three guys I walked to school with every day for five years, is the Bugman, a professional insect collector, and he could have taken me out lamping for moths in Nunhead Cemetery. I could have gone bat ringing with Henry the Batman. Henry the Batman works for the Bat Conservation Trust, and he offered me a night of bat capture in Wiltshire. I could have gone badger watching with Martin the badger bloke. Martin is a volunteer with the Radnorshire Wildlife Trust, and his special concern is badger conservation, but I feel ambivalent about badger watching. I'm not just ambivalent because of New Labour MP Ron Davies, for whom 'badger watching' was a euphemism for cottaging. It's also because of a pal of mine who used to be the host at a residential centre for writers. Most weeks, on the last night of the course, he would offer to take a susceptible and attractive young woman out into the woods on a 'badger watch', for which purpose he just happened to have this handy blanket . . .

'Did you ever see any badgers?' I asked him.

'Funnily enough, no . . .' he replied.

In the end I decided that there was one creature of the night that I wanted to encounter, or perhaps re-encounter, more than any other. And that was the nightingale. For years I've been convinced that a nightingale saved my life. There was one night, alone and lonely, beaten and fucked over by my own stupidity, marriage in ruins such as those you might have seen in Dresden on the night after the firestorm, career going downhill from what I had imagined was already an unassailably low point etc.

I was walking, as I did almost nightly, across Newhaven Bridge on my way to the Harbour Station, gazing at my ancient Docs and the turned-up cuff of my jeans, when I heard what I thought must be a nightingale, singing in a scrubby bush outside the Railway Club in Newhaven.

The Railway Club used to be one of the best places to drink in Newhaven, and it might still be, but it has always been one of the least likely spots to encounter beauty on Planet Earth. It's a single-storey building, which looks like it might have been built from asbestos panelling in the 1930s. On one side, the brightly lit entrance to the ferry port; on the other, the mouth of the Sussex River Ouse, running between piles of gravel and scrap; behind the club, the smashed windows of the disused engine shed. And on the verge between the Railway Club and the A259, a bush, a buddleia bush maybe; and, somewhere in there, a nightingale singing just for me.

It was about midnight, I guess, and what the birders call the liquid notes of the song made me look up from my shoes. I stopped and listened. It was a sound of pure loveliness, all the lovelier for its unlovely, unlikely surroundings. A tear may have run down my cheek. I was reminded of my insignificance by all the impersonal beauty in the world. And I felt better, a lot better. I lifted my head. I shook off the worst of the horrors, and clawed myself back into a state of ordinary misery. I couldn't carry on, but I carried on, thanks to the nightingale's song.

But time passes, and you come to realise that the memory plays up. I guess I've become less convinced that the sound I'd heard was an actual nightingale. I'm not sure what else it might have been, that hopeful blessed song; I doubt it was a recording, for example, or someone hiding in the bush with a whistle; but could it really have been a nightingale? In Newhaven? Outside the Railway Club? Nature is rubbish; that's why I generally prefer the BBC Wildlife Unit in Bristol to do my bird spotting etc. for me. And even then, I'm not *that* interested, as you may be coming to suspect.

But I wanted to know what it was I heard that night, and to imagine that wildness can still find its way through the glaring lights of civilisation, if Newhaven counts as such.

So I asked my friend Richard if he would take me out to hear the song of the nightingale. After all, Richard runs dawn chorus walks in spring. He takes the interested people of Presteigne out into the local woods to hear what might be waking up at 5 a.m. on a May morning. I thought that it would be fairly simple for Richard to find me a singing nightingale. I imagined, since I live in the least populated part of Great Britain south of the Scottish

Highlands, that nightingales would abound. In fact, I've always imagined that since there are hardly any people here, the whole place should be swarming with otherwise elusive creatures. Not so, apparently.

'Nightingales?' said Richard, scratching his chin. 'Hmmm. Let me work on it.'

'Aren't there any round here?'

'Not that I know of. I'll get back to you.'

A few weeks passed until I heard from him again. Then, one evening, he called.

'I think I've found some nightingales. They're at the Cotswold Water Park.'

'Really? That's miles. Why aren't there any round here? It's nice and quiet here, I'd have thought.'

'That's like asking why you don't get ostriches in Bromsgrove. It's just outside their range, that's all.'

'I'll pay petrol,' I said, 'if you take me to the Cotswold Water Park.'

'Cheers, Ian. And is it OK if I bring Mary C and one of her daughters? Mary says she's always wanted to hear a nightingale sing.'

'Gladly.' I like Mary C. She's a bit older than me, I guess, and she's an old-style Trot: union organiser, ex-WRP* member. I'm an ex-member of the RCPGB (ML)†, and where I used to regard Trots as interventionist scumbags, now I think that anyone still clinging to far-left views after Tiananmen Square is

---

* Worker's Revolutionary Party.

† Revolutionary Communist Party of Great Britain (Marxist–Leninist). We liked Albania, but nowhere else.

naïve at best. Inevitably, Mary C and I will bicker in the car, which I for one look forward to; but I don't think Richard feels the same way. I think Bird Song Guys must like a quiet life.

When Richard picked me up, Mary C and her daughter Blanche were already in the back seat. It was a beautiful early-summer evening. Richard tried to explain about the habits of nightingales as we drove towards the Cotswold Water Park.

'They only really sing in the dead of night when they are looking for a mate.'

'They're LBJs, aren't they?' I asked, smugly.

'What's an LBJ'?' asked Blanche.

'The fascist President of America who launched an illegal war against the people's liberation struggle in Vietnam,' said Mary C.

'Yes, to some extent,' said Richard. 'But LBJ is also a birders' term. It means Little Brown Jobs.'

'It means they're not much to look at,' I said. 'It's the only thing I know about bird watching really.'

'So this time of year, when they are nesting, you only really hear them at dusk and dawn,' said Richard.

'They are crepuscular,' I said, 'like cats.'

'I thought that meant like when the sun breaks through the clouds when it's been raining,' said Blanche.

'No, darling. It means twilight, if Ian would just use non-exclusive language . . .' said Mary C.

'So do you think the bird I heard singing in the bush by Newhaven Railway Club was a nightingale?' I asked.

'Have you joined your union yet?' asked Mary C.

'No, not yet. I keep meaning to.'

'Well, you should.'

'I know.'

'Places like the Newhaven Railway Club wouldn't even have been there if the workers hadn't organised,' said Mary C.

'But I still think it's unlikely that it was a nightingale, even if the club is organised on sound socialist principles,' said Richard.

'What else could it have been?' I asked.

'Oh, quite a few birds sing at night. Blackbirds, thrushes, robins even.'

'Really?' said Blanche. 'I thought it was only nightingales.'

'Oh no. They're just the most famous ones.'

'And the most romantic. A nightingale sang in Berkeley Square,' I said, 'so I see no reason it shouldn't have sung outside Newhaven Railway Club.'

'It's unlikely that the Berkeley Square singer was a nightingale, either. They are quite shy. And not so common any more.'

'What are our chances of hearing one?' asked Blanche.

'Well, it's sod's law, isn't it? You never see the thing you've set out to see.'

I know this already. We all know this, with a dull inevitability. You know this too. We are not going to hear a nightingale. That's why the BBC Wildlife Unit guys take fifteen years to record things, because most wildlife has never had media training, and they won't play the game, apart from meerkats, who've got an agent. And yet, despite the doomed nature of our quest, we continue.

'Are you a twitcher, Richard?' asked Mary C.

'Oh no. I'm a birder. It's a different thing.'

'What's the difference?' asked Blanche.

'Well, a twitcher is someone who wants to see rare birds. So, for example, there's a blah blah bird* near Southport at the moment, so the twitchers are all heading up there to tick it off on their lists. A birder is someone who is more interested in behaviour, or population numbers, that sort of thing.'

'Oh,' said Blanche.

'Tonight, we are all birders,' I said.

'Hooray,' said Blanche.

The car climbed Birdlip Hill, over the top of the Cotswolds, and down into the Water Park, which is a large area of old gravel pits near Cricklade. Richard seemed to know his way around.

'I stayed here last year,' said Richard. 'In a timeshare thing.'

It all seemed very American, and not at all wild. There were houses, newly built from local stone, lurking behind trees, and disguised to look like anything other than what they were, i.e. cutesy olde worlde cottages with the paint still wet. We drove past one of those modern pubby slash hotel slash eatery-type things, also brand spanking new, but built from local stone and designed to look like a mill conversion.

We pulled up an unmade track behind a settlement of these Hobbity horrors, to where a dozen or so cars were parked up. To judge from the state of the guys in the car next to us, everyone else in the car park was a fisherman. They were loading incalculable amounts of stuff into collapsible wheelbarrows. The actual rods seemed to be the least of it. There were baskets and boxes and vast umbrellas, and crates of beer and cool-boxes and

* Richard did tell us the actual name of the bird, but none of us can remember what it was, other than that it was rare.

sleeping bags and camp-beds. They were clearly setting up for the duration.

'This is the place,' Richard said. We got out of the car, to find ourselves in a cloud of midges; and, close over our heads, another cloud, composed of swallows, swooping around catching the midges. Clearly, for the swallows, this was a good place to eat, as there were so many midges it was difficult not to breathe them in. Richard got out his monocular, which is like a miniature telescope.

'Look at the swifts,' he said.

'I thought they were swallows.'

'Oh no. Come and look through the monocular . . .'

'If I went into a shop and asked for two monoculars, would that be a pair of monoculars?' I asked him.

Richard made me carry his tripod, which was not light for a chap well into his middle years. I consoled myself by remembering that this tripod was as nothing compared to the stuff the fishermen had to carry. We nodded our good evenings at the latest batch to arrive and start unloading their gear into the wheelbarrows, and we set off to walk round the nearest of the lakes. To get to it, the path followed a very young Thames. A sign said that we were in fact on the Thames Path, which I swear I'd walk the whole length of one day if it weren't for this damned indolence.

Light was dropping from the sky. Our eyes started to adjust. Our ears started to tune in to the twilight chorus.

'Listen!' said Mary C.

Away in the distance, we could hear an unmistakable sound.

'Cuck-oo. Cuck-oo.'

'Wow,' said Richard. 'That's the first one I've heard all year.'

'You certainly hear them round us,' I said.

'Not for years, I haven't heard one,' said Mary C.

'I've never heard one before,' said Blanche.

'Like nightingales, they breed over here and over-winter in West Africa,' said Richard. 'And, like nightingales, they are increasingly rare.'

'Why?' I asked.

'No one is sure. Lots of birds that over-winter in Africa, like warblers, are doing quite badly. The problems could be there. Or they could be here. Deer could be eating the undergrowth where nightingales live, for example.'

'Not cuckoos, though,' said Blanche. 'They live in other birds' nests . . .'

'I hate cuckoos,' said Mary C. 'They make a great model for capitalists.'

'Listen . . .' said Richard, straining his head. 'Hear that?'

We hushed, holding our breath.

A few trees over a bird was singing a song of yearning loveliness.

'Is that it?' said Blanche.

'No,' said Richard. 'That's a black cap. It's a really beautiful singer.'

'It is. Really it is,' I said.

'It's getting late in the year to hear nightingales,' said Richard. 'They only really sing for six weeks or so. And, as I say, only really at dusk and dawn for most of that time. The dead-of-night singing is only until they find a mate. And they are much rarer than they were. Last I read, the population was estimated to be down ninety per cent on forty years ago.'

'So if it was a nightingale singing in the bush next to Newhaven Railway Club . . .'

'Which I don't think it was.'

'And given that that was twenty-five years ago, that means the chances of hearing one right here are . . .'

'Are zero,' said Blanche.

'No, but suppose it was a nightingale. Ninety per cent in forty years. That means the chance of hearing one, since I last heard one twenty-five years ago, has fallen by . . . hang on . . . er . . .'

'Come on. There are definitely some here,' said Richard.

You have to hand it to Richard. A lesser man would have just told us that one of the songs we could hear, all of which were very beautiful, was a nightingale. But not he. He has standards. As the last of the light leached away from the sky, Richard would stop, and tilt his head, and listen, and then say, 'No.'

And we'd walk on round the lake.

It was a beautiful night. Overhead, the last of the swifts screamed and swirled away into the dusk.

'Are they roosting?' asked Blanche.

'No, not they. They fly hundreds of miles in a day. They never come to earth except to breed and nest. They are miles away now, chasing food.'

'What happens to the chicks while they are gone?' asked Blanche.

'Well, they fall into a kind of a catatonic state. Their parents could be gone for days, chasing after food, or just surfing on storm fronts,' said Richard.

'Wow.'

'It is incredible . . . oh . . . look . . .'

Richard made us all have a go on his monocular. Out in the lake, a pair of crested grebes were frolicking in the gloaming. I'd seen them before on the Broads, and had read about them late into the night in Arthur Ransome novels. It reminded me of my evening with the Eloi, and sitting by the side of Ranworth Broad, watching the lights from the yachts at anchor reflected in the still water.

Here, the lights came from the fishermen. Every fifty yards or so, a fisherman had taken up residence in a small bay, each marked with a peg, showing that it was an official pitch. Each of the fishermen had at least two rods out in the water, as well as voluminous empty keep-nets; but they also had those vast umbrellas, which were really open-sided tents; bivouacs, I guess you'd call them. At the back of each of the tent-brollies, each of the fishermen had set up a camp-bed, and each of them had a small stove with a kettle hissing ready for tea, a lantern, and a chair to sit in and nod while nothing much happened. I could suddenly see the attraction of the thing. I might go out there one night. I'd take a book rather than fishing rods, but I could appreciate that reading by lantern-light, hearing the early-morning rain on the cavernous roof of the tent-brolly, watching the grebes court and the swifts swirl, just sitting and listening to the night, all of that, would be a good thing to do. Perhaps I could start a new hobby: not-fishing-at-night.

'I never knew that fishermen were all so good-looking,' said Mary C, and I had to admit that, by the light of their gas lanterns, they did have a kind of craggy charm.

Richard stopped to ask a couple of the fishermen who were chatting together if they'd heard any nightingales.

'Yeah, they're here alright,' said one of the fishermen, in a local accent.

'I heard them at dawn this morning, over by the entrance to the car park.'

'Oh great,' said Blanche. 'We've walked all round this lake . . .'

'But it is very beautiful,' said Mary C. 'It's worth being out and listening.'

Which was quite true. It was. The grebes had gone with the last smudge of light in the west. Only the fishermen were left by the lake. Richard said that meant that our chances of hearing a nightingale had fallen to close to zero. We stood by the five-barred gate by the entrance to the car park where the fisherman had told us to listen. But there was nothing. Richard said he heard a robin; his ears are sharper than mine; all that I could hear was silence. Even the nightingales were tucked up and silent.

'There's just one more thing we could try,' said Richard.

'What's that?'

'Well, I've got some recordings of nightingale song on a CD in my car. Sometimes, if they hear another bird singing, they'll respond.'

So we went back to Richard's car, and he found the track of nightingales singing, opened his car door and played it loud. There was no response. Of course there wasn't. We all knew there wouldn't be.

We stood and listened to the lovely sound. There is a kind of throat-clearing first; four or five notes of not terribly pretty whistling. And then the true song breaks out; a song of love and yearning, heard in the night only for a few weeks of the year,

here and there, now and again, if you are very lucky, or a professional sound-recordist prepared to sit out for the whole of the
fortnight of night song; like the guy who had recorded the song
that we were listening to now.

'Is this the song you heard in Newhaven?' Mary C asked me.
'I can't tell.'

The memory had gone. But to hear the black caps, and the
blackbirds and robins; just to listen in the darkness, truly for the
first time; it was worth not hearing what we'd come to hear to
hear that. And to feel the stillness of the wild night; to tune in to
it. That was worth it. And whatever that bird had been singing
in that lonely bush in the middle of industrial Newhaven, I was
doubly grateful. Because it had made me come on this night
walk with my friends, open-eyed and open-eared, and full of
hope that it is still possible to catch a glimpse of the wild, or
even to hear its song, where the lights have not become so bright
as to make the world fit only for the tame.

FULL OF FIRE

The mixtapes are still going, and Neil and I are still talking, as we've been talking all night. I've tried to persuade him to get the guitar out, but he is probably one tin beyond making coherent chord shapes, and, if truth be told, my voice is probably one spliff of home-grown bud beyond being able to hit its sweetest notes.

I'm still puzzled by the stuff that Neil has never heard. I mean, admittedly I've never heard more than about a bar of the Clancy Brothers singing anything since I was a kid, but that's because I have great taste, and if I find myself in a position (for example, driving from Belfast to West Cork and listening to Irish radio) where I might be in the slightest danger of hearing the Clancy Brothers sing so much as a diddley diddley dee, I keep my hand poised by the off button. Nor is the stuff on my mixtapes exactly leftfield. It's not as though I'm expecting Neil to distinguish between, say, Throbbing Gristle and Einstürzende Neubauten.

'I like this,' he says. 'What's this one now?'

'Er . . . this is Al Green. It's called "Full of Fire".'

'Yeah, this is good. I've never heard anything by this guy before.'

'How . . . I mean . . . what have you been doing with your life?'

'Is he well known?'

Where do you go with this? If you're me, you launch into an account of the life and career of the Reverend Al Green, culminating in the story of the fabulous occasion when I stood with my friend Gary Holland in front of the main stage at Glastonbury as Al ran a revivalist meeting, interspersing his greatest hits with some old-time preaching.

'So every time Al Green shouted "Can I get a witness?" me and Gary shouted back "Yes!" and "Praise the Lord!" It's the best church service I've ever been to.'

'Do you actually go to church, Ian?' asks Neil, clearly sceptical that I have much ecclesiastical experience against which to judge watching Al Green at Glastonbury on any kind of scale of liturgical excellence.

'Yeah, I do a bit, as it goes. Not every week, but more than Christmas and Easter. If I'm in the mood, I like it very much. An old-fashioned sung Evensong is my favourite.'

'Do you believe in God, then?'

'Yeah, I do really. Or, I've had a series of experiences which I call God.'

Neil scratches his belly.

'That's the most pretentious thing I've heard all night.'

'Thanks. But I do believe. I call myself C of E on forms, and I mean it too. I have my own weird theology, and the C of E is full of people with their own weird theologies. It suits me . . .'

'Ach, I was brought up a Catholic. In Norfolk. I don't believe any of that shite now.'

'I was brought up as a kind of secret atheist. My parents didn't believe, but they pretended to. I sang in the church choir when I was little, and my parents probably write the same thing on the forms that I do, but I sort of believe it now, and they certainly don't.'

'How can you believe in all those fairy stories?' asks Neil.

'Well, because they're fairy stories.'

'Hello?'

'But that's why we read fiction, or great fiction anyway. Because it's true. Just because something's a fairy story doesn't stop it holding great truth.'

'No, but you don't believe it in the same way you believe in the existence of all your shite pop music.'

'No. I know pop music is great. Objectively. I can prove it. The God stuff involves faith, and is thus subjective, and thus can't be proved. But that just makes it a subjective truth. A matter of taste . . .'

'Ah, that's what I've not got.'

'Taste?'

'Faith.'

'That's what I got given, one night . . .'

'One night?'

'Under the circumstances, it was inevitable.'

'And had you been inevitably smoking dope?'

'I had. Settle back in your ruined armchair, and I will tell you . . .'

'Sometimes it helps to concentrate if I close my eyes.'

'Of course.'

'And snore a bit . . .'

'It was 1986 . . .'

'What was?'

'The night when I found my faith.'

'Oh, right.'

'It was 1986, and I was living on my own in an old artists' studio up in the hills behind the quaint old Sussex town of Newhaven.'

'Quaint? I caught the ferry there once. It's a shite hole. How come you were living there?'

'It's a long story.'

'I thought it might be.'

'Shhh. I had left my first wife and our daughter Charley for my lover. And my lover had left me for Jesus.'

'Bastard.'

'I was.'

'Not you. Jesus.'

'Er . . . no. Me. My first wife, Rowan, earned lots of money working for American Express in Brighton. I earned £48 a week writing up the results of horse races in bookmakers' shops. All the money I earned went to fund the Mood Index Continuum, the insane ten-piece anti-capitalist funk/pop-reggae/free-jazz/noise/country-punk band for which I was lead singer and co-writer, and in whose cause I was willing to sacrifice anything, especially the happiness and security of those around me.

'My lover played in the band. She sang like Françoise Hardy, and I'd always loved her voice. The anti-capitalist love songs I wrote for us to sing together were increasingly about being in love with someone who sang anti-capitalist love songs in a funk/pop-reggae/free-jazz/noise/country-punk band.

'We had been at school together. I'd gone away; she'd stayed at home. If I hadn't wanted to be a middle-class wanker and gone poncing off to university, maybe we would have dated, married, had our own family. Doubt it. It wouldn't have worked, and I wouldn't have had Charley. Whatever.

'Ten years after school, we ran away one night after a gig in Eastbourne; ran away, but not quite together. I walked out on my family and went to stay in a junkie house in Brighton; my lover left her partner and moved back in with her mother. She would catch the train into Brighton in the evenings, and we'd sit in the Nightingale pub opposite the station, and hold hands, and talk about our guilt; because just as I had left Rowan and Charley, she had left behind a long-term boyfriend, a true life, a shared property.

'Then, one cold night on Brighton Station, six weeks after running away, she got off the train with her, as I was about to discover, no longer ex-boyfriend; and, holding his hand, she told me it was over between us. Because I wasn't a Christian. Behind my back they had been secretly attending a Baptist church together, and had done the whole born-again bit. After fifty minutes, they caught the train home together. They were married a fortnight later.

'This was a bit rich, I thought, so the next night, after finishing work, I bimbled along to my local church and asked to see a priest. I was in bits. My local church was the extraordinary St Bartholomew's, built to the dimensions of the Ark, gilded and pimped up with mystery almost to the point of Roman Catholicism; so much so that one of the junkies I was house-sharing with used to go to Mass there on Sundays, believing it to be an actual Catholic church . . . er . . . which it is, in a way . . .'

'No, you've lost me,' says Neil.

'Anglo-Catholic, not Roman Catholic. Very high C of E. And in Brighton, the high C of E is an exercise in the highest possible camp, as you might imagine. The priest was a slim-hipped and fragrant young man in a cassock and a biretta, and a whiff of incense followed him as he half trotted and half genuflected his way up the aisle. I told him of my plight. I'd sung some anti-capitalist love songs with a girl towards whom I'd had a slight romantic attachment since school and with whom I considered myself to have fallen in love, at least in part as a consequence of singing the bloody songs. Now she'd left me for Jesus, saying that she could never be with someone who wasn't a Christian, and had gone off to marry her ex, who had just converted to Evangelical Christianity. The young priest sighed, and rolled his pretty eyes.

'"What does she mean, Father? When she says that she loves Jesus?" I asked.

'"Well," said the priest, "I really don't think it matters what she meant. I really couldn't give a stuff. And neither should you. You should be doing something about your wife and child, idiot, and not worrying about anything else. You just left your wife and child. What are you going to do about it?"

'So, the first time I went to see a priest, the guy talked truth at me; a glaring truth, one which has only become more painful over time. That counted for something, even then. It was pouring with rain; I walked back to the junkie house, and as I passed under a streetlight, it went out, and I thought, yeah, that's about right.

'When I got home, my Geordie junkie Catholic landlady was waiting for me.

'"Ian," she said. "I hope you don't mind, but ah've had a miscarriage in yer bed."'

'This never happened,' says Neil.

'It did. I swear it did. She said it was the only room in the house clean enough for her to have the doctor in. And then she said, "But don't worry, like. I've changed the sheets."'

'Which was neighbourly of her,' says Neil.

'So then I moved out of the junkie house; and I moved into an artists' studio, in the middle of the South Downs.'

'Behind Newhaven, anyway . . .'

'Yep.'

'So this is really only the start of the bit about the night where you found your faith?'

'Yes . . . no . . . I had to give you a bit of background, so that you could understand my state of mind.'

'Stoned.'

'I admit that. I admit I was stoned. I was very stoned. Ever had Nepalese Temple Balls?'

'No. I just drink beer.'

'Nepalese Temple Balls are mad.* They make you think things. Mad things. After two nights on the stuff, I thought I

---

* They really are. They are spherical balls of cannabis resin, and they are bonkers. To be avoided, if ever you come across any, unless you are looking to have a really strange time.

could shoot bolts of electricity from the ends of my
fingertips . . .'

'At . . . ?' says Neil.

'My enemies.'

'OK . . .'

'So, yeah, I was stoned out of my tree on Temple Balls . . .
and living alone in what amounted to a shed with no heating,
hot water, or cooking facilities. And only one other house in
sight. But the entire north side of the studio was a huge glass
wall, so I could lie shivering and fully clothed in bed and read
and look at the stars.

'I read about religion. I started where any self-respecting
drug-crazed failed musician would start, with the Christmas
Humphreys book on Zen, because it's in a Van Morrison
song. Then I read this mad born-again thing about how
rock music is essentially Satanic. Then I started reading seriously, anything I could get my hands on, smoking Nepalese
Temple Balls and sitting in a transparent shed in the hills,
and reading stuff all night. I read Paul Johnson's *History of
Christianity*. I read and liked Don Cupitt's *Sea of Faith*; it
talked about how to be a Christian and an atheist, all at the
very same time. I liked Nietzsche a lot. I'm not sure he
liked me, though.'

'You didn't think of reading the Bible, then?' asks Neil.

'Ooh, no. I wouldn't like that,' I say.

'Why not?'

'Well, apart from Jesus, I don't like the characters. Anyway,
Nietzsche says that if you want a happy life you should believe,
but that if you want a true life, you should investigate. I want a

true life, with an occasional measure of happiness as a consequence. I was investigating . . .

'I read *Walden* by Henry David Thoreau, and imagined myself living next to a pond, and growing oats and shit. I wore black. I smoked Temple Balls. The only sound system I had was an old mono cassette player; and I had one tape, a C60, with the first Jesus and Mary Chain album taking up most of it, but with 'Portuguese Love' by Teena Marie* taped off the radio on the end. I spent as much time as my wife would allow me looking after Charley, so I was commuting into Brighton almost every day, mourning the self-inflicted loss of my daughter, and trying to make up for what I'd done, and smoking and reading all this mad stuff, and thinking about God, pretty much all the time. For about three months, I lived like this.

'On the nights Rowan let me look after Charley, I'd catch the last train out of Brighton back to Bishopstone station, which was about a half-hour walk from the studio. The walk from the station was on a road that led back from the A259 coast road, winding up into a combe in the Downs through the old village of Bishopstone proper, and then on to the little hamlet of Norton, where the studio was, in the garden of a big old house called "Hunters Moon" . . .'

'Sounds nice.'

'It would have been, except it was being squatted by another bunch of junkies, with whom I seemed to share a weird affinity at that time . . .'

'Well done.'

* I still love this song. I might take it onto *Desert Island Discs*, now I come to think of it.

'I know. I was a stoned hermit living in the garden of a squatted house where the smack-head inhabitants saw me as being much too odd to deal with. Anyway, on the walk back to the studio, the quickest way was to take a shortcut through Bishopstone churchyard, and across an overgrown meadow to the house. There was an old path; you could still see it through the long grass, though I must have been one of only a few people keeping it open. This particular night . . . I may have been more stoned than usual. I may have been being sent mad by Nietzsche, because if it doesn't send you a bit mad, then you're not reading it properly. It was certainly full moon; and it was raining, but that rain that isn't really rain, more like walking through a cloud.'

'That's what they call a soft day here,' says Neil.

'Except that this was a soft night. Yeah. A really soft night. There was no wind. The rain in the air was full of moonlight, which turned the night . . . er . . . Lurex.'

'Lurex?'

'Yes. Lurex. It was like walking through the Stones' wardrobe in about 1972.'

'That's a beautiful image.'

'I know. So I walked along, bathed in this Lurex night, and I walked through the churchyard. It was alive with light. I could see the old path across the meadow picked out by silver condensation on the long grass, to where Hunters Moon stood alone at the edge of the village. The whole world was silver. And at once, without any kind of premonition, er . . . I just knew.'

'Knew what?'

'That I wasn't alone in the universe. That I was part of this beauty, somehow, and it was appropriate that I was there, and loved and wanted, just there and then.'

'And . . . ?'

'That's it. Ever since then I've believed in God.'

'That's it? That's your proof of God?' Neil is agitated, and shifts his arse in the chair.

He sits up, and leans towards me.

'So let me get this straight. At a time of huge emotional uproar, whilst off your skull on the strongest dope on earth, and while reading loads of books about religion, one foggy night you felt loved? Hardly the stuff of Revelations, is it? I mean, it's not proof, is it, or even news? Stoned man finds God shock. So fucking what? It doesn't prove a thing.'

'I know, but I'm not trying to prove anything. I'm telling you about an experience which, however mundane, made me feel the actual presence of God. Surrounded by love.'

'That's not love, that's just chemicals. And fucked-up-ness.'

'It doesn't matter. Anyway, everything's chemicals. All I know is that ever since, I've been on the side of Johnny Cash and Bob Marley as opposed to Richard Dawkins and Christopher Hitchens. And that was the night I started writing anything other than anti-capitalist love songs . . .'

'Like what?'

'A journal. That was the first thing I started writing. A mad journal about what I did at night. I really can't remember anything about my days back then; just my nights.'

'What were you doing?'

'Oh, I was thinking out my theological position and writing it down. It's very interesting to read now.'

Neil looks sceptical.

'No, honestly, it is. Because it's round about then that I became the Buddha.'

Neil looks the next few on the scale up beyond merely sceptical.

'You became the Buddha?'

'Yes! For about a week.'

'For a week? You were the Buddha . . . ?'

'Yes!'

'For a week?'

'Yes. I told you.'

'What was it like?'

'It was like being the Buddha.'

'No, but what was it like?'

'It was cool. I recommend it.'

'I bet. Why did you stop?'

'Oh, I realised that I had become the Buddha.'

'And that was why you stopped?'

'Well, Buddha stopped being me.'

'Bummer,' says Neil.

'Yes and no. It was a heavy time.'

I pop one together. Neil nods sagely.

'So why don't you do whatever Buddhists do?'

'Mate, you must have misheard me. I *was* the fucking Buddha! Whatever I did, that's what the Buddha did! Like eat steak and kidney pies from the Chinese chip shop by Brighton station.'

'So why don't you do Buddhist things any more? Like chanting and that? Eating vegetables. When did you ever eat a vegetable?'

'Ah, well, that was the Dalai Lama.'

'What was?'

'Who converted me to Christianity.'

'What, you met him, and he talked you into following Jesus?'

'No. I heard him on the radio, saying that he was puzzled as to why young Westerners would become Tibetan Buddhists, and that if he was a Westerner, he'd be Christian. So that's what I did.'

'It must have been difficult to find a church.'

'It was! It really was. I'd been reading all this Alan Watts stuff on Zen. He talks about how the universe is moving from simplicity into complexity; that life is becoming more complicated, in every sense. I didn't want anything plain and simple. I wanted a really complicated church, in order that I might tune in with the infinitely complex nature of the Creative. So I plumped for the Church of England.'

'That is weird,' says Neil.

'I know. But I didn't want to be one of those I'm Spiritual Not Religious people you come across on dating sites. I wanted to try and remember what it was like to feel surrounded by love, and a bit of what it was like to be the Buddha.'

'So you joined the C of E?'

'Yes!'

'So do you love Jesus?'

'Yes! And Krishna. Krishna a bit more, if I'm honest.'

'To sum up, then,' says Neil, gathering the last of his reasoning powers from some deep hidden well within, 'after splitting up with your wife and taking loads of dope and reading loads of really whacked-out stuff, you had a weird feeling of being surrounded by the Stones' wardrobe, became the Buddha, and joined the Church of England, where you currently worship Krishna?'

'Yes!'

'Bull. Shit.' says Neil.

He has me there. I go to church to try to recreate that initial feeling of being wrapped in love by a night of immeasurable compassion. I suppose you don't really get that full-on experience in church all that often, but it seems right to try. Besides, it is my culture, the Church of England, even here in Wales, where I manage to live in one of only a handful of Welsh C of E parishes. It is where I'm from. I went as a child, sang in dark churches lit by candlelight in the choir, learnt the stories at Sunday School, dozed as the words of the Prayer Book seeped into my head. It's where my language comes from, and my deepest sense of what is appropriate in the world. So I go, half a dozen times a year maybe, more when I'm in Northern Ireland. I like going to Evensong best. I especially like going to Evensong in Lichfield Cathedral with my friend Catherine Fox.

I like going there because Cath is a hoot, and writes a very funny and brilliant column for the *Church of England Newspaper* called 'The Joy of Sexagisima', and because Catherine's husband is the Chancellor of Lichfield Cathedral, the Reverend Canon Doctor Pete Wilcox, and when I go with Catherine I get to sit in the poshest seats possible, right behind the choir, and I get to watch the dean and the precentor and the treasurer and all these great officers of the Church, and it's like being in a Trollope novel, and the choir sing lovely things, and I get to say the Lord's Prayer, which I like saying very much, and then we stroll back across the Cathedral Close in darkness for a warming drop of something, and some theological debate.

Not so much debate, now I come to think of it, as me asking Pete dumb questions, and not daring to reveal the depths of my hippydom by owning up to the weird stuff.

Till now, obviously. Morning, Vicar!

I'd been a few times with Cath to Evensong, and had come to think of myself as something of a Friend of Lichfield Cathedral, when Catherine and Pete made the mistake of thinking the same, and inviting me to be the after-dinner speaker at the Friends of Lichfield Cathedral annual fundraising bash. And I, stunned by this sweeping, sudden and probably unwarranted taking-on-board of me as a potentially respectable person, accepted with pleasure. I couldn't wait. My subject was to be 'My Life as a Travel Writer'. The fact that I've never actually travelled anywhere much didn't seem to ring any alarm bells – a pity.

They always put the speaker at these kinds of do's on the top table, so there I was making conversation throughout the meal with the Lord Bishop of Lichfield and his good lady, and the Dean of Lichfield and his highly naughty wife. Also on the table were a Lady somebody-or-other, who owned Uttoxeter race-course, and her eldest boy, who was about sixty and a Sir. The Lord Bishop said something charming about a series I'd done for Radio Four. I suspect Cath had set him up, but still. A bishop had addressed complimentary remarks to me about my work for BBC Radio Four. If anything more establishment than that has ever happened to you, dear reader, then you are probably the Queen.

The Dean's wife could both see and enjoy my discomfiture, and was quietly winding me up with a series of off-colour jokes, which were making me laugh, a lot, but she was not helping me to be on my best behaviour, which I certainly needed to be. I turned to chat with the Lady who owned Uttoxeter races. Uttoxeter races gave me an 'in'; so after dinner, when it was time for the after-dinner speaker to speak, I got up and told the story about how my eldest daughter Charley got her middle name from Wetherby races, which always goes down well. I worked in the bookmaker's shop at the time that Rowan was expecting Charley, and she phoned the shop to say that her waters had broken just as the three o'clock race at Wetherby was called under starter's orders; hence Wetherby. I told the audience in Lichfield that night that if Rowan had called fifteen minutes earlier, or fifteen minutes later, Charley's middle name would have been either Manchester White City or Uttoxeter. The audience liked this story, and they laughed. One elderly gentleman at the next table laughed so hard, in fact, that he had a stroke at this point, and collapsed onto the floor.

I didn't think it was that funny, but I'm not one to say No to laughs, however hard won.

Since I had a mike, I was able to ask if there was a doctor in the house, which I'd always wanted to do. Then I alerted the staff, after which there seemed nothing else to do but to sit back down and talk to the Dean's wife, while the numerous doctors in the place fussed over the elderly gentleman, and the staff called the ambulance. Now, the fact that an old bloke was probably dying on the floor next to us didn't stop the Dean's wife from continuing to make off-colour jokes in my ear, still very quietly. The worst moment was when the paramedics arrived to take the old gentleman away. The Dean's wife leaned towards me, and whispered, 'This reminds me; I could have been at home watching *Casualty* instead of having to be here.'

And I went, 'PAAA HAAA HAAA,' very loudly; and everyone stopped what they were doing, and stared at me, and thought 'what a foul man', while the Dean's wife sat there, all demure and butter wouldn't melt in her potty mouth. And after the ambulance staff had taken the old gentleman away, the audience turned to me with cold resignation, and I felt I had to pick up my speech from where I'd left off. To say that I'd lost the crowd is something of an understatement. It was gone ten, on a very cold night in February, and they'd had their grub, heard a mildly amusing racing-related anecdote, and enjoyed the spectacle of one of their contemporaries moving much nearer the exit door than they. They had had enough. We should have left it there, really.

And I had lost the most important thing of all. I had lost my nerve. I burbled through a few desultory *Parallel Lines* and *Longest Crawl* stories, most of which, I suddenly realised through my new-found and unwelcome faculty of self-editing, were not quite proper under the circumstances.

So then I decided to tell the story of my recent pilgrimage to Iona. I learned several things from this telling. First, and this is important, do not use 'tennis enthusiasts' as a euphemism for gay ladies at any gathering which includes a bishop. In fact, probably best not to make any reference at all to the sexuality of your fellow pilgrims, even if they *are* all ladies in couples. Second, don't get bogged down in trying to explain why you took a folding electric bike with you, or what a folding electric bike even is.

But, above all, don't attempt an off-the-cuff repudiation of the works of Dr Richard Dawkins in front of professional theologians.

It is never enough just to say: 'So, I wanted to . . . I was on Iona to find . . . to rediscover, really . . . well, mystery, and that, and show that Dawkins . . . well, he missed the point, really, didn't he? I mean, like, anyone can have a go at Leviticus . . . kna what I'm saying? I mean, obviously God doesn't care if you eat lobsters or not, does he?', which is pretty much exactly what I did say.

Anyone can have a go at Leviticus, yes, but it's not a great idea when you are standing next to an actual bishop. They are broadly in favour of Leviticus, in all sorts of surprising ways.

And I tried to remember anything about my trip to Iona that I might usefully bring out to amuse this audience, but as I'd already done the 'tennis enthusiast' thing, I could think of nothing.

I mumbled my thanks, and sat down to the kind of applause that the England cricket team gets coming back into the pavilion after being bowled out for 102 against Sri Lanka on the first day of the Test. Pete and Cath led me away in tatters, propped me up in the back of their car, and listened to me blame the Dean's wife for everything as we drove back to the Close.

That night should have taught me to lay off the theology in public, but it's hard. I'd tried to talk about why I'd gone to Iona, and if I could have articulated it properly, and not just made lezzer jokes, then I still think it could have worked.

If.

But when I was on Iona, I couldn't articulate what I was looking for, and certainly couldn't say what it was that I had found there. Looking back at my journal, I find that my first entry says, 'Iona is monster. Iona is the bomb,' which is true, but we want more, I think.

Why had I gone to Iona? To see if I couldn't recapture that night outside Bishopstone, wrapped in Lurex and love. I took my folding electric bike,* obviously, and a booking for three nights at the poshest hotel on the island. If I'd been doing the thing properly, I guess, I'd have stayed in the guesthouse at the Iona Community, but that seemed a bit full-on born-againy to me. I arrived as the light was fading, on the last boat over from Mull, and I ate beautifully cooked lamb chops, the only man in an hotel dining room which was, I swear, full of lesbian couples, all preparing to go up to the Abbey for the eight o' clock service. I should go. That's why I was here.

But it had been a long drive up to Oban, and then a long-ish boat crossing, and a beautiful but exhausting bus ride across Mull to Fionnphort for the boat to Iona. I used my folding electric bike for the last leg of the journey, which is from the ferry slip to the door of the Iona Hotel, a trip of some 200 metres, but despite this assistance I was tired. The lamb chops were tending

* Oh, alright. It's a folding bike with a electric motor. They are big here in Presteigne, which is home to the world's only electric bike race.

a fellow towards a deep and blameless sleep. So I read in the bath for a bit, and then slept. Night One of my Spiritual Quest drew to its anti-climacteric.

The next day, after a hearty breakfast of kippers, I set off to explore the island on my folding electric bike. I visited the Abbey, and looked forward to reconnecting with the ineffable later that night. I visited John Smith's grave, and wondered exactly how many people he had planned on killing as part of the New Labour project and, had he lived, if he would have killed any fewer people than his criminal disciples. Then I went for a walk on the golf course, which really is great. It's just as a golffe course might have been 300 years ago; no clubhouse, no green fees, hardly any discernible greens, just an open area of machair with some holes and tee markers. It is to modern golf what real tennis is to the lawn variety. Apparently there is an Iona Open every year, when mad fans of the authentic game come and try their modern skills and clubs against this ancient survivor. I would like to see that.

Then I went for lunch, and a bit of a kip after.

Then I had a bit of a stroll before dinner. Then I had dinner. A young family group had appeared, as well as most of the ladies in sensible shoes. After dinner, I tried to talk to a few of the ladies, but they weren't having any. So, come ten to eight, I hopped on my electric bike and bimbled back up to the Abbey. Iona really is very dark. Most of the visitors were heading up for the nightly service carrying torches, but I didn't need to, as I had a fuck-off electric bike with a big light on. The crowd parted to let me pass. As we made our way inside, a group were singing a Celtic hymn. It sounded suspiciously like Irish music, so I was at once on my guard. The place was already packed by the time I arrived.

A very young man appeared, and taught us to sing a spiritual. I found this very impressive. Usually when I go to church, I sing lustily at the few hymns I know and mumble through the rest, like most people. On Iona, they are having none of this. They rehearse you. The young man divided us into four groups, and taught us a four-part harmony before the service, so that we wouldn't sound shit while praising the Creative Universe. I thought we ended up sounding alright, but the song, a South African spiritual, sounded like nothing so much as 'Back Home' by the 1970 England World Cup Squad. I tried to concentrate, but I have to say there was an African lady of startling beauty sitting in front of me, who made me think a great deal about earthly rather than otherworldly matters.*

There were a couple of prayers and the 'Back Home' song, and then another young man told us a story, but I think I may have nodded off. I came to to find myself in the bit of church services which most people dread, viz. the 'Peace'. This is when you shake hands with and mumble at your neighbours. On Iona, where the services are highly structured, they insist that you actually talk, and really introduce yourself, rather than just muttering 'psbwthu' like we do in the C of E. I introduced myself to the African lady. Her name was Gronje, and she was from Stockholm. She had been on a few pilgrimages, including one very long one on foot from Stockholm to Trondheim in

---

* I have to say that just in case you think me an unmitigated bounder, this was before I'd met my wife, and I was single at the time, and so eligible to ogle beautiful African ladies in church.

Norway. I told her that she looked great on it, but I don't think she was terribly impressed.

And that was it. I got on my electric bike, and glided through the darkness to the end of the island road, there to smoke a fag, and to stare out over the black Hebridean Sea. Iona might well be the bomb, as I had so articulately put it in my notes, but I wasn't . . . well, I wasn't 'getting' anything. I'd wanted a supernatural charge of some kind, but it wasn't coming. Instead of thinking about the infinite nature of the Divine, and my place within it, all I'd done was titter inwardly at being asked to sing 'Back Home', and tried to pick up a gorgeous Erykah Badu-alike Swedish lady. The problem, I was only too painfully aware, was with me rather than the Divine. Still, what can you do? I rode back down to the Abbey, and pushed my bike through the grounds so that I could see. Once, the windows of this Abbey would have been luminescent with candles carried by monks on their way to vespers and compline. Their job was to pray for the world, which seems worth a go.

And once, Iona was one of a handful of places in Northern Europe where learning still survived after the withdrawal of the Romans. It was a tiny flickering candle of scholarship in a dark age. St Columba arrived here from Ireland with twelve companions in 534 CE, to set up his great monastery, and from here his followers evangelised Scotland and Northumberland. The monastery on Lindisfarne was established by monks from Iona. For 1500 years, people have bent their heads in prayer, in this place, in these nights. I felt the gravitational pull of historical wonder, but the ineffable was still nowhere to be glimpsed.

There must be ghosts here. I believe in ghosts. Pete Wilcox back in Lichfield had told me about an encounter he'd had with a poltergeist when he was Vicar of Walsall; and also about a colleague of his who'd gone through the whole *Exorcist* thing, the voices, the bile, and all the rest of it. Priests believe in spirits, of course, and in driving away the terrors of the dark, those ghouls and demons and vampires that the night lets in to a corner of our imagination. All the best ghost stories are about the unseen.

I've never seen a ghost, and it might only be imagination, of course, but I've been in places where it was uncomfortable to be; one that was so uncomfortable that, trying to sleep there alone, I became spooked like a highly strung racehorse, and I bolted into the night and went to crash on a friend's floor. I can still remember the feeling in that place: evil, I'd have to say. But I wasn't picking up vibes in the graveyard of Iona Abbey at half-ten on a very very dark night. I wasn't picking up anything at all. I went back to the hotel to read in the bath before falling into deep sleep.

Night Two of My Spiritual Quest was drawing to a close.

On Day Three, after more kippers, I went back to the golffe course and looked at the spume running up the beach, and wondered if you could count the bubbles as they reached the shore. Probably not, I concluded. Another excellent lunch followed by another stroll on the beach and a refreshing after-noon nap set me up for my last dinner on Iona. A few of my fellow guests were laying off the booze to prepare themselves for the Quiet Service at the Abbey, but I thought that was going a bit far. I rode on my electric bike through the darkest night yet up to the Abbey. There were no stars; the day had been grey, and so the night was really starless and Bible black; prayer-book black, anyway. The torches of the congregation and the spotlight on my electric bike were the only lights to be seen. It was Night Three of My Spiritual Quest, and I was getting impatient.

I liked the Quiet Service. There was little or no born-again malarkey. There was a prayer, and then a period of silent togetherness. One of the lovely young people led us in a little meditation. 'We are what we are in silence,' he said. Outside, through the windows of the Abbey, the clouds had broken to reveal a scrap of moon.

So, what am I? Or what was I at that silent moment? After a couple of days of eating great food, walking, riding my electric bike, reading in the bath, lots of sleep and a church service every evening, I was feelin' chillaxed. I was perhaps overkeen on seeing what Gronje was doing after the service, which I'm sure isn't quite the thing. But in no sense had I reconnected with the numinous Lurex love presence which had surrounded me one night and had, ever since, made me feel that I was loved just for being here, being part of all this, and being me.

I hadn't done it properly, I suspect. The Community on Iona are as un-born-again-y as it is possible to get. They experiment with the liturgy in order to express something which I think many of them find inexpressible. They are an ecumenical matter, which, as Father Jack* would tell you, is a good thing. And they camp in the same mad place at Pilton festival every year, in a

* Father Jack off *Father Ted*.

little dell right next to the railway line on the way up to Lost Vagueness; not the most peaceful spot on the site, and always the first to get washed out. But there they are, every year, and they will be pleased to see you if you drop by for some liturgical chit-chat.

I did learn something from those nights in Iona Abbey. Which is that even if you can't always connect, it's always worth a go. All you can do is remember and reflect, and try to stay true to the handful of truths you have managed to pick up; and also to say thank you, to Whatever.

Which, as you can probably guess, is not exactly the stuff of scintillating after-dinner speeches to bishops, though I still maintain I would have stuck to my script if the old geezer hadn't chosen that moment to throw a whitey.

'And that's why I like going to church,' I say to Neil.

Neil is snoring.

NOCTURIA

Neil has come to and is off on one. If I'm honest, he trembles on the verge of being properly hammered, which, after six pints and seven out of a twelve-pack of Stella, he has every right to be. Now he is ranting about freedom. Hippies and travellers do this a bit.

'All I ask is freedom, man. Freedom to do my own thing. I'm not harming anyone. What harm am I doing Them? All I want is a few beers, and to go fishing, and to come over and see Mac sometimes. That's all I ask. Freedom. Freedom to grow a bit of weed. I mean, it doesn't do any harm, does it? What harm does it do? I earn about eight grand a year, Euros, from growing weed. It's the jam on my bread. I mean, surely even long-term invalids are entitled to a bit of jam? But you try telling Them.'

'What's up with you, by the way?'

Neil looks puzzled.

'In what sense?'

'Well, why do you get invalidity benefit?'

'Oh . . . it's my hip, I think. And that's another thing. I can't work. You know that. But all I get is hassle. When all I want is to be free.'

'How aren't you free?'

'I am, but I want to keep being free. They are scared of freedom.'

'They certainly are.'

'They are scared of dreams. But how can a man dream, if he isn't free?'

'I don't know how They can sleep in their beds, man,' I say. And I don't.

I don't really know who They are, but I certainly don't know how They sleep. When They get into Their beds, do Their wives ask Them if They had a nice day?

Do They yawn and stretch and say, yes, thank you, dear. I authorised the renewal of the British Nuclear Deterrent today? Or: no, quite routine really, dear. Launched a few unmanned drones into a Pashtun wedding party, but otherwise fairly dull. And do They reach out and click out the light, and fall into a blameless slumber? Or do They stare wide-eyed at the wall all night, longing for sleep to come?

Sleep will come, in the end, no matter what is on our consciences. It has to, or we'd die. There is a Venetian family who carry a prion disease similar to CJD, called fatal familial insomnia. Those who succumb go into a state of perpetual wakefulness. They sweat, their pulse and blood pressure rise dramatically, and they never sleep again. It's a degenerative disease; it takes a little over a year to go from the initial night sweats to death. And the whole of that time, the victims are awake, and aware of what is happening to them. Sleep, it turns out, is not the same as death at all.

Most living things sleep, but we all do it differently, and for different reasons. Horses only need three hours' sleep, whereas the bat goes for the full nineteen, like Minnie. Small mammals seem to sleep because it saves them energy, whereas in more complex animals, like tigers, or humans, sleep provides recovery for the brain's cortex. The cortex is the lumpy stuff on the outside of the brain, and it has lots to do. It needs a rest, in the way that the parts of your brain which are running automatic functions simply don't. The bit of your brain that is cognitive might be asleep while the bit that controls motor functions might be awake; hence sleepwalking. If you go without sleep, your heart keeps beating and your gut keeps digesting, but lack of sleep directly impairs the cortical functions.

So if you lack sleep, your creativity is affected, but not your ability to perform mindless, routine tasks. If you stay up for twenty-four hours, you would find it hard to paint a masterpiece, but still be able to read the *Daily Mail*, for example. Speech is affected, and the range of your vocabulary shrinks; so your novel, like your masterpiece, is also best put on one side if you are sleepy – but you should still be fine with the *Mail*. The human ability to empathise is severely impaired, and so sleep-deprived people are more likely to be irritable and suspicious than their better-rested neighbours; once again, this seems to fit the profile of a *Daily Mail* reader quite neatly. Perhaps if *Mail* readers got more sleep, they'd be less incensed.

There seems to be a natural pattern to sleep, called the circadian rhythm. Humans seem to like about eight hours a night, but we also have an increase in sleepiness in the afternoon, known to science as the 'Disco dip'. It is quite natural and normal to want a nap in the afternoon, especially after an ill-judged couple of pints at lunchtime. Teenagers need more sleep, because they are idle layabouts, for whom a clip round the ear is too good. Our 'internal clocks' are set by 'zeitgebers', or 'time-givers', which leads me to suspect that the Germans got up earlier than we did, and left their towels on the nomenclature. Zeitgebers include light striking the eyes, or simply the aware-ness of clock time, so, to some extent, our clocks actually set our internal time. The most important zeitgeber is melatonin, 'the hormone of the night', which is produced by your pineal gland, the 'third eye' of the mystics. This is in the middle of your fore-head, and it seems to release melatonin during hours of darkness, (rather than during sleep). Melatonin may influence your repro-ductive cycle, as well as sleep patterns.

Darkness and sleep have lost the necessity of their connection with the advent of the light bulb. People used to go to bed with the setting of the sun, and get up at its rising. But this doesn't mean people needed more sleep; the evidence is that pre-modern people still slept eight or nine hours a night. So people would tend to have two sleeps, with a period of up to two hours' wake-fulness in the middle of the night. They would lie in a state of watchfulness, or say their prayers; sometimes they would eat and drink. A common piece of bedroom furniture in fifteenth-century well-to-do homes was the aumbry, an early kind of mini-bar, to hold food and drink in order to stave off night starvation.

What I have suffered from night starvation over the years! I have been a martyr to it. At about two in the morning, pork pies, which have little appeal in the afternoon, seem to call to me from the fridge, or even from as far afield as the all-night garage in Leominster, which is fourteen miles away. Carefully secreted bars of special ladies' chocolate, whose existence bothers me not at all by day, seem to beg to be unearthed from their hiding places in the depths of the night. Cake is an especial menace at night, in my view. It should be locked out with the cat. As night starvation leads to night fridge-emptying, so night fridge-emptying leads to weight gain, which is, in turn, one of the main reasons why people snore.

Snoring is another thing that has made me lead many disturbed nights. Apparently, I snore quite loudly. I'm told that people as far afield as Mortimer's Cross need to wear ear protectors when I get snoring. I'm told that, in 2007, my snoring gave rise to disturbances in the Church Stretton Fault, which in turn led to a small earthquake in Bishop's Castle. So I'm told. I never hear it, of course, because I'm fast asleep. But my sleeping companions have all ended up poking me, quite hard, and this wakes me up with a start, which puts me in a poor temper. Which just makes me hungry. Snoring is linked to neck fat. Bulldogs snore more than other dogs, and so it is with a well-made Englishman like me. It can be dangerous; it's called sleep apnoea when you stop breathing for a bit. Apparently it's what killed Grateful Dead guitarist Jerry Garcia. That sound that we thought was the Dead tuning up was apparently old Jerry catching forty winks behind the stage.

Apart from snoring, the main thing that wakes women up at night is their husbands getting up for a piss. The most common reason for waking at night in both men and women between fifty and eighty is 'toilet'. A less common reason might be 'lava-tory'. Presumably, after eighty, you just stop bothering to get up, and leave it to the nurse. It is thought that men need to go to the 'toilet' more after fifty because of 'benign inflammation of the prostate', which is great. Women wake up and go to the loo because their husbands wake up and go for a piss. Nocturia, it's called, and two thirds of people get it.

I get it, heaven only knows. I'm up and down like a bride's nightie these days, and knowing that it's due to benign inflam-mation of the prostate doesn't help me settle back down. No matter what I drink, there I am, two, three times a night, pissing my heart out. I have learned a sobering fact since I started spending a large part of my nights pissing. This is that men are all covered in piss. You stumble to the 'toilet' (or lavatory), trying not to wake everybody up. You don't wear pyjama trou-sers, so you are bare-legged. You point into the bowl and a great fountain of piss issues forth, which hits the back wall of the bowl, bounces back, and covers you in a fine pissy mist. You need to be bare-legged to feel it; it's like warm spray on a Dodecanese beach moistening your knees and shins. You could sit down. You should sit down, especially if you haven't turned the light on. If you haven't turned the light on, you will be pissing up the wall, and over the floor, and over the seat; and your wife, woken by your constant fucking pissing, will get up and sit in your piss.

It doesn't matter where I am. All night, it's piss piss pissing piss. At home, it's bearable (for me, you understand; less so for wife, daughters, stepdaughters etc.). In a shared hotel room, it's not so good, because you haven't got your piss routine together;

you biff into things, and trip over the bags, and you have to put the light on, and nobody's happy except you while you're pissing. Worst of all, I find, is when I perform at festivals, and have to camp. I have a chi-chi little one-man tent, and a state-of-the-art sleep mat, and a smashing bag. I get in my little tent at the end of a day of singing and recycling jokes, and I snuggle up quite comfy, and can drop off while all around me are drumming and listening to Scandinavian death metal. But two hours later, I'm desperate for a piss. And my snug tent, though easy to carry and erect, does not allow a man to so much as kneel up. And I can't get dressed and go to the pissers, because they are a ten-minute walk away, it's pissing with rain and there are 100,000 pissed mentalists between me and the blessed act of pissing. And I can't piss out the door because I'm surrounded by tents full of drummers and Scandinavian death metal enthusiasts. These days I take an empty four-litre water bottle, and half fill it by morning. You have to choose a water container with a wide neck, or aiming becomes all but impossible, and you either get chafing trying to stuff your cock up the neck of the bottle, or you get piss all over everything.

The first year I did Glastonbury after my fiftieth birthday was the first year I was truly confronted with this problem. I had been to many festivals before, and had slept right through without ever needing to get up. But this particular year there was no escaping it; I was awake, I had to go, and I had to go now. And there was nowhere to go. The rain was beating on the roof of my little tent. My wellies were tucked inside the fly door. There was nothing else for it. I grabbed my left welly, and pissed into it. And fell back to sleep.

In the morning, the accursed Glasto rain was still falling. I woke up, got out of my tent, got dressed as quickly as I could – and put on my wellies. Yes indeed. Even I could see the funny side of this. Later on in the day, when I'd dried my feet and changed my socks, I was sitting in a backstage bar with my friends Sir Gideon Vein and Matt Barnard, and I told them what I'd done. They thought I was very stupid. I swore them to secrecy. Later on that evening, I was walking through Theatre Camping when someone shouted at me, 'Oi! Piss in Boots!'

Such is fame.

I don't apologise if you are over fifty and reading this in bed. This is your cue. Get up now. Really empty your bladder. Squeeze out every drop. Don't be lazy; you'll pay for it later. Nurses recommend that men with persistent nocturia drink nothing after lunch except occasional sips of fruit juice; and you've ignored that excellent advice, haven't you? So, go on, get up now, and give it a real good go. With any luck, you'll get through to four-ish.

Everyone gets night erections, which really is great. Nobody is sure why, but they do. So men over fifty wake up with a stiff-on, and need to go for a piss. Even if they sit down, the wall is in danger of a spraying. Women get enlargement of their clit-oris, and their vaginas slightly lubricate; again, nobody is quite sure why. It could be something to do with our dreams, I guess.

Henry James said that if you write a dream, you lose a reader, so I'm going to lose three readers as I recount three recent dreams. First, I am walking through the Greenwich Foot Tunnel deep in conversation with a large and lucid parrot. We are looking for somewhere to piss. I wake up. And need a piss.

Next, I am in a Soap Box Derby, racing against Lulu and Martin Amis. Martin is laughing. We crash into a giant inflatable public lavatory, and all decide to have a smashing piss. I wake up. And need a piss. Lastly, I am fighting in a war. I am a dashing cavalry officer, and I have rescued Charlotte Gainsbourg from a herd of maroon sheep. Charlotte is wearing little except a dress made from pages torn from the *Daily Telegraph*. She gazes adoringly into my eyes and asks me if I know somewhere where she could have a piss . . . and so on. My dreams are soaked through with piss like a sponge.

Dreams were not always about piss. Neuroscientists now think that dreaming is essentially the cortex's way of processing a day's worth of rubbish; it is defragging itself. But for our ancestors, dreams were pregnant with meaning, meaning external to the dreamer. It was how the Gods communicated with Man. In the twentieth century, psychoanalysts, in particular C.G. Jung, became interested in deriving new meanings from our dreams. Dreams were how our unconscious mind communicated with us. Jung believed that our dreams contain 'archetypes' which pattern our existence, archetypes which spring from a collective unconscious, a shared place where we dream together.

I've done a bit of Jungian analysis, and I found it very interesting. I learned to disregard the stuff about piss; even to see it as a useful way to wake up so that I could write my dreams down. There were things that I learned in Jungian analysis which have stayed learned, no doubt about it. The neuroscientists might be right, that it is just a dumping of images, necessary for our mental health, but an instinct tells us that our dreaming must have meaning, if only for ourselves.

Back when I was the Buddha, I saw meaning in everything. Because I was, as you may have deduced, a little bonkers, I decided that these meanings were external to my consciousness. Even when I stopped being the Buddha, and my nights slowly became normal again, I was still susceptible to believing that the world ran on occult lines, which I could control.

A few months after the time in the artists' studio, when I spent my nights looking out through my glass wall at the stars and being Buddha, I was back living in a proper bedsit in Brighton, and was starting to go out at night to ordinary good things like pub quizzes. A few months later still, Rowan told me she had a new boyfriend, who also happened to be one of my closest pals on earth. I was happy for them. Another few months later, I was in love with somebody new, who I'd met at one of the pub quizzes. This turned out to be Lily, Minnie's mum. A few months later again, Lily and I were living together, and making big plans. Somehow, a year had gone by since I had left Rowan and Charley one night for a soon-to-be-born-again-Christian. In that time, all kinds of nights had passed, and I had come from strange nights of near madness and terrifying beauty back to quiet nights of quiet stars; nights of love and rest and hope, of forgiveness and new chances.

One night I had a vivid and terrifying dream. The fillings of my teeth were being pulled out, one by one, by a sharp wire hook. It was an image that stayed strongly with me the next day. After work, I went into WH Smith's on Churchill Square in Brighton, and went to the mumbo-jumbo section. I was looking for a book on the interpretation of dreams, and all I could find was a gypsy's dream book, which gave pre-psychoanalytical readings of dreams as prophecy. It gave interpretations which assumed that dreams had meaning outside of the individual's consciousness. I looked up dreams about teeth, about losing your teeth, about having teeth pulled. They all came to pretty much the same thing. It was the worst kind of luck. In fact, it was quite explicit: dreams of tooth pulling presaged the death of a loved one. I put the book back on the shelf in disgust.

Two weeks later, Rowan died.

After that, nights were never quite the same.

THIS WOMAN'S WORK

The last unlabelled CD mixtape from the damp glove compart-
ment of my car is going down much better with Neil than the
previous, more characteristically cheesy selections. This one is
straight-ahead rawk music, which I'd made just to prove to myself
that I still liked actual rock bands. Some things from my far-distant
youth, like the New York Dolls and Blue Öyster Cult; a few
newer things (well, newer to me) like Dinosaur Jr and Super
Furry Animals. Neil is greatly cheered by this, and pops a tinnie.

I try him with another of my central theories, that everyone
of our generation is either a mod or a rocker.

'Which are you, then?' Neil asks me.

'Since I've just been playing you Roxy Music and The
Impressions, I would have thought it obvious . . .'

'You're a mod?' Neil laughs.

'Of course.'

'You're telling me that, if you had the choice between a
beautiful fuck-off motorbike and a poncey scooter, you'd choose
a scooter?'

'Of course I would. You get to the nightclub without oil on your beautiful handmade Italian suit. You gobble up purple hearts and dance all night, and then get into work the next morning wide-eyed with amphetamine madness; but still with no oil on your suit. A scooter wins every time.'

'I worry about you,' says Neil, tipping his nth tinnie down his highly relaxed gullet.

'You still ride bikes, Neil?' I ask.

Neil looks sad.

'No, man, not for thirty years . . . not really since my big motorbike smash.'

'I didn't know you'd had one.'

'Yeah, man. That's when I did my hip. Thing was . . .'

Neil is filling up.

'What is it, Neil?'

'My best mate was on the back.'

'Was he hurt?'

Neil shakes his head.

'I don't know. He was killed. I hope it didn't hurt.'

'Shit.'

'Yep.' He gulps at his beer, wipes his cheek with his sleeve.

'What happened?'

'It was a wet night. I came off on a corner, and hit a tree. Don't remember much really. I came round a few days later, and they told me my mate was dead.'

'Shit!'

'And he was my best mate since we were kids. It was always me and him.'

'What was his name?'

'Martin.' Neil shifts in his armchair. 'I was in hospital for three weeks. When I came out and went home, nobody wanted to know me.'

'Why?'

''Cause everybody said I'd killed Martin.'

'That's shit.'

'Yeah. It is. After a year of everybody ignoring me, I came out here.'

'And never rode a bike again?'

'No, man. Never again. Never been home, neither.'

Sometimes, I guess, things hurt so much, and are so hard to heal, that there is no going back. The world changes beyond all recognition, just by taking one person away from it.

I know this.

One night in 1987, a few weeks before my twenty-ninth birthday, Lily and I were making our way up to bed. It was just before midnight. I can't remember what we'd been doing; just enjoying being together, I guess. I'd brought some tea up to bed, maybe. I know we were happy. The phone rang, and I answered from the bedroom extension, despite it being so late. I had no reason to hate the phone ringing late; I was still getting work as a singer, and it could have been any number of muso pals offering a gig. In fact, it was Rowan's friend Kiera, to say that she had been round Rowan's flat that evening, and that Rowan had just had a fit, and had been admitted to hospital. Charley was asleep upstairs, Rowan's boyfriend was in Ireland, and what should she do?

Lily knew. She is a nurse. Dealing with crisis has been her life. She said that she would drive over to Rowan's flat, and sit with

240

Charley, while I went up to the Sussex County to see how Rowan was. So that's what we did.

I found Rowan alone in a brightly lit corridor, on a hospital trolley, covered by a single sheet. It was clear that she was unconscious, rather than asleep; something in the way that she was lying, perhaps, or in the laboured way she was breathing. I held her hand, and told her Charley was alright, but I could tell that she couldn't hear. A nurse came to find me.

'I'm her husband,' I said to the nurse, and I was. Our divorce was due to have been heard a week later.

Rowan, Rowan, my poor wife. There she lay on the trolley under fluorescent lights; the Chelsea girl, the best-looking girl from our time at university, the liveliest, naughtiest girl I'd ever known, the leader of the girl-pack, my first real girlfriend, mother of my child. My wife. It didn't matter what had happened. She was my wife. I was her next of kin. The nurse brought a doctor, who told me they were as certain as they could be that Rowan had had a brain haemorrhage, a sub-arachnoid haemorrhage, and that I should expect the worst. But I didn't, because you don't.

It was after three when I left the hospital. I walked alone through the streets of Brighton; down Edward Street, up and over Queen's Park, down to the Level and out along the Lewes Road. My memory is of empty roads, and silent streets, lit by that part of the spectrum that only sodium can reach. Perhaps there were people about, or taxis taking people home; I remember only emptiness. There were no parents to give me comfort, no friends to play with, no bands to sing with, no lovers to hold on to, no nightingales to give me hope, and no sense, at all, of being part of a loving universe. I was, finally, alone with the night. I tried to think about what it was necessary and appropriate to do.

You might wish for your death to come suddenly in the night. Four a.m. is the time that most old people die; in Larkin's poem 'Aubade' it's the time that he wakes up every night to wait for his death. You might wish to go to bed one night and, at around 4 a.m., while you sleep, to slip into death. The association between sleep and death is an obvious one. In France in the seventeenth century beds were sometimes made too short to lie down on properly, because lying down is the nearest thing to death, and by sleeping sitting up, we somehow kept ourselves safe; kept ourselves distant from death.

You might wish to drop down dead, suddenly, because then you wouldn't suffer. I would urge you to reconsider, if there are people in the world who love you.

I arrived back at Rowan's flat, where Lily was waiting up for me. Charley slept on upstairs. We talked about what to do, who had to be contacted, the processes that it would be necessary to put in place. Lily, as I've said, is a nurse. She knew what a sub-arachnoid haemorrhage might mean. If Rowan lived, she would need months of rehabilitation. She might never walk again. Her personality might change beyond recognition. Lily saw, as I did not, that all our plans and dreams for a life together had just been radically changed. It was hard for her to be the first to really see what all this meant.

In the morning, after I'd taken a surprised Charley to school, we began making the phone calls and arrangements that would make everything better. Charley was to stay with my parents for a few nights; they were to pick her up from school that afternoon. I called Rowan's boyfriend in Dublin at nine; he turned up on the doorstep of her flat just after one. Rowan's brother and sisters arrived, from London and Gloucestershire. Friends came round to the flat. Daylight brought hope. When Rowan's brother visited the hospital, she sat up, and demanded a piss.

Those will probably be my last words, too.

In the evening, Lily drove me over to my parents' place to see Charley, and to tell her that her mummy was very ill. Then back to the hospital, to sit with Rowan's boyfriend and her family until we couldn't stay awake.

The following evening, the same.

And then the next evening, we drove to my parents' place again. I sat Charley on my knee, and held her tight, and I told her that I was very sorry, but that her mummy had died that afternoon, and she was coming to live with me now. Charley pushed me away, jumped from my lap as though she had been stung, and pelted up the stairs into the bathroom, where we could hear her being sick. I started up the stairs after her, but she shouted at me to leave her alone. I heard her say through the bathroom door, 'You must be brave, Charley. You must be brave.' Then we wrapped her in a duvet, and took her back to our flat, where she somehow managed to sleep between me and Lily. I don't think either of us managed it.

In the months following the death, there was lots to sort out. By great good grace, since Rowan and I were still married at the moment of her death, there were no custody issues to sort out. Charley would live with me, as soon as it could be arranged, and in the meantime would stay with her aunt. Lily was in an impossible position, an overnight stepmother and partner to someone who was suddenly deep in mourning for his ex-wife. Not ex-wife. Wife. Dead wife.

Somehow, we got things sorted. It took a few months, but we got it sorted, up to a point. We moved from Brighton to an isolated house in Radnorshire. Charley came home, and started a new school. Lily fell pregnant with Minnie. I sold second-hand records on the local markets. We made new friends. Rowan's family would visit us; Charley's cousins would come to stay. Our most frequent visitor was Rowan's boyfriend; we would walk on the hills, and remember her together. The days weren't so bad. The emptiness and beauty of Radnorshire soothed us.

It was the nights that were unbearable. For months, they followed the same pattern. I would wake at about two with excruciating pain in my head. To call it a headache makes no sense. They say you can't remember pain, but I can. It felt as though every night an axe had split open my skull, and been buried in my brain as far down as my eyes. The pain was so intense, it made me vomit up the contents of my gut, every night. Then I would be starving hungry, and I would go downstairs and eat pretty much the entire contents of the fridge. Only binge eating stopped the pain. Then I would go back to bed. In the mornings, the sheets would be soaked with acrid sweat. It was exactly as though I had pissed the bed. I was too exhausted to move; anyway, if I lay still, I could stay warm in the pool of liquid that had poured out of me in my sleep, but if I moved I would be lying in freezing sweat. Lily would get Charley ready for school, and walk her down the hill to the bus stop, and then come home, lever me out of bed, and change the sheets before going shopping for more food.

All of the doctors I saw, and I saw plenty, and all of the tests they ran, told me that there was nothing wrong with me. Which was clearly untrue. One day, I got a locum, one of those old-fashioned country doctors with an ashtray full of fag butts and a copy of *Farming Today* on his desk. He referred me to see a psychiatrist. The psychiatrist sorted me out after just a couple of appointments. The terrible head pain, the vomiting, the ridiculous night sweats all cleared up. I had been mimicking what I subconsciously thought of as the symptoms of a brain haemorrhage. Let *me* die. Let it be *me*. Everything would be so much simpler. After all I had put Rowan through, it was *me* that deserved to die, not her. She deserved to be happy, not fucking dead. The psychiatrist's suggestion was simple; I just needed to stop trying to sort things out and make everyone happy, and do some crying.

It worked. I cried. I got my sleep back, the one thing in my life at which I had been consistently great. Although my weight had ballooned, I could live with the extra few stones. Life was back on its bumpy tracks, because I'd found a new way to get through the night.

Seven years later, I had graduated from Lancaster University, and now Lily was a student there. Lily and I had been unable to contain the forces that Rowan's death had unleashed, and were living apart. Charley and I were living in a two-up two-down in Lancaster. I was working part-time in a second-hand bookshop. I was trying to write seriously, but I was also back singing with The Mood Index Continuum, even though there were now only two of us, and no girls allowed, except Dee, who came and sang backing vocals for us, and who wouldn't have accepted me as either a client or a lover anyway. Nights had fallen into a familiar routine. After dinner I would write. Sometimes I'd have a gig, or a rehearsal. After the gigs, I'd go back to a friend's recording studio, smoke a little spliff, listen to music until about two, and then go home and read what I'd written earlier. Three nights a week, Minnie stayed with me and Charley. On those nights, friends would often come round to mine after the pub. It got so that I would be disappointed if nobody knocked on my door at about half-eleven. Mostly, these late-night callers were young postgraduates, split half and half between philosophers and historians of science. They came to mine to have a blow and a laugh, but often we'd get to talking about their work. To this day, I know more about the ethics of virtual sex and the history of prosthetic penises than is healthy.

Lily and I were still trying to do things together with the girls. One weekend we took the kids down to West Wales to stay with Perry Venus and his wife Shinaid. Perry and I had played a round of pitch'n'putt together in Aberaeron. On the way back, while we were stopped at a Little Chef outside Wrexham, I became convinced that I was having a heart attack. I had pain in my left shoulder, which worried me. I very quickly became aware of other symptoms: my heart rate was going up, and I started breathing very quickly. I couldn't stop panting. Then my arms started to tingle. I knew what that meant. Death. Instant death. Falling down dead. Fucking up the lives of all those left behind. The ultimate cop-out, an act of complete cowardice.

Leaving Charley an orphan at fifteen. That's what was happening. I begged Lily to call an ambulance, which she did, even though she knew what was really happening. I was having my first panic attack.

In the hospital, they showed me my ECG, and mapped it against an utterly normal print-out, and demonstrated that they were identical.

'But what about the pain in my shoulder?' I asked the doctor.

'Have you been playing golf by any chance?' he asked me back.

I was very embarrassed. I was just as embarrassed three months later when it happened again. Then six weeks later. Then once a month, then once a fortnight, once a week. Then a panic attack every other day.

One night, walking late through Lancaster, on my way back from a rehearsal, I was struck by the worst attack I'd had yet. When you're having a panic attack you don't think, 'Oh bother, I'm having a panic attack.' You think you are dying, dying right here and now, and you are scared. Very scared. You prepare to run; you produce a rush of adrenaline, such as that you might get from sitting in the front seat of a rally car, a rally car that is about to crash and burst into flames. You breathe fast, in gulps, because you need a lot of oxygen in order to get away from death. Breathing in too much oxygen makes your hands and arms tingle. And so on. It's only later that you realise you've had another panic attack.

So, gripped by fear, I hammered on the door of a friend's house; I could see from their lights that they were still up. They took me in, sat me down, made me tea, and sent me home in a taxi. That was the end of my non-panic moments. From that night on, for the next two years, I inhabited fear. Unremitting fear.

Sleep was impossible. Every night in bed I tried and failed to calm my pulses. Up till then, I'd had no idea how many pulses the human body has. I'd now say there are dozens. All through the night, I lay aware of all those pulses as my blood twitched its way round my body. Whether I had the light on or off, whether I read or just lay in bed, the pulses banged their rhythm of impending death. I could almost hear the adrenaline squeezing into my heart. I would move my position over and over again, so that I couldn't feel the pulses, to see if I could bring life to my tingling hands. My mouth was dry with fear. I drank and drank, and still my mouth felt like I'd been sucking cotton wool. Nothing worked. The fear had taken over.

The fear said, 'You are dying. Now. The doctor said you're not dying, just fucked up, but that was at yesterday's surgery. Now, at two, three, four in the morning; it is now that you're going to die. Now now now. It is certain – this next breath really is your last.'

The adrenaline squirts; the dozens of pulses tighten and bang harder.

No wonder I'm a coward. No more adrenaline for me, thanks. I've had quite enough.

In Philip Larkin's last major poem, 'Aubade', he stares in the night at 'unresting death':

> Making all thought impossible but how
> And where and when I shall myself die.

I understood that impossibility. Larkin's poem ends with a DNA trace of hope: death is inevitable, but life goes on. I didn't share that drop of stoic optimism. My death was inevitable, and it was coming any second now, but life wouldn't go on, because Charley would be alone, and not even have a daddy, and what would she do when she found the body? How could I do it to her, now, this moment?

I was a haunted house. There was a ghost inside me, scaring me out of my wits.

Ghosts are terrible. We are right to fear them.

As with most haunted houses, people tended to avoid me.

The doctors wanted to avoid me too, but they couldn't.

I went to the surgery three or four times a week. The doctors would take my blood pressure, and listen to my heart, and reassure me that I was fine, and I would believe them for a few minutes; but when I got outside the fear of instant death would take over again, and I would go home, almost certainly to die. Then the doctors sent me to heart specialists, not because they thought there was anything wrong with my heart, but because they thought that the specialists could do what the doctors could not, i.e. persuade me that there was nothing wrong with my heart.

The best thing the doctors did, though, was give me pills.

Oh, blue remembered pills!

Oh Valium, oh temazepam!

Valium was the best, of course. The cares of the world drop away, leaving you wrapped in a drug-induced blanket of loveliness. Valium was the only thing that could take away the taste of fear in my mouth, or stop the ticking pulses counting away the last few seconds of my life. Valium is great. But it's a bugger to get it on a repeat prescription, even though I would much rather have had a Valium problem than live with the fear. But the appalling responsibility of my doctors meant that I learned to save my Valium for the very worst moments. This left me with temazepam, wobbly eggs to our Scouser readers. Mazzies rock, because they work. I knew that if I took a mazzie, I would sleep, no question. My pal Big Doctor Dave, a rocker and biker boy to the core of his huge being, was appalled that I was using mazzies to sleep.

'It's a waste,' he grumbled. 'The point is to take them when you wake up, washed down with a four-pack of Special Brew. THAT's how you do mazzies.'

But I needed those nights of relief from the prospect of the unresting death. Mazzies seemed to induce unconsciousness, rather than real sleep, but I'd take unconsciousness if I couldn't have true rest. The problem was, the pharmacology is quite clear: if you take too many over time, you build up resistance, which means they stop working. And I needed them to work. So I followed the best-practice advice. I took my mazzies two nights out of every three, because without them nights were still unbearable. My nights took on another new pattern. For two nights in a row, I would take my mazzie, and pass out. Although I would be woken in the morning by the flood of adrenaline and the banging pulses, at least I avoided the 'furnace-fear' in which I had spent all my pre-mazzie nights. Then night three would come round, and I would lie awake, my mouth parched with fear, my heart trying to hammer its way out of my chest, fighting my true desire, which was to call 999 and weep. I think now about the wartime Mass Observers, lying under suburban dining-room tables, waiting for the Doodlebug's engine to stop, and for death to come now.

I also took beta-blockers and anti-depressants, which take longer to work, but probably do more good than mazzies or Valium. And one night, driving over the brow of a low hill, and seeing the sun set over Morecambe Bay, I remembered the Lurex love; I remembered that the universe does love me, even though it might have an odd way of showing it sometimes. And I got into therapy, where I learned that there really was something wrong with my heart.

It was broken. I was crippled by a metaphor. But the pills and the prayers and the psychoanalysis put the metaphor to rest, and the broken pieces of my heart came back together.

So slowly, over a couple of years, I got better. Really better. The ghosts have been chased away. And now, because the folksy truths of pop songs say everything best, I'm all cried out, but love heals the wounds that it makes, thank you for asking.

Better for thirteen years, so far. Sleep is back, as good as it always was, except for the pissing. Death is still inevitable, but not imminent, not tonight, anyway. (Touch wood. I still find it hard to write.) Life really does go on after us, and that's how we can face death; of course it is. It's the greatest miracle of all; that in the midst of death, we are in life, and we can continue to live, despite the inevitability thing.

I still get anxious moments, especially when the phone rings after nine, but I know I'm better because I've finally got a proper heart condition, and it hardly worries me at all. I found this out when, three or so years ago, my heart started going spazz on a regular basis, and I didn't think to trouble the doctors, as any heart problems I might appear to have are all clearly imaginary. I was on the phone to Lily one afternoon, and I said I was still getting weird heart things, but they didn't worry me one bit.

'Like what?'

'Well, the rhythm of my heart goes insane. It speeds up. It stops. It goes THUMP! THUMP! THUMPETY THUMP! then it goes ticktickticktickticktick. It's mad! I must be stressed about something.'

'What have you got to be stressed about?'

'I don't know. But I must be. It'll be my subconscious.'

'How often do you get this?'

'Oh, most days.'

'Have you got it now?'

'Oh yes. Had it all day. But I won't get fooled again . . .'

'Is your doctor's still open?'

'I don't know. Why?'

'If it is, I think you should go now.'

So I went. Luckily, I took my book and my reading specs. I just caught the doctor as he was coming to the end of evening surgery. I explained the symptoms. He listened to my chest.

And phoned for an ambulance to take me to hospital. Result!

I was worried when my heart started to calm down as soon as they got me in the ambulance, because it seemed to confirm to me that I was still a mentalist. After those years of living in the grip of fear, those nights of waiting for death, I would much rather have a minor heart condition than the return of the panics. I was suddenly scared that it was all coming back. I told them in the ambulance that I had a history of panic attacks.

'Does this feel like that?' the paramedic asked me.

'No,' I said.

'Well, I don't think it is a panic attack.'

By the time I arrived at Hereford County Hospital, it was dark. I wasn't allowed to walk. They wheeled me up into the emergency cardiac ward, and nurses started to gather around me. My heart had calmed down. I must say I was feeling a bit relaxed. For someone with a history of health anxiety (call it hypochondria, I don't mind), the prospect of a night in hospital surrounded by nurses and doctors and consultants is always a peaceful one. And I had my book, and my reading specs, after all. I was trying to get through the Booker long list, which a magazine had sent me in order that I might come up with some betting advice for their readers.

To my surprise, however, an emergency cardiac ward is not the place of peace that I had always imagined. It was full of sick people. Sick old people. Some of them were unconscious. Some of them had weeping relatives by their bedsides. Some of them were groaning. It is most unsettling when you're trying to read and make notes about what might represent a value bet for literary punters.

Worst of all was the gentleman opposite, who the nurses told me was in his nineties. He'd had a fall, which the medics suspected might have been caused by a stroke. They wanted him to stay in bed, but he was having none of it. As soon as the nurses turned their backs, the old geezer was trying to escape. He would pull back the sheet, and swing his legs over the edge of the bad, and shout for Kathleen. His wife? A daughter? I don't know. What I do know is that every time he tried to get

253

out of bed, his backless hospital gown rode up to his waist, and I could see his whopping great big old bollocks. I tried not to look, but I couldn't help but peep over the top of my book. I'd never seen the like.

I'd been admitted just at the end of the evening routine, and was triaged by a busy nurse. She asked me amongst other things how my bowels were moving, which surprised me, but I guessed it was a heart thing, so I told her about the touch of diarrhoea that I'd had over the last few days. She told me that they would therefore be putting me in a private room, in case I had a bug. Selfishly, I was glad that I would no longer be confronted with the old man's voluminous nadgers every time I turned a page.

A doctor came and examined me. He agreed that my heart now seemed normal. I explained my symptoms. He read the note from my doctor. He said that I probably had primary atrial fibrillation, and that I would be fitted up with a wire for a week, so that they could try and record an episode, and confirm the diagnosis. He said that he would keep me in overnight, but that I could probably go in the morning, after the consultant had seen me.

The nurses told me that I had missed the evening meal, but they brought me a cheese sandwich and a cup of tea. I told them that apart from my book and my reading specs, I'd brought nothing with me, so they gave me a toothbrush and a flannel. They told me that the private room was nearly ready for me.

'Do you think I could go out for a breath of fresh air?' I asked them.

'Well . . . really we should get a porter to take you outside in a wheelchair.'

'Oh, I'm allright . . .'

'Well, it's your responsibility,' they said.

So I went down through the hospital to the entrance, where the last visitors were leaving the hospital; and where, just outside, mums-to-be and ancient invalids sat in their dressing gowns smoking fags. I joined this merry throng. There is a special devil-may-care atmosphere amongst groups of hospital smokers. I sat on a bench next to an old guy with a bag of piss up on a stand. He gripped the stand with one hand and smoked with the other.

There was a flurry of activity opposite where we were sitting. The visiting stragglers were asked to wait. Security guys in day-glo visibility jackets were putting down barriers to close off the access road. In the sky, we could see the lights of a heli-copter. Its chattering drew closer.

'Air ambulance coming in,' said the old bag-of-piss-on-a-stand guy.

As the helicopter came down, a thing of noise and light, a team came out from the main doors of the hospital by which we were smoking, and hurried across to it. Everyone did that head-ducking thing. The paramedics on the air ambulance handed out a stretcher, which the team from A and E put onto their trolley and hurried inside. The paramedics hopped back into the helicopter, which shook itself up to speed and pushed off into the night sky.

'Marvellous, really,' said the old bag-of-piss-on-a-stand guy. 'And all done by charity. Cigarette?'

'No, thanks. I roll my own.' I put together another fag. 'What are you in for?'

'Oh, you know,' he said, indicating his piss bag with his ciggie. 'Just the usual. You?'

'Dicky ticker. Shouldn't be smoking really.'

'Load of nonsense. Little bit of what you fancy does you good.'

'Yeah, a little bit. Not like I do it.'

'Smoking seems to be dying out,' he said. I laughed, and he smiled at me.

'I remember when you could smoke in this hospital,' he said.

'So do I. Last fag I had here was the night my daughter was born,' I said.

'Really?'

'Really. She was an emergency Caesarean. They wouldn't let me into the theatre.'

'Would you have wanted to go?'

'Not really.'

'So you went and had a cigarette?'

'Yes. In the smoking room. It was quite small. There was a girl in there, very heavily pregnant, and I had a fag with her. It was only about twenty minutes before the nurse came and told me that I had a baby daughter. Who was very small.'

'Was she?'

'Three pounds two ounces.'

'That is small.'

'Her name is Minnie.'

'You like a joke, don't you?' said the old bag-of-piss-on-a-stand guy.

'I do, really,' I said.

The world changes beyond all recognition, just by bringing one person into it.

A thought strikes me. I nudge Neil, who is starting to nod.

'That's why pop music is great, Neil,' I say.

'Wassat?'

'I say, that's why pop music is great. They say that things like opera glorify the human spirit, but I don't see it myself. Pop music gives us voice.'

'What time is it?'

'There's this Kate Bush song, called "This Woman's Work". I can't believe it isn't on one of these CDs. Not the Kate Bush version. The live Maxwell* version. Kate is the bomb, Maxwell says. And it's this song, written by a woman, but for a man to sing, because it's about this guy waiting while his wife . . .'

'What is?'

'This Kate Bush song I'm telling you about. "This Woman's Work". Everything in that song happened to me.'

I should be crying, but I just can't let it show.

'It's late, Ian,' says Neil. 'It's really late.'

---

* An American R'n'B singer. His version of 'This Woman's Work' is on his *MTV Unplugged Live* album.

SOMETHING OF THE NIGHT

My ex-sister-in-law Emi is a keen cyclist, who lives in Hackney and works in Covent Garden. Not only does she ride her bike into work, she rides it around at lunchtime to go and pick up something to eat. She told me this story last summer.

'I go to this falafel place off St Martin's Lane. Best falafel pitta bread in London. I always go on my bike, and I always chain it up to a drainpipe while I go in and get my falafels. So, to do the chaining up, I have to bend over. One day, I'm bending over chaining up my bike, and this limo pulls up next to me, with frosted-glass windows, and I'm like, who's this? Some kind of VIP. And the window rolls down, and it's him, isn't it? Michael Howard. And because I'm bending over, I'm right by the window, and he gives me this smile. Woof! I tell you, Ian, he's got it. I felt myself blushing, and I kind of smiled back, and we had this . . . moment. No kidding. I've had the hots for him ever since.'

'Did he have something of the night about him?'

'Oh yes! No wonder he can hang on to his beautiful wife. Lucky bitch, I'd say.'

Perhaps this is what Ann Widdecombe meant, when she said of Howard that he had 'something of the night' about him, though I somehow doubt it. It was right towards the end of the Major Government, when the Tories were getting ready to go back to their constituencies to prepare for unemployment. Howard, then Home Secretary, had appeared on *Newsnight* after the controversial dismissal of Derek Lewis as head of the Prison Service. Paxman asked Howard the same question ('Did you threaten to overrule him?') twelve times. Howard refused to answer a straight question with a straight answer, but ducked and shimmied around it. Howard didn't overrule Lewis. But did he threaten to overrule him? Howard wasn't saying.

Six days later in a speech in the House, Ann Widdecombe, who was Minister of State in the Home Office with responsibility for the Prison Service, said of her then boss that he had 'something of the night about him'. Everyone knew what she meant, but why? Was it because he was, as Emi asserted, something of a lady-killer? Was it to do with his miserable appearance? Or was it, heaven forefend, because Howard comes from a Romanian background, and Miss Widdecombe was making an allusion to Dracula, and vampires? Later that same year, 1997, Howard stood for leadership of the Conservative Party; and legend has it that it was Widdecombe's assessment that did for his campaign.

Whatever she meant, it was the start of Widdecombe's rehabilitation in the eyes of the public. She was one of the most hated figures in the old Tory party, but after her jibe she has slowly come to be seen as . . . not cuddly exactly, but a good sport, maybe. I imagined, as lots of people seem to, that 'something of the night' was a quote from somewhere; Shakespeare, probably, or maybe one of the Romantics. But it appears to be Widdecombe's own phrase.

But what did she mean? He has something of the night about him. It can't mean that he induced feelings of restfulness and calm, of quiet evenings spent in front of a blazing log fire. She means, doesn't she, that Howard is a wrong 'un. A bad lot. That he is dark, darkness always being a bad thing. And that he is occult, unfathomable, covert, shadowy. That there is an absence of light.

I said at the beginning of this book that during its making, I came to feel that there was 'something of the night' about me. I have, on occasion, given way to my dark side, more than I would have wished. I have been occult to myself, hidden from my own view, cloaked in secrets that I didn't know I was keeping. And I am a creature of the night. I've been more creative, more aware, more myself, even, when the sun goes down and the stars come out. Ninety per cent of this book has been written after dark. I'd sleep all day, if circumstances allowed, and sit up all night, writing, smoking, reading and thinking. And singing too, when I got the chance. I don't sing anti-capitalist love songs any more. Now I like to sing Burt Bacharach and Jimmy Webb songs, because I believe more in love and less in politics than I used to.

Doesn't mean I'm not still obsessed with politics. I stayed up all night at my parents' house the night before Lewes Bonfire and watched Obama win the US election. And I wouldn't dream of going to bed on a British election night until I was certain that I knew what was happening. I love election night;

sitting with my wife or my daughters watching hopes fade, dreams collapse, careers made and unmade.

All those nights, 1974, 1979, 1983, 1987, 1992, 1997, I stayed up until the sun was thinking about rising, praying that the Tories would lose. Even in 2001, I still wanted them to do badly. But then came 2005 and 2010, and I stayed up all night praying that the murderous Labour Party would slink away and hide itself under a rock, even if it meant that the Tories came back.

I don't watch political TV quietly. I shout at the screen. I talk to the presenters. Election night is worst of all; I sit with the blinger, channel-hopping between the BBC and ITV, groaning at the platitudes of the politicians who they drag on to spin their party's result, whatever it may be. I shout at them, mimic their voices, take the piss out of their hair . . .

On election night 2010, I sat with my wife watching as the exit polls came in. The main thing I wanted was to see Labour punished, but I also had hopes that the Greens might get in in Brighton. I had once been an activist in the Brighton Green Party. I had helped write a policy document, and had knocked on doors, and posted leaflets through the letterboxes on the Lewes Road. It would be nice to imagine that if Caroline Lucas did get in in Brighton, I might have popped a leaflet through a door one night in 1986 that had changed somebody's mind, and won her a vote all these years later.

I always start by watching the BBC, because that's what I do. It's a habit. From the BBC, I hop around. Can't say they have the better coverage, because although they have all that Peter Snow gadgetry and graphics, ITN get some great guests on. So

I channel–hop all night, trying to find out what's really happened. In 2010, I sat on the sofa with my wife, and took control of the blinger, as I am a man and head of the household. It is my clear responsibility to hold the TV blinger.

The election shows had started at ten, and no one was believing the exit polls. The first results were favouring the Tories, but the Lib Dems weren't showing as strongly as expected. I hopped around, hoping that on one of the channels I could find the truth. On ITV they had Ann Widdecombe as one of the pundits, and I'm sorry to say that my wife and I both said pretty much the same thing as she was introduced: 'Ooh! Doesn't she look nice! That frock is smashing. I like her new hairdo. It really suits her.'

We were both a bit ashamed, and tried to listen to what she had to say. These days, now that she is no longer a politician, and I am fifty-three, I find her comments robust and often funny. And then the bloody phone rang. It was 11.30. I had a good idea what it would be about, but I still don't like the phone ringing at night; besides, it was election night, when I'd planned to be watching the telly until four-ish and admiring Ann Widdecombe's new do along the way. It was all hugely inconvenient.

'Hello?'

'Oh, hello, and would that be Mr Marchant?'

'Yes. Hello.'

'Oh, this is Sister Fidelma from the Waterford Regional Hospital. Mr Marchant, I'm terribly sorry, but I have to tell you that unfortunately your father passed away at 11.25 this evening. Just a few minutes ago.'

'Oh. Oh dear.'

'I believe you got a chance to speak to him this afternoon.'

'Yes I did.'

'Well now, I'm sure that was a great comfort.'

'Oh, I hope so, sister.'

'Will you be coming over now?'

'Well, I can't come for a few days. It's the Electric Bike Race Weekend here in Presteigne . . .'*

'I see . . .'

'And I'm doing the commentary. And I've got a couple of gigs . . .'

'Well now, we all have to do what we have to do . . .'

'I've already booked a flight for Monday.'

'Oh, I'm sure that will be fine.'

'So . . . thank you for calling.'

'Oh well, Mr Marchant. Our prayers are with you at this sad time . . .'

'Yes, thank you.'

'And with your daddy. He was a character, wasn't he?'

'He certainly was. Well, thank you for calling . . .'

'Are there any questions you'd like to ask?'

'Not really . . .'

'I don't think he suffered.'

'No?'

'No. He was in no pain.'

---

* We really do have the world's only electric bike race here in Presteigne. Presteigne is to electric bikes what Wimbledon is to tennis. It's called 'The Tour de Presteigne' and it takes place in May. Google us, and come along; we'd be pleased to see you.

'Good. Well . . . thank you very much.'

'Well, God bless, Mr Marchant. As I say, you're in our prayers.'

I was starting to feel nervous that she was about to play me the new Westlife single.

'Thank you for calling. Goodnight.'

I put the phone down.

'Dad dead?' asked my wife.

'Yes. What's happening?'

'Not much. There might be a recount in Edgbaston.'

A few minutes later I said, 'Could I have a cup of tea?'

'What!?'

'Well, my dad has just died.'

'Oh . . . you terrible man.'

'Go on.'

It's not every day you get to play your 'My Dead Dad' card, and I was determined to get a cup of tea out of it.

I hadn't seen my dad for over four years. In 2006 I went to visit him in Florida, where he had been living for fifteen years or so. He had an American wife, Martha, who I had met a few times and liked. He'd been diagnosed with lung cancer in 1999, and had had a lung removed. He had diabetes, and a spot of prostate cancer, too. But he knew that the lung cancer would get him one day, that removing the lung was only a postponement. That trip had been our last chance to talk stuff through. His wife went to visit her daughter in West Virginia, so my dad and I could bond. We spent a fortnight in one another's company, and it was enough.

We fought all day, and late into the night. When I went to bed, I would lock the door, just to feel safe. He ranted that I only hated him because I'd been told bad things about him. He was right that I had been told bad things about him, for most of my life, but they didn't stop me loving him, because I didn't believe them, and he was my dad. When, as an adult, I came to see that the things I had been told were true, even then I still didn't hate him. I just wished I'd had another father. One who loved me, and loved his grandchildren. Not much to ask of a parent, really. No matter how much we tried to talk about stuff, it could not be resolved; mostly because my dad was a vile man. He really was. I know writers are supposed to show and not tell, but I can't be bothered, and if I did show you some of that stuff, you'd only go, 'What a vile man.' And you'd be right.

At the end of the visit, I lied to him about the time of my flight. He ran me up to the airport in Orlando, four hours earlier than I needed to be there. I sat in a coffee bar, and I wrote to his wife, telling her I wanted nothing more to do with him; and that, furthermore, I wanted writing out of his will, since all he cared about was money, and I wanted him to see if he could take it with him. My sister had done something similar ten years previously; so had my uncle and aunties. I was just the last person that he had driven away, apart from his American wife. I flew back from Florida to Gatwick and called The Old Feller, my stepfather, to tell him I loved him, and that he had always been my real father anyway; and that was that. I didn't hear from my dad, and nor did I expect to.

Until February of 2010, when he phoned up out of the blue. I was away, so he spoke to my wife for almost an hour. They'd never met. She told me that he couldn't have been more offensive, unpleasant and insensitive if he'd wanted to. I told her that

that was him trying to be nice. I was angry that he'd found my phone number. A few days later, he called again, and we spoke. He told me that he was leaving his wife in the States and going to live in Ireland, in a place called Tramore, near Waterford. He said he'd never been there, but he couldn't stand the US any more. He'd been fighting with his wife's family, and wanted out. Ireland was the only place he could imagine being. I told him he was stupid, but that he could call me when he got there, if he wanted. He didn't. I forgot him.

On the day before the election, May the 5th, I got a call from a medical social worker in Waterford, telling me my dad was severely ill, that the cancer had come back, and that I should consider flying over at once. He'd given her my number, and told her I was his next of kin, the bastard. I told her that it was inconvenient, because I had three shows over the course of the coming weekend, one of which was my annual stint as the Murray Walker of electric bike racing. I think she thought me a bit callous. She said, 'You must do what you think right.'

I arranged to fly out on Monday the 10th to see him. The next morning, election day, the head of the palliative care team at Waterford Regional Hospital called me, and told me my dad wanted to speak to me.

'Put him on . . .'

So I got to speak to my dad on his death-bed. He could hardly breathe. He said that I had to love him, as I was his son, and I'd 'come out of his body' (in common with countless squillions of other little spunky homunculi). He told me that he was leaving an estate valued at £250,000, but that I wasn't getting any, and 'neither are your girls'.

He said, 'I know I've not been a perfect father . . .'

I said, 'Well . . . who is? I'm certainly not a perfect father.'

'Hah,' my dad gasped. He had got what he wanted to comfort him into the next world.

'I'm facking glad to hear you admit it,' he said. 'At last . . .'

I had given him some kind of absolution. My lack of perfection as a father was the only explanation he felt he needed for his own shortcomings. He asked me to say that we were mates, so I did. We weren't, not ever, not once. I told him that I could be there the next day, but he said it would worry him because of the money.

'Who'd pay?' he asked. 'Me or you?'

Then he said, 'But you talking to me is worth a million dollars.'

Then he became agitated, and said he couldn't talk any more. I said I'd call the following morning to see if he felt able to talk. Instead, Sister Fidelma from the palliative care ward phoned me, to say my dear old dad had died.

During the course of the night, as the inconclusive results came in, I grew angry.

'I can't believe he named me as his next of kin! And I told him we were mates! I can't believe that he forced me to give him some comfort. Fucking bastard.'

'It's just common humanity,' said my wife. 'You'd do it for anyone, wouldn't you?'

'Yeah. Anyone else.'

In the morning, I began the process of sorting out what I was prepared to sort out. I spoke to an undertaker in Waterford, who quoted me for a funeral including an oak coffin with brass handles.

'No no no. Don't you do cardboard coffins?'

'Oh well, we couldn't go that far now.'

'What do you do for tramps?' I asked.

'Ooh, we get money from the government for people like that, to ensure they get a decent burial.'

'No wonder your economy is up the spout . . .'

He was nicer to me than I deserved, I suspect. He fixed everything up. Daddy was cremated, alone, unmourned, on Saturday 8 May at the Island Crematorium outside Cork. It was Minnie's twenty-first birthday, which dad wouldn't have known or cared about if he had still been alive.

That night, I spoke to Martha, dad's fifth and final wife, on the phone from West Virginia. She was upset, but resigned.

'Ah loved him, but he loathed everything and everybody. He had a narcissistic personality disorder. I hope you never get that.'

I told her that although I clearly had a narcissistic personality, I felt that it wasn't disordered. Now I think I know what she means.

I took the flight on Monday, from Luton to Waterford.

My dad had taken a holiday flat in a modern block overlooking the beach at Tramore. His landlord, Pat Doyle, had been a help to my dad after he arrived in Ireland, and now he was a huge help to me.

He picked me up from the airport, and was kind enough to drive me round. We went to the hospital to collect some paperwork, and then on to the Community Care Centre to register the death and collect the death certificates. Then we called at Thompson's undertakers to collect the ashes. The place was one of those cute-as-pie Irish pubs that serves beer, but which also functions as a shoe shop, or a barbers, or, in the case of Thompson's, a funeral directors. My dad loved all that stuff. He had a sentimental attachment to the Ireland he had seen depicted in Oirish pubs and *Finian's Rainbow*. That's why he'd chosen Ireland as a place to die.

He loved traditional Irish music. My mum loved Nat King Cole. They lived together until I was ten. Every day, they fought to get their records on the turntable. When he was home, dad would always win, and the house would be full of the sounds of the Clancy Brothers or The Dubliners. He liked rebel songs, especially. He loved standing up in pubs and singing 'The Wild Colonial Boy'. He despised Nat King Cole, who he said was saccharine shit. He told me I needed to learn to appreciate real music, such as 'The Fields of Athenry'. In his last days, he became a huge fan of Daniel O'Donnell. When he drove me up to Orlando airport for our last goodbye, he played his Daniel O'Donnell tapes the whole way, because he knew it was killing me.

Pat Doyle tried to talk to me about my dad as he drove me around Waterford, and then out to the coast at Tramore, six miles away.

'He was OK, your dad. I liked him.'

'I'm glad. He could be charming.'

'I had no complaints against him. He turned up here in March and rented the apartment. Loved going down the pub for a sing. He was a good craic, your dad.'

'Yes . . . he loved Ireland.'

'I tried to do my best for him, y'know?'

'Yeah, I know you did. I really appreciate all this.'

'I hope you don't mind my saying, but you didn't get on?'

'Not really.'

'It's a shame. To end up like this.' He indicated the cardboard box full of ashes on my lap.

So Pat Doyle took me to the apartment he had rented my dad in Tramore, and left me there for two nights. There was a great view along the beach towards the giant sand dune the locals call the Baldy Man. I put down the cardboard box containing dad's ashes, and made myself a cup of tea. And smoked a few fags, and watched Sky News as Cameron and Clegg began the last hours of their negotiation. Took myself out for dinner. And then came back to my dad's flat, and started to sort through his things.

There wasn't much: a suitcase full of clothes, a jewellery box of old-fashioned cuff-links and collar-studs; a small TV, now tuned to BBC News 24. There were some papers piled on his desk; I didn't quite have the willpower to start going through them yet. I sorted the kitchen, and then his clothes. Most of them I put aside for the charity shop, but I kept a few T-shirts and some jeans. I kept the curtains open, and watched as night closed in from the east over Tramore Strand; but when the sun had gone down, the windows turned into mirrors of black and gold, and they showed me packing up food, trying on shirts, and watching the telly.

When it was time to sleep, I got into his bed. I guess it smelled of him, but I couldn't say, as I had no memory of how he smelled.

In the morning, I explored Tramore. It's a long curving surfing beach, though the lady in the surf centre told me the surfing wasn't all that really. I walked as far as I could, three or four miles. On the beach, I found a spiral stone, and carried it to the top of the Baldy Man, and left it in the marram grass on the low sandy summit.

After dinner on my second night, I sat at his desk and started on the papers. There were a few bills, and some bank things for me to parcel up and send to Martha. What interested me was what he'd considered precious enough to pack up and bring with him to Ireland from the States. The things he had wanted by him while he was dying, as he had surely known he must be.

There was a bundle of old napkins from American casinos, on which he had kept records of winning combinations of numbers on the Florida State Lottery, which seems to have been his only great interest in life. He was trying to work out a system.

He had a Tijuana bible* in a leather wallet. This particular example was based on a Blondie and Dagwood cartoon. Blondie shags a neighbour in graphic detail while Dagwood is away on business. In eight frames, each reproduced on a separate and ancient photograph, the dirty story is played out. He must have had this for years, I guessed from the state of the photos. He must have liked it.

He had all the papers from his divorces.

He had a tattered wallet in blue vinyl, with 'Britain's First Decimal Coins' in worn gilt lettering on the front. Inside, Britain's First Decimal Coins were displayed on a card. You can buy one of these on eBay for 99p if you'd like to see what it looks like.

He had a tenth of a Kruggerand in a plastic holder, which I sold for fifty quid at a jeweller's in Hereford.

---

* Pornographic cartoon books, which were produced between the 1920s and the 1970s.

There were two meticulously kept account books, dating all the way back to 1976. In these he had noted every penny he ever spent; on shopping, on car maintenance, on grandchildren's Christmas presents. I'm looking forward to auditing these accounts, and mapping them against his life. It will tell me more about what he felt to be important than he ever did while he was alive.

Other than the pornographic cartoons, he had no photos. No photos of his five wives, his two children, his five grand-children, his lovely, kind parents, his funny, warm brothers and sisters.

I bundled up the papers and sorted out what was for Martha, what for the bin, and what for me to keep. I left the flat and walked down the hill to his local, but I didn't feel like talking. I drank a Guinness and went for a walk down the beach. Out in the Irish Sea, on the horizon, the lights of ships slipped past. It was a clear night, and a long level sandy beach is a good place to walk in the dark.

On his death-bed, my dad had said one true thing. I did come out of his body. I am his spunk walking; that's why he couldn't quite leave me alone, despite it being all I had asked him for.

From looking at his papers, and from talking to my mum, my sister, my stepmothers, my aunt, my uncles, I know one thing for sure about my dad. He was what used to be called a socio-path. He had, there can be no doubt, something of the night about him. The traits of sociopathy: glibness, superficial charm, a grandiose sense of self-worth, the failure to accept responsi-bility for one's own actions, the lack of realistic long-term goals, the promiscuous sexual behaviour . . . I have too many of these traits, there's no getting away from it. Something of the night. Here is everything that is worst in my nature.

Everything that was worst in my dad's nature turned from a twisted weakness into a deep sickness that took him over, and drove away everyone who ever loved him, but whom he was unable to love in return.

I stood on Tramore beach. I listened to the surf and watched the lights out at sea. I remembered Martha's warning, about the disordering. I remembered again the one thing he taught me. I am the son of a sociopath.

Every night I pray that I won't turn into him.

RAY OF LIGHT

It is late. Neil is right. It is very very late.

It is so late that shortly it will be early. It is still clearly night, but soon people will be starting to get up. Neil will not be amongst their number. He is fast asleep in his chair. A trail of drool runs down his chins. Neil is making a sound like an espresso machine trying to blow up a whoopee cushion.

I'm cold. If you are a lark, your body is at its coldest at about 4.30 a.m. If you are a night owl, it's about 5.30 a.m. I look at my watch, and I'd say that was right. I'm shivering. The wood-burner has stopped putting out heat. My body clock is trying to tell me to wrap up warm and sleep.

I'm not ready. I'm cold, but I'm not sleepy. In fact, I'm wide awake. I get up and put on the kettle. I take my tea outside, and pull my fleece close around me. Even Billy has given up, and gone off to sleep somewhere.

My cortex is finding different ways to defrag itself. I'm daydreaming in the darkest hour, the one just before dawn. I'm daydreaming about the night.

So – I'm still doing the gigs. And I'm still about as successful as ever. In the summer of 2010, I was compering a performance space cum tea shop cum fancy-dress hire venue called 'The Village Hall' at the Secret Garden Party festival outside Huntingdon. I was down to work from midday on Thursday till eight on Sunday night, playing a comedy vicar. I was also hired to do two sets with Your Dad.

The boutique festival's boutique festival, is Secret Garden Party. If you like a pretty festival, then SGP could be your thang. It's very North London; the only person I met outside of the crews who wasn't from North London was living in Bristol, a student at the university, but originally from Crouch End.

The Eloi are here; it is their place. While grizzled festival veterans like myself, or Pete Mustill or Chas, might be seen as cool at Glastonbury, here we are regarded as rather distasteful. The Eloi wear fancy dress, and promenade past the umpteen stages, the countless food outlets, the limitless shopping opportunities. It is a twenty-first-century pleasure garden. Vauxhall, the best known of the eighteenth-century pleasure gardens, was lit at night by 15,000 lanterns; there must be ten times that here. Between 1662 and the mid-nineteenth century, Londoners would stroll about the illuminated avenues of Vauxhall, and watch circus acts, or listen to music. There is something about the dandified Eloi that reminds me somehow of the eighteenth century.

They are at ease, untroubled by Daddy's suffocating business, or Mummy's increasing closeness to her pilates teacher Wendy. Here all is sweetness and light. Few of them are drunk, even last thing at night. Mostly, what they are on is ecstasy clones. All night, they drift past our venue, on their way to somewhere else. We don't take it personally, because they drift past every other venue, still on their way to somewhere else. We work hard to make them sit at our tables, drink our proper hippy chai and hire our fancy-dress costumes. To pay all the weekend's wages, including my fee, we need to keep four people queuing at all times at our tea tent. At the level of show business at which I operate, it's not about keeping bums on seats. I dream of playing venues with seats to keep bums on, but, alas, for me it's about how much chai and lemon drizzle cake you can move over the course of a weekend.

We did spoof weddings and played telepathic bingo. We had a Chief Brownie, who played games with our visitors. We had a large Australian swing dance troupe who came by each night to give free swing dance lessons to the promenading Eloi. We had a permanent knitting circle.* We had bands, spoken word, street theatre, beat-boxing, giant Jenga, a free raffle with valuable antiques as prizes, a real dog show, because dogs are allowed at SGP – and still the Eloi drifted past, smiling beautiful smiles; stopping sometimes for five or ten minutes and then moving on. Our venue is very pretty; it sparkles with fairy lights. It's a nice place to pause from the endless all-night parade. We work until late to keep our queues long and happy; it can be done, but it's hard.

One of our crew is a guy called Max, a video-maker, aged twenty-five or so. Here, he's working as part of our tea tent team. I like Max very much; he's the son of a pal of mine, so

---

* We are supposed to be the Village Hall, after all.

I've known him for years. Cool, is Max, self-possessed and together. I asked Max what we needed to do to stop our punters from drifting.

'They, we, are the internet generation. We're used to clicking and moving on, because there's always something better a few clicks away.'

'So it's like a website? If you give them content, they'll stay.'

'That's right. In a world of infinite choice, content is king.'

It is the Eloi's primary right, the right to make choices about their behaviour as consumers. And there's no doubt that the expansion of choice has given us lots to choose from. Now the opportunity to make choices is the great political choice of our time. We pity China, because its citizens have fewer choices than us. We're all existentialists now. The snag is, the possibility exists that this state of choicefulness might leave us facing up to actually making a choice. Which is hard, because what if we make the wrong choice? So we re-examine the choices. There must be a better choice, and it's just a click away.

We didn't have choice in my day. We took what we were given and disliked it. My first festival was Reading '74, when I was sixteen. I went with my mate Andy, because he was the only other person whose parents would let him go. There was only the one stage, in front of which you sat drinking all day, in a compound big enough to hold 30,000 people behind a high wall of corrugated iron. We sat there and watched a sequence of dull bands. It was shit, by the standards of today's festivals. I can't even remember who was on save for Friday night's headliners: Hawkwind, then at the height of their pomposity. Andy and I sat in the dust, surrounded by beer cans, watching Stacia, the six-foot-tall exotic dancer who used to gyrate in front of Hawkwind's legendary light show.

Reading '74 was shit, but it was my first real taste of the nights I'd been longing for. This was what adulthood had in store. Paradise, if slightly postponed. No matter that most of the bands were dull, that the only intoxicants we had were four tins of warm Guinness each, and that no girl was going to come anywhere near a couple of dweebs like us. Paradise was just the possibility of sex and drugs and rock and roll, which were all my brain and body needed, and which were suddenly realistic prospects. Childhood was over. From now on, I was a grown-up, and I could sit all night in a dustbowl with piss-head bikers from Harpenden and drink Guinness from a can and listen to Hawkwind to my heart's content. Things could get started from here.

Those were the days when dancing was largely *verboten* in hip circles. I certainly can't remember anyone dancing at Reading '74 other than Stacia, and she was being paid. I went a lot to gigs in Brighton between 1972 and 1976, largely at the Dome and at the Students' Union at Sussex University, and dancing wasn't going to happen, not at the earnest events to which I was witness. At the Students' Union, indeed, there were cushions strewn about on the floor, so you could lounge like young Roman nobles, and listen to Quintessence, or whatever. At the Dome in Brighton, people would sit in ranks, and watch Procul Harum, or Rory Gallagher, or Soft Machine or Focus or Golden Earring, and may God help me one day forget the bass solos. Dancing was done by a whole other group of people. Skinheads. Suedeheads. They liked reggae and soul music, but there weren't that many of them, not until you got lower down the school.

So no one much danced the night away, not in the English provinces in 1974. You sat about. You listened respectfully. You clapped, stood up at the end for the encore, and walked out into the night to catch your train home and to discuss whether or not Wishbone Ash were right to use Orange amps.*

It was horrible.

Now, my night-time paradise bears little relation to the one I saw in prospect at the 1974 Reading Festival. Then, sitting for three solid days and nights in front of a stage and listening to Hawkwind seemed like heaven. Now I would rather hammer hot pins under my fingernails than spend a night at the Reading Festival. Paradise is slippery.

I was once with a friend on a ten-mile beach of white sand, fringed with coconut palms, sitting on his tail-gate, drinking ice-cold tins of Carib Beer, smoking some righteous ganja, and listening to Augustus Pablo playing on the pick-up's radio. We looked out over the blue Caribbean, sparkling and full of pretty girls, and my friend turned to me and said, 'Man, this is paradise, isn't it?'

And I said, 'Oh no. Paradise isn't like this at all. In paradise, night is falling on the Charing Cross Road, and the rain is easing off. By the light from a bookshop window, I see a copy of *Uncle and the Battle for Badgertown* by the Rev J.P. Martin priced at five

---

* Hawkwind, Quintessence, Wishbone Ash, Golden Earring and Soft Machine were shitty 70s bands. Rory Gallagher was a blues guitarist, and he was quite good, but sadly no longer with us. Procul Harum were a 60s band, past their prime when I saw them, who were named after my pal Ash's cat. This is now official.

pounds, which I buy. I read it on the steam-hauled journey home from Paddington to an un-Beechinged Presteigne, where my beautiful wife is waiting for me by the fireside, with a pot of tea and some lovely buttery crumpets and my trusty old pipe full of this admirable ganja, and an evening of bibliographic chat in prospect, and just the tick of an old clock and perhaps the hoot of an owl to send us up the stairs with some proper cocoa and into dreamland. Then, at eight in the morning, we wake up and . . .'

'You've got it all thought out,' said my friend.

Oh yes. My ideal night. Not at all what the Eloi are after, I imagine.

On the Saturday afternoon at SGP, when I was pretending to be a vicar and trying to coax the Eloi into the Village Hall to play telepathic bingo and eat cake, a beautiful half-naked man spun up to me on his bike. Tall and tanned and not as young as he once was, but still lovely, my friend Ed had spotted me through the uninterested throng.

We hugged, despite his tanned bare loveliness and my scratchy 1950s Co-Op vicar's suit. Ed is a yachtsman, a builder, an explorer, and an all-round sweetie.

Ed had just been paragliding in Bolivia* and now he was at SGP to do a spot of building. He'd built a floating gay disco out in the middle of the lake around which the festival is set up.

'How do you keep it stable?'

'Ah ha,' said Ed. 'Boatbuilder, me. And I've been working on the blimp . . .'

---

* Or something. That sort of thing, anyway.

A huge white floating blimp was anchored at one end of the lake, but tonight it would be propelled into the middle to be torched.

'It's just paper on a frame,' said Ed. 'It'll look amazing.'

The fire show was due to start at nine, and venues all over the site emptied out as the Eloi hurried to find a place by the lake. To my delight, but to Pete Mustill's horror, we cancelled a folk act who were due to play in the Village Hall to let people go and watch some fireworks. Pete was on our crew as paterfamilias and chief electric-bike engineer, and the prospect of a huge fireworks show somewhat marred his evening.

Pete and Chas and I stood together by the lake and watched the spectacle.

The blimp was spotlit from the banks of the lake as it was floated out into the middle and ignited with torches. From three different places around the lake, dozens of hot-air lanterns were filled with hot air and released into the night sky. They always look good, but dozens at once were rather wonderful.

Behind me, a bloke said, 'That'll be fun, come harvest.'

'Why's that?' said his mate.

'They're made from the stuff of coat-hangers, and they shit up combines if they run over them.'

And then as the lanterns climbed almost beyond sight, proper fireworks, peonies, dahlias, chrysanthemums, were launched from the burning frame of the blimp.

'But what does it mean?' Pete asked me, and I could see his point.

It was very pretty, like the Eloi, but nothing else. Not much content, really. The Eloi smiled and drifted away.

Fireworks, then, need to be about something if they are to justify their existence. They need to celebrate something, whether it's somebody's wedding or the landing of King Billy in Brixham. They need to be about light banishing darkness. About a joyful explosion of seed. The SGP fire show was very pretty, but it wasn't about anything.

Not even fire and light.

Our fire festivals which occur around late October and early November, such as Halloween and Bonfire Night, are relics of the pagan festival of Samhain. It marked the gateway to winter, when nights grow longer and days shrink away. Fires would be extinguished and relit from a ritual bonfire, to make sure that they would be strong against the lengthening night. The barrier between our world and the invisible world of spirits was at its most permeable; so fires were lit to keep malevolent forces at bay. Our ancestors offered fire and light that the darkness might not overwhelm the day. We offer up fire and light because they are pretty. There is no danger for the Eloi. There is no darkness strong enough to overwhelm the unblemished sunshine of their days.

'Were there fireworks at the Isle of Wight?' I asked Pete.

'Other than Hendrix, no,' said Pete. 'At least . . . I can't remember if there were. We were all a bit fucked . . .'

In 1970, Pete and some of his biker pals, including my good friend Ash, turned up at the Isle of Wight Festival, and insisted that they were running the backstage area. No one had the nerve to tell them otherwise, so that's what they did. It was the biggest festival that had ever been held; it's estimated that half a million people turned up. The organisers were overwhelmed, as must have been evident to anyone who noticed that the backstage area was being run by a bunch of self-selected lunatic hippy bikers from Essex.

'Did you ever do Stonehenge?' I asked Pete.

'No. We went to Afghanistan for a year after the Isle of Wight. The festival scene all seemed a bit tame after we got back.'

'I did,' said Chas. 'A couple of times. It was fun.'

The Stonehenge Free Festival probably still stands at the head of the Pantheon of Legendary British Festivals. It started in hope in 1972, and ended with the British State smashing hippies' windows in at the Battle of the Beanfield in 1985. At its height in 1984, 65,000 revellers turned up at the stones, to celebrate the summer solstice and to listen to rubbish hippy bands. For a long time after the brutal suppression of the Free Festival, the authorities were nervous about letting anyone near the stones at summer solstice; but now they have relented, and thousands of people go to Stonehenge in June. You cannot actually get up and touch the stones, but you can, if you are very lucky and the morning is clear, see the sun rise behind them. You can't listen to the music of Here and Now, Ted Milton and Blurt or Cosmic Dave any more, which is probably no bad thing, and the whole occasion has become a bit tame.

It's at the winter solstice that the spirit of the Free Festival comes most nearly back to life. Anyway, although we know very little about Stonehenge and what it was used for, it does align more accurately to the winter than the summer solstice. It makes sense. Winter solstice is the date you really need to know, because that's when the world is at its most horrifying, since the sun has been losing its power for months, and it looks like the night has won, and will inevitably overwhelm the day. Winter solstice is when the day starts to fight back against the night. Winter solstice at Stonehenge is the best place to see the dawn, to mark the end of night.

I went alone. Nobody wanted to come with me because it was nearly Christmas, and everyone was busy. Besides, it was freezing cold and wet and horrible. I didn't take a tent; I planned to arrive about midnight, have a wander and see if there was anyone I knew, grab a few hours' sleep in my car, wake up at about six and head up to the stones.

At summer solstice, the roads around Stonehenge become all but impassable; arriving at midnight for the winter solstice was much quieter. Such traffic as there was was parking up along the perimeter track, which was lined with living vehicles; buses, horseboxes, ambulances and even an old fire engine, all converted to comfortable living spaces. This was the remnant of the crusty culture of the 80s, the ghost of the Peace Convoy, proud survivors. A very few people had even set up tents, which given the foul weather I could only admire. It was tipping down. There were bonfires lit as I drove along the potholed perimeter road. It had been raining all day, so the potholes were turning into ponds, which the traffic was trying to skirt around, churning the verges into mud. Around the bonfires were groups of hippies who looked as though they had retreated from Stalingrad, wrapped in blankets. Some of them were drumming, which all hippies think they can do, but they can't, because they are hippies. A few of the groups around the bonfires were playing host to loud sound systems playing house/trance/dubstep/grime etc., and the most committed of the travellers were wobbing about in time to the music.

Torches flickered along the track as people made their way back to their vehicles, or looked for an accommodating bonfire. Most of the revellers would be planning to stay up all night, to pat at drums and wob about to drum machines, until the pivotal moment which we had all gathered to see.

The potholes were getting deeper as I drove along the track to find somewhere to park up, and the car was thinking about getting stuck in the muddy verges. I parked on a firmish bit of verge, opposite a converted ambulance with hippies dancing round a bonfire to the doof doof doof of trance/house/dub/old skool/grime etc.

It was after parking the car that I realised that I had failed to bring a torch. Or my wellies. I could risk trying to pick my way up the track in darkness, to see if I could avoid the worst of the mud, but actually I was knackered and didn't fancy my chances of not getting covered. I pushed back the driver's seat, wrapped myself in a blanket, and fell comfortably asleep, doof doof doof notwithstanding . . .

And woke at 7.30.

Horror! I should have been awake at least half an hour before. Solstice is at 8.23. Already light was tinting the clouds. I tumbled from the car, pulled on my coat, and started hurrying down the track towards the dreaded tunnel into the actual site. The site opens at about 7.30, and then only for an hour and a half, and I'd just come to.

Goddess must have been on my side that morning, because I hadn't gone ten yards down the track when I heard 'IAN!!' in the loudest voice imaginable, and coming smiling down the track towards me was the greatest of the hippies, the truest of true believers, the great Panit Dave, dyslexic sign-writer,* insane genius, Beanfield veteran and beautiful man. Of all the people I needed to run into in the world at that exact moment, it was Panit Dave. He hugged me and banged my back.

'Ian, you cant! What the fack are you doing here?'

'I've come to see the solstice. I thought you didn't do Stonehenge any more?'

'First time I've been back in twenty-five years, since they smashed up our vans.'

'Where are you living?'

'In Richard's fire engine. I've just come back from the stones to get some booze.'

The fire engine was parked about fifty feet from my car, which I pointed out to Panit Dave.

'We were there all night, you stupid cant! Why didn't you come and find us?'

'I hadn't brought my wellies. Or a torch . . .'

'You are a wanker. 'Ere, 'ave some of this.'

He had grabbed a bottle of Laphroaig from the fire engine, and was insisting that I had a pull. This seemed a good idea in the absence of tea.

'Thank fack I'm 'ere to look after you! Right, let's get up to the stones.'

We walked across a field towards the stones, which were silhouetted against the rising light. Panit told me his van was

---

* He's called 'Panit Dave' because he can't spell 'paint'.

parked up in a field in Somerset, and that he'd only decided to come at the last minute because Richard his neighbour had decided to do the solstice, and had offered Panit a lift.

The great henge of stones was full of drumming hippies, and dancing hippies, many of them with garlands of ivy around their necks. Dave shouted greetings at everybody:

''Appy facking solstice, you cants!'

There were maybe a dozen security guys to look after the five hundred or so people who'd turned up. I wanted to talk to them, but Panit doesn't like security guys and they don't like him, so I saved them for last. A few of the hippies came up and said hello.

'It's my dad!'

I tell them that I'm not their dad, I'm one half of Your Dad.

Lots of people were hugging the stones. A few of them started ululating. I looked at my watch. It was 8.23, and the long night was over. The moment of dawn took place behind heavy clouds, but we knew it was there. People lit up spliffs, which were passed round. The security guys didn't seem to mind.

Panit introduced me to Clarissa, who was garlanded in ivy and mistletoe.

'I'm a pagan,' she said. 'This is our church, and we're only allowed in once a year.'

'Because you can't come up to the stones at any other time?'

'That's right. You must come and touch them.'

So I did. I put both my hands on the nearest of the upright stones.

'Can you feel the earth's power? That's why the stones are here. To channel power,' said Clarissa.

'Well . . .' It was very nice to be at a morning party under the shadow of the stones; very nice, come to that, to be in amongst the stones at all. But nobody knows what they are, or what they were for. Yes, they are probably aligned to the winter solstice, and there are reasons why it might have been built that way, but we were ascribing modern motives to people of whom we know nothing. Which is fun, actually.

I talked to one of the straightest-looking men I've ever met, in his mid-forties maybe, with a nice smart haircut. He reminded me somewhat of the Tory MP for Leominster. He would have been quite happy at the Friends of Lichfield Cathedral do, except that he was dressed in white druids' robes.

'I've just been initiated,' he told me. 'I've always been a pagan, and I just wanted to take it a bit more seriously.'

'I don't suppose you can tell me about the initiation?'

'Not really, no. It . . . celebrates the cyclical nature of life.'

This didn't seem the moment to expound my theory that life is helical, rather than cyclical. It would have been like dissing Leviticus to a bishop.

I gave Panit the slip, and chatted with one of the security guys.

'How do you find it?' I asked.

'Well . . . it is a bit bizarre.'

'What sort of things would you normally do?'

'Well, things like car rallies and that.'

'Oi, leave my mate alone!' shouted Panit at the security guy. I smiled, and rejoined my chum.

A famous hippy wandered past, one of the ones that television crews often light on at these kinds of events. He calls himself

King Arthur, as he believes himself to be Arthur's reincarnation. He dresses appropriately. He's not one to go lightly out of character, is Arthur.

'Appy birthday, Arthur, you cant!' bellowed Panit. King Arthur inclined his head at Panit.

'Is it his birthday?'

'Course it is. Winter solstice is King Arthur's birthday. Didn't you know that? I thought you knew every facking fing . . .'

The security guards started to marshal the assembly towards the tunnel which leads out onto the perimeter track. They close the site at nine, and reopen it at ten to members of the general public who might want to visit the henge on the day of the solstice, but who were too panty-waisted to join us for the moment of dawn, and who didn't care that they couldn't touch the stones.

Panit made sure he was one of the last to leave. The security guards were starting to put back the rope which, except for this hour and a half in the year, separates the stones from those who want to hug them.

'It's our sacred facking place, Ian,' he said, 'and we should 'ave the freedom to come and touch the cant whenever we want.'

Then Panit Dave took me for a spliff and a whisky coffee in his mate Richard's fire engine. It was a good way to end the night.

The sun was up. The night had gone. From this moment on, the days would be starting to lengthen.

And now the sun is coming up behind the Mountain, though its rays have not yet reached down into the valley below us and touched the little West Cork town where Neil and I had met twelve hours earlier. And I am sleepy. I grab my blanket from the car, and take it back into the house. Neil is well away. The sitting room rocks to the sound of his snoring. There is a sofa in the kitchen. I move some more bits of Neil's fishing tackle, and lie down, wrapped in the blanket from my car.

I won't sleep for long.

In an hour or so, after I've closed my eyes for a bit, I'll get up and slip into my old car. I'll tuck my bit of grass under the driver's seat. I'll release the handbrake, rather than start the engine, because I won't want to wake Neil. I'll roll a little way down the Mountain first. I'll leave the CDs for Neil, so I'll turn on the radio again. The presenter will talk to Niamh in Cork about *The X Factor*, and play some Westlife records.

Then I'll drive the 300 and some odd miles back to Belfast through the autumn sunshine. I hope to be home before night.

ACKNOWLEDGEMENTS

With grateful thanks to Catherine Smith, Iain O'Neill, Georgina Slater, Richard Jarman, Rachel Francis, Finbar Francis, Isaac Francis, Panit Dave, Sussex University Library Special Collections, my colleagues and students in the School of English at Birmingham City University, the Linen Hall Library in Belfast, Christopher Charles Ambler, Pete Mustill, Alison Parry, Juliet Orbach, Deirdre Rusling, Monique Roffey, Steven Moger, David Hibling, Ian Willson, Richard 'Bugman' Jones, David Westmore, Kate Stonestreet, ECWM, EJMM, VCM, SKS, Saleel Nurbhai, Jean and Ralph Foxwell, Paul Williams, Richard Pitts, Rhys Pitts, Pauline Clarke, Ian Whiteley, Nik Morell, Jay Tate, Dr Sean Holden, Julian de la Motte Harrison, Paul Warwick, Mary Compton, Blanche Pope, Peter French, Katherine Wood, Abra Lazarus, Dr Catherine Fox, Reverend Canon Doctor Pete Wilcox, Tony Green, Matt Barnard, Annette Mills, Jillian Stuteley, Josephine and Simon Felton, Clodagh and Laurie Howes, Dr 'Doctor' Hannah Howes, Quinten Manby, Emi Manby, Dr Seiriol Morgan, Dr Dave

Littlewood, Shevaughn Williams, Holly Blackwell, Jolyon Jenkins, Martha Marchant, Steven and David Furnell, Max Fielden, Andy Lievens, Bob Rowberry, Annette Green, David Smith, Colin Midson and the late and much loved Richard Panton.

Without the loving and unhesitating help of my friends Sara Ivanovich and Bob Machin, I could not have finished this book – you know what you did, and I will never forget.

This book, and all my nights, are dedicated to my wife, Hilary Marchant, without whose love and patient correction of my sometime's erratic use of the apostrophe, nothing would be possible.

NOTE ON THE AUTHOR

Ian Marchant is a writer, broadcaster and performer. He is originally from Newhaven in East Sussex, and now lives with his family in the not-entirely-real county of Radnorshire.

Before taking up writing books, he sang in various unimaginably obscure bands, wrote up the results of horse races in betting shops and ran a large second-hand bookshop on the Charing Cross Road. He currently teaches creative writing at Birmingham City University and with the National Academy of Writing.

Something of the Night is his seventh book.

For supplementary material and more information on the author please visit www.ianmarchant.com

SIMON &
SCHUSTER

London · New York · Sydney · Toronto · New Delhi

A CBS COMPANY

IF YOU ENJOY GOOD BOOKS,
YOU'LL LOVE OUR GREAT OFFER
25% OFF the RRP ON ALL
SIMON & SCHUSTER UK TITLES
WITH FREE POSTAGE AND PACKING (UK ONLY)

Simon & Schuster UK is one of the leading general book publishing
companies in the UK, publishing a wide and eclectic mix
of authors ranging across commercial fiction, literary fiction,
general non-fiction, illustrated and children's books.

For exclusive author interviews, features and competitions log onto:
www.simonandschuster.co.uk

*Titles also available in **eBook** format across all digital devices.*

How to buy your books

Credit and debit cards
Telephone Simon & Schuster Cash Sales at **Sparkle Direct** on **01326 569444**

Cheque
Send a cheque payable to *Simon & Schuster Bookshop* to:
Simon & Schuster Bookshop, PO Box 60, Helston, TR13 OTP

Email: sales@sparkledirect.co.uk
Website: www.sparkledirect.com

Prices and availability are subject to change without notice.